"Truly this is humanity's last stand: we can let [...] and its accompanying systems of oppressions choke the planet and [...] one another, or we can rise up to support locally-waged struggles for justice linked with defending humanity. We need an anthropolitics more than ever."　　　　　—from the Introduction by Mark Schuller

Advanced Praise for *Humanity's Last Stand*

"*Humanity's Last Stand* is an electrifying work that dissects a range of interconnected problems—climate change, ultra-right nationalism, and global inequality—and proposes concrete steps to avert total catastrophe. This highly readable book is prescient, if not premonitory. It is essential reading for anyone interested in our species' long-term survival. Anthropology at its finest!"　　　　　—Roberto J. González, author of *Connected: How a Mexican Village Created Its Own Cell Phone Network*

"Mark Schuller's approach to the convergent crises pushing us toward human catastrophe and planetary disaster should be taken to heart. With admirable conviction and commitment to radical empathy and pragmatic solidarity, he makes a bold argument for a publicly-engaged anthropological imagination that contributes a holistic understanding of and concrete solutions to urgent global crises."　　　　　—Faye V. Harrison, author of *Outsider Within: Reworking Anthropology in the Global Age*

"Schuller's brilliant book is critical reading for all of us who work to envision, and bring into being, a socially and ecologically just world. Grounded in a politics of solidarity built through the understanding of, and dismantling of privilege, he mobilizes a new vision for what an 'anthropological imagination' can afford us in terms of activist practice and radical empathy."　　　　　—Paige West, editor of *From Reciprocity to Relationality: Anthropological Possibilities*

"An urgent and much- needed contribution to our world in crisis. Schuller lays out crucial groundwork for how an anthropological reimagining of global social, political, and economic relationships can save us from ourselves. In clear prose, he shows the public how anthropology can be deployed as a way to create more empathy in these troubling times."　　　　　—Jason De León, executive director of the Undocumented Migration Project, author of *The Land of Open Graves: Living and Dying on the Migrant Trail*

Humanity's Last Stand

Humanity's Last Stand

Confronting Global Catastrophe

MARK SCHULLER

Foreword by Cynthia McKinney

Rutgers University Press

New Brunswick, Camden, and Newark, New Jersey, and London

Library of Congress Cataloging-in-Publication Data

Names: Schuller, Mark, 1973- author.
Title: Humanity's last stand : confronting global catastrophe / Mark Schuller.
Description: New Brunswick : Rutgers University Press, [2021] | Includes bibliographical
    references and index.
Identifiers: LCCN 2020019374 | ISBN 9781978820883 (hardcover) | ISBN 9781978820876
    (paperback) | ISBN 9781978820890 (epub) | ISBN 9781978820906 (mobi) |
    ISBN 9781978820913 (pdf)
Subjects: LCSH: Social movements. | Social justice. | Environmental justice. |
    Anti-globalization movement. | Human rights—Anthropological aspects. |
    Empathy—Political aspects.
Classification: LCC HM881 .S336 2021 | DDC 303.48/4—dc23
LC record available at https://lccn.loc.gov/2020019374

A British Cataloging-in-Publication record for this book is available from the British Library.

♾ The paper used in this publication meets the requirements of the American National
Standard for Information Sciences—Permanence of Paper for Printed Library Materials,
ANSI Z39.48-1992.

www.rutgersuniversitypress.org

Manufactured in the United States of America

To my students, who are also my teachers on this world they are forced to confront

Contents

Foreword

CYNTHIA McKINNEY

I was green, before I was a Green. I grew up playing in the creek across the street from my house; the woods through which I trekked to school whenever I missed the school bus were my biology class. Snakes and lizards and frogs and ticks populated my lab. And, so naturally I would never approve of turning Mother Nature, herself, into a profit center. After all, it's the air that we breathe, the water that we drink, and the earth that nourishes us. I have never accepted any reason whatsoever for any activities that pollute or contaminate the air, water, and soil that humankind and other animals need for life. For me, all life is important.

And that's what makes Professor Mark Schuller's call to action so important. In *Humanity's Last Stand*, Schuller asks us to think at an entirely different level (for most grassroots activists): he asks us to think at the anthropological level. In short, *Humanity's Last Stand* is a call to arms to elevate our thinking to the species level, or, he cautions, the species will face extinction. When I was first sworn into Congress, I was readily embraced by the office of Congresswoman Patricia Schroeder who had been dubbed *"America's* Congresswoman." When her staffer came to give my staff an orientation on life on "The Hill," one of her sayings always stuck with me, "The bankers always win." And I would modify that a bit for this context and say, "In the end, Planet Earth will always win"; Schuller reminds us that humankind may not. And therein lies the urgency of his message.

At this very moment as I write, a mere few milliseconds (in geologic time) from the global climate change protest called Global Climate Strike, it is acknowledged that the earth is experiencing momentous changes: decreased geomagnetic field, magnetic pole shifts, discoveries of extinctions and emergences of species, and climate change.[1] Add to these phenomena the impact of the sun on the climate of the earth, and the science seems to carry us from theory to speculation.[2] Thus, it seems to me that while much more is known today about climate than, say, a hundred years ago, there is much more now known, also, about what is not known. And I gather from the current climate debate that that's a lot!

The reality of human degradation of the human habitat is unquestioned. What is questioned is the extent of anthropogenic climate change. On September 26, 2019, five hundred scientists and professionals from Europe, Brazil, Canada, Australia, and other countries sent a letter to the United Nations secretary-general stating that there is no climate emergency: "Our advice to political leaders is that science should strive for a significantly better understanding of the climate system, while politics should focus on minimizing potential climate damage by prioritizing adaptation strategies based on proven and affordable technologies." The title of their submission to the United Nations was "There Is No Climate Emergency."[3] This came after a November 29, 2012, letter to the United Nations from 125 climate scientists challenging a statement made by then–United Nations secretary-general Ban Ki-moon that "extreme weather caused by climate change is the new normal." Ban Ki-moon went even further later, stating that the science was clear: "We must reduce our dependence on carbon emissions." The 2012 open letter was sent as a challenge to all of the secretary-general's statements.[4]

While I don't take a stand one way or the other on *anthropogenic* climate change, I have long opposed the unbridled despoliation and worse that has been done to our environment. And I do believe that humankind's uneven distribution of access to Earth's gifts is a large part of the problem. Also, straying away from Indigenous "ways of knowing" and living also contributes to this readiness to render our environment toxic *to some people.*

The problem is that those who are largely responsible for human habitat despoliation are the ones who are not being asked to pay for their crimes against the rest of humanity and Planet Earth. I view as positive forward movement laws passed in some countries that accord a right to a clean environment to humans and a right to not be polluted to Mother Earth.

As I was reading *Humanity's Last Stand*, several thoughts crossed my mind. But foremost was the question I asked myself throughout: for whom has Schuller written this book? I believe this book is most effective for those who are newly awake to Earth's climate issues and are wondering how we human beings and the planet came to be in this condition. Arguing for an "anthropological imagination," Schuller believes that this particular outlook is the best way for human beings, divided systematically for the last four hundred years, to overcome both their real and their fabricated differences. Thus, an anthropological imagination begs humankind to look at itself through a *species*-level lens. Schuller believes that such a lens, then, lifts all human struggles, especially justice struggles, to one common denominator—justice—that binds us all together. Because all "the good guys" want justice.

While reading Schuller's book, I was reminded of the courage of Robert F. Kennedy, who ventured into deepest, darkest Cape Town, apartheid South Africa, and told the young people he addressed that he had traveled around the world from Congo to Russia, Peru, and the United States and pleaded that the struggles—all detailed differently in the local—shared a common goal in the global. He issued a call to young people in South Africa to join that global struggle for justice and dignity and to "take the lead for a new order of things." He reminded us that there is a role for even a single person: "Each time a man stands up for an ideal, or acts to improve the lot of others, or strikes out against injustice, he sends forth a tiny ripple of hope, and crossing each other from a million different centers of energy and daring, those ripples build a current which can sweep down the mightiest walls of oppression and resistance."[5]

Schuller asks nothing less of today's generation than Bobby Kennedy did in 1966; however, two years after giving that speech—almost to the hour—Kennedy would lie dead on a hotel ballroom floor after he had just won the prize of the California presidential primary, on his way to the White House. Kennedy's assassination was the first time I shed tears. At that very moment, both the best and the worst of U.S. leadership were manifested and indicated the challenges that "we, the people" had before us in achieving this "anthropological imagination." Kennedy represented the absolute best example of leadership of that generation; those who conspired to kill him to protect their very powers that he was rallying all of us of his generation to challenge represent the absolute worst in the leadership of that day. In fact, the absolute worst leadership of that time chose to kill ("expose, disrupt, or otherwise neutralize" in the language of the Federal Bureau of Investigation's founding documents) the young leadership of that time in what became known as the COINTELPRO program of the U.S. government.[6] U.S. intelligence activities at that time included assassination plots of foreign leaders as well as real assassinations of dissenters to the common injustices of that time. I've seen and studied what the 1960s U.S. government COINTELPRO countertransformation repression did to the Black Power, antiwar, "New Left," Puerto Rican independence, and American Indian movements.[7]

Which leads me to today.

We know what the problems are; and we know what the solutions are. Yet the necessary ingredient—behavior change—is missing.

The College Fix reports on an effort to bridge the cultural gap on a U.S. college campus by hosting a discussion on "White Consciousness." No matter how one might approach the topic (with enthusiasm or with skepticism), the results should be shocking: that is, on a campus of thirty thousand students, fewer than ten attended the workshop, and of that number, two were journalists, two got extra credit from their professors for attending; the remaining five of the total nine present were from the Young Americans for Freedom campus chapter who showed up out of curiosity, according to the news story.[8] And while we celebrate the nine who came for whatever reason, how are we going to accomplish building a movement on anthropological imagination with such numbers? Or better still, what kind of engagement do we need if we have only such small numbers?

I have long wondered how to build a trans-partisan movement in the United States based on our shared values, grounded in our diversity. As I was reading *Humanity's Last Stand*, I thought about Dr. Martin Luther King Jr.'s "Letter from a Birmingham Jail," in which he laments the not-very-helpful role of so-called white moderates during the civil rights era.[9] Yes, an anthropological imagination would have catapulted the civil rights era, I believe, to the list of most successful U.S. movements in modern times. Thus, Schuller's call in *Humanity's Last Stand* to understand how white supremacy works in real life and in academia. But our conundrum again revolves around how to deprogram hundreds of years of programming. Donald Trump proclaimed that the U.S. "system is rigged." And I maintain that the people have also been rigged in order to maintain a rigged system. Now, just understand that the global system (of apartheid) has also rigged outcomes so that a few people, approximately one billion around the world, are winners and the rest languish for generation after generation in a system not meant to benefit them. (For example, I currently teach in a part of Asia that was colonized by Great Britain, and the students I teach have never had the opportunity to *play* with a doll that *looks* like them, reaffirming their looks!)

So, how do we unrig ourselves?

I have decided to dedicate my ruminations for this book to a very dear friend whom I have not seen in more than a decade. Her name is Tracy. And I believe she did exactly what Schuller recommends with his idea of us all adopting an "anthropological imagination." I never will forget Tracy literally screaming and crying at me trying to get me to understand why she was so terrified.

Tracy said, "I gave up my white privilege, and I'm terrified of what that means for me."

First, some background: Tracy was way cool, counterculture, and way green—just like me, but even more so. She had converted her diesel Mercedes to run on used restaurant grease. So she would go from restaurant to restaurant and collect their used cooking oil, filter it, and use that instead of gasoline to run her car! I just thought Tracy was too cool to be true. But for some reason whites seemed less comfortable around her than nonwhites. And one day I found out why.

Tracy understood that she had been "rigged" (to put it into today speak) and that as a white person in the United States she enjoyed certain privileges that I could never understand or access. But just like Tracy had decided to transform her car to become "solutionary," she had also transformed herself. Not only did she recognize her white privilege, she acted in ways that acknowledged and shed her hidden privileges—whatever they might be. That also entailed speaking truth to the powers that be inside organizations—yes, even the so-called socially progressive ones— that didn't want to hear what Tracy had to say. I am only just now understanding the profundity of what Tracy really meant on that last day that I saw her. She had created for herself a world without white privilege—she was terrified, but she did it. She was building her bridge to a more perfect world as she walked on it, and she didn't know what dangers lurked just around the bend. But what she did realize was that she was alienating a lot of her white colleagues by exposing the contradictions in their own behaviors. In my opinion, Tracy was a pioneer and forged a path that many others are now attempting to re-create.

There are people who are doing the heavy lifting and the hard work against this particular type of rigging that has been ongoing since the dawn of capitalism and the "creation" of the "white" race. Anibal Quijano, writing specifically about the *American* experience, called it the "coloniality" of power; he wrote that capitalism is the main global structure for control of labor.[10] The life work of Jeffrey Perry has been to curate the work of Theodore Allen, whose epic two-volume *The Invention of the White Race* chronicles the creation of the "white" identity as a method of social control after black and white laborers in the colonial United States joined together in solidarity to press for employment/labor reform.[11] Perry writes, "On the back cover of the 1994 edition of Volume 1, subtitled Racial Oppression and Social Control, Allen boldly asserted 'When the first Africans arrived in Virginia in 1619, there were no "white" people there; nor, according to the colonial records, would there be for another sixty years.' . . . 'White identity had to be carefully taught, and it would be only after the passage of some six crucial decades' that the word 'would appear as a synonym for European-American.'"[12] Importantly, Perry focuses his work on the role of white supremacy as a retardant to progressive social change and therefore views the struggle against white supremacy as a key part of any effort to create progressive social change.

Tracy understood what Quijano, Perry, Allen, and Schuller were studying and writing about—some writing only in academic journals. But it was her lived experiences and her critical thinking that allowed her to arrive at the same conclusions as these most eminent thinkers—that transformation is possible. And that gives me hope.

I'm wondering how many Tracys are out there, already having done some heavy lifting in their own lives in order to save humanity and this earth as we know it. Writing this made me realize how much I miss Tracy and how I had neglected my friendship with her for too long. So I searched for and found an old email address for her and clicked the send button. She responded almost immediately. She has relocated to the East Coast and is happily partnered up with a young man she's known for most of her life! And she is happy.

While Schuller grounds his call for an anthropological imagination within the current issues regarding climate change, he is smart enough to realize that no change at all will occur if we human beings are not able to act with compassion that "give[s] rise to the power to transform resentment into forgiveness, hatred into friendliness, and fear into respect and love for all things."

Now, that's a reality that's worth struggling and sacrificing for.

Preface

As I write this Preface, it's been over two and a half months since COVID-19 was declared a pandemic.

This book already feels out of date now. It is impossible to predict what human life will be like when the book is in print. Hopefully, by the time you read this, there will have been a reckoning, lessons learned about our world, our society, ourselves.

As of today, COVID-19 has infected over six million people worldwide (6,229,408)—and that's only what we know about, people who have been tested. So far, the disease has claimed 373,973 lives. In the United States alone, 1,799,747 cases have been confirmed to date, killing over 100,000 people. At 104,702, this is more than all U.S. deaths—military and civilian—in *all* wars, both declared and undeclared, since World War II (102,684). And the number of deaths keeps growing.

The virus spread as quickly as people within today's global economy. As of this writing, neither a cure nor a vaccine has been found. The public health goal has been to "flatten the curve" by limiting contact, from what was incorrectly called "social distancing" to stay-at-home orders and shutting down all but "essential" workplaces. Experience from other countries has shown that a hands-on, active approach from a central government anchored on clear messaging and consistent enforcement, and robust and equitable testing and response, has stemmed, slowed, and in some cases all but stopped the disease, yet the United States did not (and as of this writing does not) have that sort of plan in place. We have much to learn from local experiences everywhere.[1] COVID-19 should have ended the "debate" on universal health care, not just out of empathy but also out of principled, collective self-interest: truly the best way to protect me is to protect you.

Yet even the wildly inconsistent measures taken to slow transmission to within the ability of the public emergency health response to manage it from state to state—number of hospital beds, respirators, and life support—had an immediate impact on the economy. In the past few days, the number of unemployment claims in the United States topped 40 *million* people. This impact is greater than the October 1929 stock market crash that triggered the Great Depression.

Meanwhile, as tens of millions of people were forced to drastically change their way of life quickly, turning a closet into a makeshift office or getting creative with whatever was left in the pantry, the overindulgences of consumer capitalism seemed distant—going to grocery stores risked exposure, and the shelves were often empty of basic necessities like toilet paper or flour. Driving past malls offered eerie premonitions of what archaeologists of the future might surmise about our lifestyle: our mating rituals, our sacred objects, our sorting mechanisms.

And people did adapt . . . in the meantime, global carbon emissions went down 17%. Bypassing corporate food conglomerates, more people turned to cooperatives, farm shares, and "victory gardens." Mutual aid groups—Puerto Rico's life support after Hurricane Maria[2]—sprouted in hundreds of communities across the country.

Even forced to stay at home with limited contact, our human lives are already connected to one another. Especially in our response to catastrophes like COVID, our consumer choices impact other families. In an effort to protect their families from exposure, many people turned to online delivery services, while workers at Amazon protested working conditions that put them at direct risk of contracting COVID. They demanded their right to take sick time because of the pandemic without being fired. Meanwhile, in the first month of the pandemic, Amazon founder Jeff Bezos's net worth climbed 24 billion dollars—and it continues to grow.

As these brief examples highlight, disasters like COVID are not the "great equalizer." Disasters unmask social inequalities normally allowed to remain hidden to many in order to maintain ideological appearances. We need bottom-up analysis that centers *specificity*, building on the lived embodied, raced, and gendered experience of the people most impacted.³ For example, for many women confronting intimate partner violence, being shuttered at home risks their further isolation and abuse. Trans or nonbinary individuals often face greater challenges of returning "home."

The disease, while "color blind," has disproportionally impacted people who literally can't afford to work at home while middle-class professionals—disproportionately white—*can*.⁴ Who is picking up potentially infected trash, or recycling our growing number of cardboard boxes? The people performing the most dangerous labor for companies deemed "essential," making at or near minimum wage, are disproportionately African American or Latinx, often immigrants, including undocumented people. Inequities in the health care system map onto the mortality rate, which also corresponds to patterns in residential segregation. African Americans are disproportionately getting COVID-19, and even more disproportionately dying.⁵

Blackness—more to the point, *anti*-Blackness—is lethal in other ways, as this book attempts to show. I am writing this Preface as the country is publicly reckoning with its legacy of racial injustice. In one incident a white woman was asked to follow the established rules for Central Park and leash her dog. Christian Cooper, an African American bird watcher and board member of the local Audubon Society, pointed out that the area was a sensitive habitat for species of rare and endangered birds. Angry at being called out for not following the rules, Amy Cooper (no relation) dialed 911 and reported a dangerous Black man, weaponizing her white supremacy. The incident, recorded, could have become violent—the NYPD has a long history of violence against Black men.

Not two days later, Memorial Day, when the U.S. COVID death toll approached 100,000, in the similarly "liberal" city of Minneapolis, police officer Derek Chauvin held his knee on top of 46-year-old suspect George Floyd's neck for 8 minutes, 46 seconds. This was *not* Chauvin's first deadly use of force.

"I can't breathe!"

Floyd's words, echoing Eric Garner's, who was killed six years ago by an NYPD chokehold, became a rallying cry for justice. The local community, having emerged from the pandemic stay-at-home order the previous Monday, came together to share their outrage. According to my organizer colleagues who were there, the first night's protest was large, multiracial, passionate, energetic, and peaceful; no one was hurt, no property damaged. The full extent and explanation about what happened next—with reports of looting and violence impacting many communities—is only becoming clear, as I am writing this just a week later. The "Minneapolis Uprising" as it is already being called has inspired solidarity protests against institutional racism within the police state in dozens of cities across the United States and even around the world.

Minneapolis mayor Jacob Frye has since confirmed that the people damaging property across the city were *not* residents of Minneapolis. Melvin Carter, the mayor of St. Paul, Minneapolis's "twin" city, reported that nearly all were from out of state. The commissioner of public safety confirmed the presence of white supremacist groups, who put calls on their social media for their members to loot businesses in order to incite violence and trigger a reaction. Some even spoke of a "civil war."

It worked. President Trump tweeted, "when the looting starts, the shooting starts." The national guard was sent in, license to kill. And just today, the commander in chief called upon the U.S. military to intervene. The coordinated actions of the open white supremacists and the occupant of the White House have made it clear that the struggle in the United States right now is about humanity or profit, human lives—*Black* human lives—versus the police-military nexus needed to uphold the inequalities foundational to racial capitalism.

I apologize if this is too blunt to begin a book, not giving time to catch your breath. I would have loved to be wrong about the ways in which these struggles are already connected. But for people of color, particularly Black people in the United States, it's been about, in Floyd's words, not being able to breathe, whether from toxic waste dumps put in their segregated neighborhoods, not having enough respirators for victims of COVID-19 because the hospitals on Chicago's South Side were shuttered a month into the pandemic, being choked by law enforcement, or being teargassed as the tweeter-in-chief's incitement of violence emboldened people who *still* say they are not racist to shoot.

This book has been the most challenging, most gut-wrenching, soul-searching, ambitious writing I have ever attempted. This was a labor of love and truly arising from a powerful community of social justice warriors.

First and foremost, this book is inspired by and dedicated to activists in a range of collectives, too many to mention in the pages that follow. Three organizations in particular, named here, are especially inspiring. I've always donated royalties (whereas, except for the documentary, they've never amounted to much), and never named them, as I've always considered it an obligation, the very least I could do. Given the urgency of this book I feel compelled to name them this time around: The Red Nation, Organized Communities Against Deportation, and Black Youth Project-100.

The idea first germinated in a grad seminar with the late Cedric Robinson, who has also inspired a generation of scholars, sprouting during the Iraq War protests with Queergrad making connections between issues, the focus of the Voices for Global Justice collective at the community radio station, then directed by Elizabeth Robinson, who maintained contact as my career advanced, always asking insightful questions on air. My former colleagues at York College, particularly the team reviving the African American Resource Center and the late Mychel Namphy, planted the idea in firm ground. Colleagues at NIU, in anthropology and what is now nonprofit and NGO studies as well as collectives working on a community organizing training (called "POWER") and the faculty union, both fertilized the garden and pulled the weeds. Quakers in New Paltz, Flushing, and Chicago held this in the light. My activist/academic colleagues in Haiti, particularly the Faculté d'Ethnologie and the Saturday Supper Salon, gave the ideas sunshine and water.

Formalizing this writing, my career owes a debt of gratitude to both the Society for Applied Anthropology and American Anthropological Association for the receipt of the Margaret Mead Award. I didn't feel worthy of the award then—still not sure, but it compelled me to work to earn it. This was the push needed, and I blurted out the first words and core thesis at the 2016 awards ceremony.

Making this a reality, the sabbatical provided by Northern Illinois University—and the opportunity provided by, in all honesty, the failure to begin long-term ethnographic research in Cuba during the first year of the Trump administration—provided me time to spend doing the research and the first chapter drafts, in fits and starts.

I was fortunate to have conversations with colleagues who have critiqued, questioned, and sharpened the analysis. Thank you to participants of the NIU "Mash up" and seminars at the University of Pittsburgh Department of Anthropology; University of Illinois Department of Anthropology; SUNY New Paltz departments of anthropology, women's, gender and sexuality studies, and Latin American studies; and the Treinta y Tres conference hosted by NIU's Center for Latino and Latin American Studies. I especially want to thank Kathleen Musante, Sarah Bray, Ellen Moodie, Jessica Greenburg, Ben Junge, and Christina Abreu for making these fruitful exchanges possible. I subjected my students in Anthropology and Contemporary World Problems course—twice, in 2018 and 2019—to drafts. Their comments, questions, discussions, and anonymous feedback were invaluable.

I owe particular thanks to individuals making this book possible: Karl Bryant, Betsy Wirtz, Barbara Rose Johnston, Dawn Pinder, Laura Heideman, Jonathan Katz, Edwidge Danticat, Gina Ulysse, Marlie Wasserman, Kimberly Guinta, Jeremy Grainger, Manolia Charlotin, Mamyrah Dougé Prosper, Cynthia McKinney. Thanks also to coauthors Darlene Dubuisson, Jessica Hsu, and Elizabeth Wirtz for sharp analyses in blogs.

Many people offered useful references: Jason Antrosio, Dana Bardolph, Michael Blakely, Leo Chavez, Melissa Checker, Jason de León, Shirley Fiske, Ruth Gomberg-Múñoz, Faye Harrison, Barbara Rose Johnston, Peter Kaufman, Tania Levey, David Lewis, Michelle Marzullo, Jeff Maskovsky, Leila Porter, Kurt Rademaker, Felix Riede, Payson Sheets, Deborah Thomas, and Tiffany Willoughby Herard.

Providing necessary critique were several people who read chapter drafts, and some the entire book: Maya Berry, Andy Bruno, Karl Bryant, Orisanmi Burton, Heide Castañeda, Dána-Ain Davis, Nick Estes, AJ Faas, Ruth Gomberg Muñoz, Hillary Haldane, Anne Hanley; Laura Heideman, Josiah Heyman, Trude Jacobsen, Melissa Johnson, Heather Lazrus, Sandy López, Julie Maldonado, Beth Marino, Emily McKee, Dawn Pinder, Gina Ulysse, Jacqueline Villarrubia Mendoza, Simón Weffer, Jennifer Wies, Jessica Winegar, Betsy Wirtz, and Kevin Yelvington. Needless to say, any errors were a result of my stubbornness. Thank you to the anonymous peer reviewers for their extremely helpful insights, and Rutgers editor Kimberly Guinta has the patience of Job sifting through rantings and finding the useful core underneath.

Two people in particular have sustained me. Betsy Wirtz, literally held me up and believed in me and this book when I couldn't, or when I couldn't bear to read yet another horror story. Karl Bryant was there literally at the beginning to the very end. I hope this book justifies the wounds to your soul.

This has been the most difficult book I have ever written. It is ironic that when it finally goes to press, copy edited, with final changes made, the future is uncertain: Will the civil war have begun? What is the role for principled solidarity in defending humanity on the other side? What is demanded of those of us who still have hope in humanity now is the courage to put our bodies, even and especially white bodies, in between those with guns—open-carry, white supremacists, and the blue line alike—and those defending Black lives. We need the courage to imagine that this new order can outlive the current crisis, that sustaining a solidarity economy is possible. That we don't go back to business as usual "when this is all over." An anthropolitics based on the contingent, specific humanity in our differences might then be possible. But first and foremost, we need the courage to love ourselves, and love one another.

Humanity's Last Stand

Introduction

Careening toward Extinction

The fight for equality must be fought on many fronts—in the urban slums, in the sweat shops of the factories and fields. Our separate struggles are really one—a struggle for freedom, for dignity and for humanity.

This passage of a telegram from Martin Luther King Jr. to César Chávez from September 22, 1966, offers an important lesson for today's activists, as struggles for justice are becoming increasingly global. It is one of the first articulations of what can be called an anthropological imagination.

Every day it seems another crisis is coming to light, each more urgent than the next. It is easy to feel overwhelmed. Within a generation, getting news went from having daily broadcasts and newspapers to being subjected to a literally constant barrage of information. The "news cycle" is rapidly losing its meaning. In addition to several twenty-four-hour news stations with constantly scrolling headlines, news websites now employ clickbait, sensationalized content to entice readers to click on a link to a particular website, sponsored by paid advertisers. Social media platforms track—and predict—our every move, eerily foretold by the movie *Minority Report*. How can one possibly keep track of what's actually going on or tease apart fact from "fake news" or "alternative facts"?

The year 2017 was marked by catastrophe. Within the span of a single month, three consecutive hurricanes battered the Caribbean and the U.S. South. The people most impacted were poor, immigrant, elderly, people of color, or those living in poorer nations or colonies.

People in the frontline communities of Houston are now paying for the damage to their city caused by the fossil fuel industry headquartered a few miles away that benefited from easy-money deregulation only days before Hurricane Harvey, category 4, hovered over the area beginning on August 26. Not two weeks later, Hurricane Irma, category 5, slammed through the Virgin Islands and Dominica before ripping along the northern coast of Cuba and heading north to Florida and Georgia. On September 20, Hurricane Maria, also a category 5 storm, devastated Puerto Rico. Many of the island's 3.4 million residents were without power and water for months. The United States played politics with the death toll: while the federal government initially counted 64 dead,[1] Puerto Rico's governor Ricardo Rosselló belatedly accepted a figure almost fifty times greater, 2,975. Maria was the worst hurricane to hit Puerto Rico in eighty-nine years. The science connecting climate change to the increasing destructiveness and longevity of hurricanes has been clear for quite some time, even as the U.S. administration seems hell bent on a policy of denial.

At the same time, not since the 1960s civil rights era have white supremacists been so active, openly marching and committing acts of violence and aggression in Charlottesville and other cities across the South. On August 12, 2017, white nationalists gathered near the University of Virginia to protest the removal of a Robert E. Lee statue, chanting, "You will not replace us" and "Go back to Africa." Many present referred to Dylann Roof—a young white man who murdered nine Black worshippers at a Charleston church two years earlier—as a national hero. Another white nationalist rammed his car into a crowd of counterprotestors, sending several to the hospital and killing one, thirty-two-year-old Heather Heyer. Rather than condemning the violence, President Trump equivocated, blaming "both sides" while calling Black athletes like Colin Kaepernick a "son of a bitch" and attempting to bully the NFL to fire individuals for exercising their First Amendment rights to free speech. This mobilization of hate was repeated in October when three white supremacists from Texas opened fire following white nationalist Richard Spencer's speech at the University of Florida.

President Trump, elected on a platform of white supremacy, xenophobia, isolationism, Islamophobia, and more than a hint of disdain for women and their bodies, has ushered in a whiplash of terrifying social policies. While he hadn't yet been able to take away gains in health care overall, funding for women's health, particularly reproductive health, has already seen a dramatic cut. In addition to working to privatize our public education system, Education Secretary Betsy DeVos has rolled back programs focusing on prevention and response to violence against women on college campuses. Attorney General Jeff Sessions formalized frightening policies deporting undocumented residents. Undocumented individuals from Mexico, Central America, and Haiti have committed suicide or fled to Canada, while the Supreme Court finally allowed Trump's "Muslim ban" to be enforced. This happened in the first week of December 2017, on the heels of the Republican-led Senate's eleventh-hour, razor-thin majority vote in support of Trump's tax reform, the greatest redistribution of wealth upward in the history of U.S. tax law. Trump's pardon of Arizona sheriff Joe Arpaio, who was brought to justice following his illegal and inhumane treatment of undocumented people he kept in tents sweltering in the desert sun[2] sent a clear message to the world about the Trump administration's priorities, as did the conditions attached to a six-month extension of the Deferred Action for Childhood Arrivals program that grants limited rights to children of undocumented residents.

One can never catch up; barely a year later these particular assaults on humanity and dignity have been buried by many more. Millions of women (and some men) were retraumatized by official dismissal of concerns about Supreme Court nominee Brett Kavanaugh's multiple counts of sexual assault. Kaepernick *did* lose his job, literally becoming a poster child for Nike.[3] Deportation turned uglier as families were separated. Two children from Guatemala, seven-year-old Jakelin Caal Maquin and eight-year-old

Felipe Alonzo-Gomez, died in U.S. custody in December 2018. That same month, caving into right-wing pundits' bullying about the border wall, Trump announced a government shutdown that impacted 800,000 federal workers and millions of recipients of federal program resources. And the shutdown was felt worldwide: the website offering global climate data for scientists was down.

Seeing Our Connections

This short intro is already past tense, history. And it's a lot at once. It's how people experienced it, as simultaneous urgent crises. Many people I know have become overwhelmed, traumatized, hopeless. Speaking to these real and imminent fears, Toni Morrison said, moments of crisis are "precisely the time when artists go to work." These times have also energized writers of all sorts: activists and scholars as well as artists. The current moment calls for bold thinking and fresh analysis that doesn't shy away from asking the big questions. I'm writing this book because I believe that humanity is better than this, or can be. That we don't have to give in to our fears. It's now or never for us to act. The earth is sending loud and violent warnings that the current capitalist system is unsustainable.

It is also precisely during periods of "crisis" like these that the fog of ideology is easier to lift. Activist movements now are already adopting an intersectional approach, leading the way. But people who are going to one march this week against gun violence, another next week against family separation, or climate change, or women's rights to safety, or transgender people's right to exist, or science itself, risk reproducing a defensive, single-issue individualism, atomization, and compartmentalization—a "whack-a-mole" approach to resistance.

Our destinies are already intertwined, connected by legacies of colonialism, patriarchy, slavery, and capitalism. After World War II, within the United States in particular, a white "middle class" was created and sold the belief of endless growth. That growth has reached its natural limits. And the engines of growth are belching greenhouse gases, choking out other life. At some point this endless growth machine was going to come back and bite us. That time is now.

Rather than the endless whack-a-mole process of resisting, which is exhausting and burning people out, this moment calls upon us to see how we are not only connected by these particular issues but also connected to communities that are differently situated along global capitalism's process of accumulation by appropriation. Folks whose bodies, families, languages, and religions have been targeted by this system built on inhumanity are building specific networks of solidarity. People who until now have been spared the brunt of the colonialist, white supremacist, cis-heteropatriarchal accumulation machine's violence need to put our own bodies on the line. Not just by carrying signs and chanting, but by educating ourselves about the ways in which these issues that appear on the surface to be particular local struggles are already interwoven together globally. More importantly, those of us who have found ourselves on the privileged side of these increasingly terrorizing inequalities need to do the self-reflection necessary to see how our lives are complicit in maintaining these systems. And when we do act—and we must act—to dismantle this privilege, we must do so with the understanding that these systems that might have temporarily benefited the privileged few need to be dismantled from within and without. The inhumanity of the genocide of Indigenous populations of the earth to make way for settler populations, and the economic system built off this theft and the savage system of slavery, reducing the entire planet, including women's bodies, to the status of private property, is not good for anyone. It is killing the planet, just as it is killing individuals who are fleeing their homelands seeking asylum.

If we—and by "we" I do mean everyone—are serious about our struggle to defend humanity against the worldwide systems of dehumanization, in all its specific local faces, we need to see the system for what it is. To do this requires what could be called an anthropological imagination.

An Anthropological Imagination

Taken in isolation, these sudden and urgent threats to humanity, to our very species, can be daunting. Increasingly, people are talking in apocalyptic terms:

> *Are we as a species careening toward our extinction?*

> *How can we as humanity put a stop to our own destruction and the possible destruction of the planet?*

Before we can act, we need the ability to see how issues such as the Syrian refugee crisis, the mass shootings in Parkland and El Paso, and the rising tide of ultra-right nationalism across Europe and the United States are all connected. Seeing how these global issues are lived and confronted by real, living human beings and how they are connected to other issues and people can be called an "anthropological imagination." An anthropological imagination also underscores that these issues are products of human action, and therefore changeable: they are particular local manifestations of the inhumanity of our global political and economic system based on inequality and private profit seeking at the expense of the collective good.

But more than anything, an anthropological imagination helps inspire, reminding us, in the words of the World Social Forum, that "another world is possible." For this world to be imagined into being, we must also heed the warning of the U.S. Social Forum, "another U.S. is necessary." This requires us to act.

I am certainly not the first to use the term "anthropological imagination"; it has mostly been used by anthropologists to conceptualize their particular field site or writing.[4] Ilana Gershon used the term to discuss how anthropologists engage social issues.[5] It was also in the title of the 2018 American Anthropological Association conference.

And as noted in King's note to Chávez from the start of this book, I am certainly not the first to apply an anthropological imagination, seeing various struggles for dignity and humanity as one. Understanding this interconnection, today's activists practice intersectionality, a politics of both/and, not either/or. Many call for a politics of solidarity that moves beyond "allies" and into "accomplices," dismantling privilege and sharing in the struggle to the end.

I define the anthropological imagination as the ability of people to see as connected species-level phenomena to individual lived experiences, understanding particular local injustices as manifestations of global capitalism, built on the theft of Indigenous lands and plantation slavery, buttressed by patriarchy, and hence connected to one another. Products of human action, these injustices are therefore changeable. Importantly, an anthropological imagination also sees these global and species-level phenomena as lived, understood, confronted, and resisted by real human beings. We must identify the humanity in others, and the humanity in their struggle, while affirming particular identities and challenging differential privilege: an anthropological imagination inspires radical empathy and solidarity.

Understanding Humanity

To talk about our extinction is by definition talking about our species, *Homo sapiens sapiens*. This is the "Anthropos," which, until feminist anthropologists intervened, was translated as "man." The accepted scientific term is now "humankind," which, while gender neutral, lacks the political dimension of "humanity." Anthropology is its study.

Anthropology's roots go back to ancient Greece, when Herodotus—known as a historian for his analysis of the Greek-Persian War published in 440 BCE—analyzed information written about the Persian groups that the Greek armies conquered.[6] Tunisian scholar Ibn Khaldun (1332–1406) also theorized about culture and society. During the Renaissance, several European world travelers left behind "exotic" tales, and later the imperialism and colonialism of the 1800s put foreign lands in direct contact with one another, formalizing curiosity about the customs of other cultures. Formalized in this imperialist context, anthropology classified human individuals and societies along a single evolutionary line, with European physical and cultural traits (not surprisingly) ranked most evolved. Critiquing what he called "armchair" anthropology, Franz Boas, a German-born Jewish immigrant to the United States, assembled the "four fields" (archaeology and physical, linguistic, and sociocultural anthropology) to combat the dominant ideas of racism and xenophobia prevalent at the turn of the twentieth century. While Boas exhorted anthropologists to do fieldwork, this dictum was formalized, in part accidentally, by Bronislaw Malinowski, a Polish immigrant to the United Kingdom. During World War I, as an enemy combatant, Malinowski was sent to the faraway Trobriand Islands (in today's Papua New Guinea) for two years, and later he wrote about his experiences among the people there. These two "patriarchs" formalized anthropology in their adopted home countries: Boasian U.S. anthropology was set on a path toward valuing specificity and "cultural relativism"—trying to understand phenomena within a cultural context—while Malinowskian British anthropology looked for generalizable patterns and formalized "functionalism"—understanding how these cultural traits served to maintain the social order.[7] French anthropology was heavily influenced by the structuralism of Claude Lévi-Strauss, identifying ways in which culture in the minds of people reproduced mental models, including binary oppositions. All three countries had colonial skeletons in the closet, and all three attempted to reinvent themselves during the turbulent upheavals of the 1960s.[8]

An Evolution of Evolution

Anthropological ideas have found their way into popular discussion. For example, social Darwinism, sometimes called survival of the fittest, is used to justify inequality, with the argument that the current social system is a result of genetic or reproductive fitness.[9]

However, a nuanced understanding of evolution argues just the opposite. Just like the moths studied by Charles Darwin at the dawn of the Industrial Revolution, we too as a species are finding ourselves at a similar precipice. White moths had more easily hidden from prey before the soot from London factories turned buildings black and gray. Following, black moths had better cover and thus were more likely to survive. But of course, unlike the moths, the changing conditions that humans have to adapt to are largely of our own making. Foregrounding the role of humans in shaping the environment, some scientists call our geological epoch the "Anthropocene."

If anything, "evolution" teaches us that diversity, flexibility, and adaptiveness to change are keys to our survival. While certain classes, races, and genders of people have decidedly been favored in the global capitalist economic system, it is increasingly evident that our planet is sending loud and violent warnings that this system must change. If humans are to survive, we need to embrace our differences and adapt to the new conditions that we created, to welcome change.

How can we learn to live on this planet we are rapidly using up? In other words, how can we live within our means—our "carrying capacity"? While human beings have demonstrated our capacity for destruction, violence, aggression, marking territory, and massive systems of enslavement, inequality, and ideology justifying the plunder of the world's resources, we have also demonstrated in key moments that we have the capacity for collective solidarity, cooperation, and love—the love of Gandhi, Martin Luther King Jr., Che Guevara, Dean Spade, Stephanie Mott, bell hooks, James Baldwin, Valarie Kaur and Patrick Cheng, not to mention Jesus. As Cornel West and Michael Eric Dyson said, justice is what love looks like in public.[10] Or as Chela Sandoval has argued, love is the methodology of liberation.[11] It is the core of empathy, without which transforming the world will not be possible.

Radical Empathy

Obama's first Supreme Court nominee, Sonia Sotomayor, the first Latina appointed to the bench in May 2009 and only the third woman, raised a ruckus in some circles because of her use of "empathy."[12] Meryl Streep, verbalizing the strain of hope in many, put the word back into mainstream discourse in her Golden Globes acceptance speech in January 2017, less than two weeks before Trump's inauguration. Streep said that actors offer the world lessons in empathy, playing the part of someone else, experiencing what it feels like to be someone who may be different from ourselves.

Anthropology has—in its best moments—always had this same potential, to imagine how people in different cultures live and understand the world, in our promotion of cultural relativism. However, the particular urgency of today's interconnected crises requires more than just suspending judgment. We need to identify the ways in which one's identity categories within a society limit one's choices, seeing how local, lived experiences are intertwined with global, species-level phenomena. As Dána-Ain Davis and others have argued, what's needed now more than ever is not just empathy but radical empathy.[13]

What is radical empathy?

- Being able to see the humanity in people defined as your enemy by for-profit media and a seemingly endless War on Terror.
- Being able to identify with a struggle for justice that does not directly impact the community you care about or identify with connected to your own.
- Understanding that the undocumented, nonbinary gendered, Muslim, or any other person does not exist for people's moral edification or education but that "they" too are "us." That humanity itself is always (already) hyphenated. That no one gets to claim universality based on the fact that history textbooks, evening news programs, Bibles, and entertainment programs reflect a certain norm of a middle-class, patriarchal, white, Christian, suburban household as "human" and that everyone else has to struggle to claim and reclaim the status of "person."
- That we are all queer to someone else.
- That it might just be *our* way of life that is strange, that needs to change.

Radical empathy also means that we each need to be willing to stand up for others caught in the system, being denied health care, or clean water, or the right to worship, or freedom from sexual harassment or assault, or the right to safety when going to the bathroom, or the right to exist because they too are human, and because we need everyone's perspective to survive. Preventing our pending extinction reminds us all of our shared interest.

All this is to say that radical empathy is NOT an abstract, distant, privileged notion of being a "citizen of the world," or what Teju Cole called the "white savior industrial complex," being a do-gooder or a weekend activist.[14] In order to ensure my own survival, the survival of my children, and theirs, and theirs, I need to join in solidarity with marginalized groups engaging in local struggles for liberation. Because whether it is around the corner or around the world, our struggles are against the same inhumanity, only in a particular local form, just as the worldwide economic system based on profit, exploitation, and inequality limits my own humanity in particular ways.

And radical empathy can lift the fog of privilege, helping name and identify specific ways inequalities and systems of oppression are felt differentially, and how they shape everyday life.

Back in the Matrix

My own anthropological imagination began while I was an organizer in the Twin Cities in the late 1990s, including over two years at the now-defunct St. Paul Tenants Union. I saw how people could build solidarity across racial identities and forge a common interest, then work together to benefit all, an element of what C. Wright Mills called a "sociological imagination."[15] I was inspired by and learned from activists—who were what Antonio Gramsci called "organic intellectuals"—working together until we were all laid off, as the money ran out. I didn't know the word "neoliberalism" at the time, but I understood what Tenants Union members, people barely scraping by, knew in their gut: their jobs were being "downsized."[16] Corporations relocating their operations overseas in a "race to the bottom" hollowed out cities in the United States, taking their corporate giving programs with them.

Rather than starting over with another grassroots organization, I decided to go to graduate school to study the impacts of funding on nonprofits (outside the United States, they are called NGOs, nongovernmental organizations).

I have been working in and writing about Haiti since 2001. In Haiti I learned other elements of an anthropological imagination: that we are already connected, that local struggles for justice are merely different aspects of the same fight for equality, for humanity. Importantly, I saw, lived, and breathed the impacts of neoliberalism.

Ever since I returned to Santa Barbara from my dissertation research in 2005, literally in tears in the Costco parking lot because of reverse culture shock, I have referred to the United States as "the Matrix," a virtual reality simulation. Most U.S. Americans don't know where our electricity or food comes from, or our water, nor where it goes. We can get caught up in the latest "binge-worthy" reality TV show or the newest version of the iPhone, while people in Haiti pray for rain to end their two-year drought. For at least the last twenty-seven years since my Haitian colleagues began documenting it, average rainfall there went down every year. Now, every six months or so, flash floods destroy entire crops. In October 2016, Hurricane Matthew was the worst storm to hit Haiti since 1954.[17] Climate change is yet another example of the injustice befalling the people of Haiti, descendants of one of the first movements to affirm that Black lives matter, the Haitian Revolution, which decisively altered the course of Atlantic history.

Living in Haiti clarified a few things for me: In Haiti, you don't have to wonder where your trash goes. You don't have to see how the "other half" lives. The naked realities of global capitalism are all too real, and all too visible. To go to a grocery store or ATM requires armed guards. At first, I tried to buy local and skip the air conditioning. It was all too easy to blame what some called Haiti's "morally repugnant elite" for excluding Haiti's poor majority while letting people like me in.[18] As Gina Athena Ulysse has powerfully argued, quoting Edwidge Danticat, my white skin—and U.S. passport—was my "three-piece suit," invisible to me.[19] More than a three-piece suit, my U.S. passport allows me to not see the guns that guard far more than a supermarket. I literally fly over them. The U.S. military has always been trained on Haiti's poor majority, pouncing on people risking their lives in rickety boats, throwing them into dark, hidden detention centers like Krome, near Miami.

Being a *blan*—which in Haiti means both white person and foreigner—helped me to see the multiple layers of racism operating in Haiti, the difference between being marked as "other" and systematic white privilege. And being a solidarity activist in Haiti has helped me to see issues more clearly: I have come to see Haiti not as an "exceptional" case or somehow beyond the pale, but as an early warning, a canary in the coal mine, since contradictions and inequalities within the capitalist system are easier to see in places like Haiti.

One key similarity among contemporary struggles for justice is the assertion of humanity. The social movement in Haiti that in 1986 ended the U.S.-supported dictatorship asserted boldly, *tout moun se moun.* Everyone is a person. But how can we see these various struggles as directly connected? Having an anthropological imagination brings us closer to a transformative, identity-conscious solidarity politics. When we are forced to be reactive and defensive, struggling to keep up with events, and competing for tweets, airtime, and people's limited attention, or what can be called "compassion fatigue," we lose sight of our common struggles. We need to identify not just humanity, but the specific processes of dehumanization that operate as the seemingly permanent capitalist war machine targets particular groups of people. Human life is worth defending, and we should operate from that assertion. Identifying who is funding the hate, and who stands to benefit when people are pitted against one another, offers a useful counterpart to the ideological work being done by factions that want to facilitate the inhumanity of capitalist economic exchange. Having something to fight *for*, a unifying platform that is not a "big tent" or a "least common denominator" politics, something that can inspire and be easily understood and is harder to malign, has been missing for quite some time, at least in the United States.

Confronting Issues

An anthropological imagination helps us highlight the linkages between various issues, particularly when we consider an expanded timeline. By understanding just how out of step the current capitalist system is with the vast majority of humanity's time on this earth, we can also identify how issues usually confronted individually in the single-issue, whack-a-mole approach to activism are connected to this larger system. Looking at the long view, which we'll cover in the next chapter, helps challenge the grip of what seems "normal," to render the familiar strange and therefore change it.

As chapter 2 argues, current global capitalism was born from plantation slavery and the transatlantic slave trade. Once institutionalized, the cultures supporting African slavery needed an entire cultural apparatus to produce ideology normalizing it: white supremacy. While humans have always sorted people into an "in-group" and "out-group," *race* as we have come to know it was a coproduction of capitalism, solidified by elites to stoke divisions between groups that otherwise might have realized they had issues in common, and to disrupt solidarity within working classes. Successfully dismantling white supremacy requires drawing upon holism, seeing the connections between our political and economic system and the multitude of dehumanizing cultural apparatuses that prop it up. An anthropological imagination helps us value specificity—specific identities and specific sites of struggle—while gesturing toward possible points of intersection and solidarity.

Climate change, discussed in chapter 3, is one of the most urgent issues facing humanity. An anthropological imagination helps us simultaneously identify solutions to the global system and local manifestations of the problem. It is not enough to divest from fossil fuels. We must also support local struggles in places like Standing Rock, North Dakota, where Indigenous communities defended their sacred sites and their right to clean water against construction of the Dakota Access Pipeline. Protesters on the ground knew their struggle was at once global and local, about defending their local sovereignty and also stemming the tide against climate change. The pipeline had investors as well; not surprisingly, they are some of the same investors who profit from injustices in other local sites. Unraveling the larger system starts with concentrated, principled, inspired local action, and seeing how these are connected to the larger struggle. While tugging at the loose thread, we need to examine and address the connections between climate justice and the ways of life we've grown accustomed to or aspire to, given media messages we are fed that encourage consumption. Eventually we'll encounter other groups tugging at the threads of other local injustices, already knotted into a global web of foreign investors and transnational companies gaming the system.

Migration and migrants are increasingly targeted, not only in the United States, but in Europe and other capitalist centers. Several countries are confronting a wave of xenophobic nationalism. Chapter 4 offers an anthropological approach to understanding migration. An anthropological imagination helps us at once value the particularities of each case and defend the rights of people caught in the system at risk of deportation or being killed, whose lives are in the hands of mercenaries, while also at the same time attempting to identify common patterns, exploring the connections between cases, and interrogating and confronting the system that keeps people on the margins. From our species' point of view, this current system of border patrols, international conventions unevenly applied, War on Terror, and racist "populist" reaction does not fit with our propensity for mobility. However, the current system serves many interests: it reinforces borders, defines who has which entitlement to what wealth, and maintains a global economy while simultaneously buttressing inequality. Capitalism is built on upholding the settler colonial fiction of private property. At the same time, our anthropological imagination must also firmly root itself on the real experience of people who are just trying to get by, to humanize those who have been used as scapegoats, to inspire empathy. Each time someone is deported or denied asylum, it is easier for the global capitalist class and the state system they have co-opted to maintain an even tighter system of borders and checkpoints. And each time it happens, human life is devalued. To defend immigrants, refugees, and asylum seekers also requires us to take a hard look at the racism embedded in the global capitalist order.

One strategy to confront specific local injustices triggered or exacerbated by global capitalism is to defend the "public" against further encroachment by private interests. One place to draw the line in the sand, a site for this struggle, is public education, particularly at universities. Chapter 5 discusses the need to dismantle the ivory tower and decolonize knowledge, suggesting potential solutions. The discussion highlights roles universities play in the war machine, targeting and profiling minority identities, and the large shadow of student debt looming over a generation, particularly communities of color. Struggles for justice are always "inside" and "outside." This current moment of all-out war against immigrants, Muslims, African Americans, women and women's bodies, transgender people, the climate, and science itself demands that we build on the town-gown coalition that created radical ethnic studies and opened up spaces for inclusion of more diverse voices.

Humanity's Last Stand asserts and affirms that humanity's urgent contemporary crises can—and must—be solved. Pulling together the strands of the rest of the book, the short concluding chapter offers radical, yet practical, solutions for real-world engagement with activist social movements: creating new venues and media to shift public dialogue, shifting relationships of power, and informing and transforming policy.

This book aims to do for anthropology what C. Wright Mills's (1959) *The Sociological Imagination* did for that discipline. Mills's masterwork reinvigorated the field, readying sociologists for engagement with the civil rights movement and quagmire regarding the U.S. engagement in the Vietnam War. It also was useful as a text for social movements in their consciousness-raising exercises.

Unfortunately for the future of our species, we have little time to lose and *need* to act now; we need to first be able to articulate what we are fighting for. Truly this is humanity's last stand: we can let the endless growth machine and its accompanying systems of oppressions choke the planet and kill one another, or we can rise up to support locally waged struggles for justice linked with defending humanity. We need an anthropolitics more than ever.

I literally couldn't write this book fast enough. No sooner did I finish a draft of a chapter on migration than another, more terrifying twist came. After I finished a discussion of dismantling the ivory tower and decolonizing anthropology, a scandal rocked the field. When the final text went to press in March 2020, COVID-19, the disease caused by the novel coronavirus, had four days before just been declared a "pandemic," and whole cities and even countries had been placed on lockdown. By the time of publication, events discussed in this book will likely already be taught as history—if at all. Centuries from now—if we survive, that is—researchers will point to the actions of our generation as pivotal.

I also couldn't possibly be exhaustive: new issues present themselves every day. New activist collectives are coming together to unravel this centuries-old system of oppression that is tightening its grip. A fully actualized and engaged anthropological imagination can address head-on humanity's urgent contemporary crises and lay the groundwork of radical empathy and solidarity we need to face the issues of tomorrow.

We have our work to do. I hope that this book plays some small role in bringing these issues to the forefront, exploring connections, and raising people's conscience. The first step to creating a better world is to imagine it.

1

Structuring Solidarity

Uncovering Our Connections

> If you've come to help me, you're
> wasting your time. But if you've come
> because your liberation is bound up
> with mine, then let us work together.

Australian Aboriginal activist Lilla Watson is credited with expressing this core tenet of solidarity, although she prefers to share authorship with her community. Martin Luther King Jr.'s "Letter from a Birmingham Jail" expresses a similar thought: "Injustice anywhere is a threat to justice everywhere."[1] Similar expressions of Oneness abound across many faith traditions: Quakers hold that "there is that of God in all persons." Rastafari cosmology (how the world works) sees "I in I"—myself within others. This interconnectedness is also expressed in the Lakota *Mitakuye Oyasin*, translated as "we are all related" or "all my relations." Without this basic understanding, a central aspect of an anthropological imagination, even well-intentioned efforts by allies tend toward saviorism. In addition, without seeing the interconnectedness of the various struggles for justice, seeing the underlying root causes of oppression, we will always fall short of liberation, of defending our humanity. An essential component to an anthropological imagination is holism, seeing how these issues are connected.

To take seriously the urgent threats facing humanity, to survive within our means, and to stop building walls and killing each other as resources like fresh water dry up, we need to be able to imagine alternative ways of organizing human society. First, we need to directly confront how we as a species ended up here. Could we have done otherwise? An anthropological imagination, particularly an anthropological timeline, zooming out to our earliest hominid (human-like) ancestors, throws into stark relief just how different things currently are, and also that our most destructive behaviors are, in species terms, very recently acquired. For-profit media and politicians often fear monger, limiting our imaginations—as Margaret Thatcher, former U.K. prime minister, famously said, "there is no alternative" to neoliberal capitalism. However, an anthropological timeline illuminates an abundance of alternatives, focusing in on just how out of step our current system is to our experience as a species.

Global Capitalism

What *is* this system?

As is usually taught, capitalism is an economic system. Adam Smith is credited as its primary architect, in *Wealth of Nations*, published in 1776, the same year that rebellious white colonists declared independence from England. The cornerstone of capitalism is capital, wealth as investment. It is a system of production based on market exchange: in addition to depending on a currency to establish a common way to value commodities, labor is also a market exchange—as a worker, I sell my labor power, for which my boss pays me. What distinguishes capitalism from its predecessor mercantilism is the belief in free exchange. No one can compel me to work; instead I receive wages for my labor. What Smith called the "invisible hand" of the marketplace—competition—establishes fair prices for commodities and labor, and as such competition should be unfettered from government interference. In theory.

Even the most cursory glance at capitalism as practiced today shows that the system does not practice what its bible preaches. Governments intervene all the time, subsidizing certain industries, protecting and supporting them, establishing borders, policing who (or what) can enter a country. And left to its own devices, capitalism tends to evolve away from competition, where many companies vie for your business, into monopolies, where one or two giant companies absorb the rest and control the market. Rather than services or companies being owned by the state, the capitalist elites who run these companies in many real ways have come to own the state. The 1873 U.S. Supreme Court *Slaughter-House Cases* gave corporations the status of "persons," and they gained citizenship rights granted to formerly enslaved people under the Fourteenth Amendment. These Fourteenth Amendment rights were solidified in the 2010 *Citizens United v. FEC* decision: faceless corporations now have an unlimited ability to support candidates for office. And they do. Government officials who are bought know whom they have to pay back. In addition to billions of dollars in direct government support, corporations score perks such as lower taxes, endless loopholes around other laws, decreased regulation, protection from foreign competition, and the unfettered ability to create tax havens and park their capital overseas.

In other words, capitalism is rigged.

It's also a *global* system. The benefits that corporations gain in one country allow them to extend their reach across borders and affect the economies and politics of other countries as well in order to suppress the power of others and consolidate their own wealth. It's always been that way. In his 1938 Oxford dissertation in economics, Trinidadian independence leader and first prime minister Eric Williams detailed the many ways in which the capitalist economy, the much-vaunted British Industrial Revolution, depended on slave labor in the Caribbean.[2] Anthropologist Sidney Mintz, who also worked in the Caribbean, assembled historical and ethnographic data to go further: not only was the Caribbean the birthplace of global capitalism, enslaved laborers were "proletarian" in Marxist terms—working class.[3] This is to say that, also from the beginning, capitalism and racism have always been intertwined. Not only does this bring Black peoples to the center from the margins of history, it offers important inspiration for solidarity politics. Seeing the intricate connections between capitalism and white supremacy is one example of holism.

Connecting the Dots: Holism

An anthropological imagination helps us see that global capitalism is not just an economic system; it is also a political system and a moral system. It shapes gender roles and inequalities and fashions our understanding of differences, sorting people into different categories that we can call "race" or "culture"—or even "terrorist" when the need arises. Particularly urgent manifestations of this system are global climate change, increasing xenophobia against migrants, and state-sanctioned white supremacy and violence.

Understanding how these issues are connected involves a reboot of what is often described as a hallmark of anthropology: holism. How does our economic system relate to our system of kinship, our family structure, or our religion, for example? How does our patriarchal society shape our view of science, of technology, of how the world works, or how society does—or should? The idea of holism was first trotted out via old-school "functionalist" thinking—that cultural systems have an internal logic and that even the most remote and seemingly disconnected aspect of society exists to fulfill a purpose. In the hands of white apologists for colonialism, this idea was dangerously conservative, justification for the status quo.

But in the service of humanity's liberation, understanding the interconnectedness of our systems of inequality, our gender identity formation, our ideas of "race," our family structures, and our religious beliefs and practices can be essential to unmasking the inhumanity of our global economic system, and show how contemporary neoliberal capitalism influences our daily life. The field of cultural studies has taken the colonial, conservative elements out of holism, studying the cultural dimensions of neoliberalism, the ways in which postindustrial society ruptures traditional gender norms, or the ways in which descendants of slaves face a "social death."[4] Karl Polanyi warned against the social ruptures triggered by the market economy: relationships become transactional, reduced to understandings of the current "exchange value" of what we have to offer, when everything, including the human body, is reduced to the status of a commodity.[5]

One such example of the interrelation between economy and society is that the Industrial Revolution created the so-called nuclear family, divorcing the units of production from consumption. Family farms needed the labor of all members to make a living. But once crowded into cities, children became more of an expense than an asset. So, culturally, families became smaller and (white) women's labor was often reduced to unremunerated "household chores," though care work and other labor were often performed by women of color and/or immigrants (and still are, often for less than minimum wage).[6]

Karl Marx's comrade, coauthor, and benefactor Friedrich Engels argued that private property solidified men's domination over women.[7] For the 99 percent of human history before agriculture, when we were foragers (gatherers, hunters, and fishers), labor was organized along gender lines, but it appears that this role specialization did not automatically spell out inequality and patriarchy. As Karen Sacks (Brodkin) pointed out, the foraging of women and children often contributed more calories to the family diet than the men out hunting.[8] Researchers among the !Kung San (sometimes called the Dobe Ju'Hoasi), in the Kalahari Desert—the people who inspired the problematic movie *The Gods Must Be Crazy*—calculated that on average families spent twenty hours a week on subsistence, a point corrected by feminists like Sally Slocum as reflecting androcentric (male-centered) bias, notably leaving out women's labor in social reproduction (raising families and household chores).[9] Ignoring colonialism's role in penning up these contemporary "bushmen," and certainly the racial under- and overtones, some use these studies as models for how humanity lived before.

Early Marxist thinking was replete with full-throttle defenses of a simplistic ideology of liberation—that once the means of production were in the hands of laborers themselves, other social inequalities would wither away. These single-issue theorists claimed that working classes would see instantly that it was in their interest to identify with other workers and not the capitalist classes who also controlled the media and the state, and that revolution would lift the fog of capitalist ideology. The fact that the world socialist revolution has not yet taken place has been used as evidence of the failure, or at the very least the naïveté, of what Marxist thinkers dismiss as a simplistic, mechanistic "vulgar materialism."[10]

Later thinkers clarified and nuanced their critique of capitalism: Max Weber called into question the structure of power itself, how bureaucratic rationality gets in the way of human liberation, and also how people live in and understand what he called "status groups" or "subjective" classes. What is a "middle class"? Why is it so powerful that both major political parties in the United States appeal to its constituency? In strict Marxist terms this is just ideology: one is either a worker or a boss, who either sells one's labor power or owns the means of production. Marxist historian Howard Zinn called this imagined middle class "guards of the system" granted small rewards to identify with those in power.[11]

The limits of a single-issue Marxism are even more clearly identifiable when understanding race or gender. Marxists often argue that racism is a tool of the dominant class to discourage cross-racial worker identification and solidarity. While this is most definitely true, it also glosses over the very real racism and violence that even leaders within trade unions meted out on people of color to keep their own relative share of the spoils of their labor to themselves and exclude newcomers, be they Black, Latinx, or Chinese, from entry.

Holistic thinking also makes capitalism's gender inequality visible. The concept of the "family wage" assumes a patriarchal structure, wherein a male patriarch, a Fred Flintstone or George Jetson, provides for "his" family, including "Jane, his wife." The ideology of these 1960s cartoons is effective in its seeming innocence: it doesn't seem like cultural programming. However, the message is clear: the white, patriarchal family unit always has been and always will be. Not a product of historical accident.[12] Not a product of racist policies of exclusion from FHA loans and the GI Bill. Not a deliberate strategy to get women "back into the home" after they, like Rosie the Riveter, successfully staffed "heavy industry" ("man's work" like construction or manufacturing, unlike much lower paid "unskilled" labor requiring "nimble fingers" like operating sewing machines) to back up "our boys" on the front lines in Europe and the Pacific during World War II.[13] Currently women in the United States earn 79 cents to a man's dollar, though that varies across the states: average women's salaries are 90 percent of men's in Washington, D.C., and 65 percent in Louisiana. This inequality is even more pronounced for women of color: Black women receive 63 cents per the dollar of a white non-Hispanic male overall, 48 cents in Louisiana.[14] "Hispanic" or Latina women fared worse: 54 cents to the dollar.[15]

Anthropology offers a challenge to abstract, top-down, single-issue theorizing. World systems theory accounts for how disparate struggles are connected to the larger picture: they are manifestations of global capitalism. More difficult is how to start with people's actual, lived experience, how people understand their situations, and how they confront these systems of inequality. The specificities of particular localities, identities, and conflicts do in fact matter.

Being able to analyze holistically and centering local realities and lived experience are useful when working *with* and not *around* people, for us to identify from our own perspective what common cause we may have with someone halfway around the world or across the tracks. It can help us connect the dots between three seemingly disparate contemporary human crises: global climate change, rising anti-immigrant xenophobia, and white supremacy. To see these issues as connected, using a holistic lens, it helps to look into our human history.

An Anthropological Timeline

As a discipline that studies human physical and cultural remains, from ancient ancestors to modern humans, anthropology expands what counts as "history." This anthropological timeline helps us see that corporate culture is not the only way society can be organized. We need to draw on this deeper look into the human past to learn how to manage the increasingly evident limits on our natural resources. One lesson in sustainability can come from how human beings survived for 99 percent of our history. Foraging people are often called hunter-gatherers, though women's "gathering" contributed 70 percent of human diets.[16] Human beings adapted and thrived not because of our propensity for competition and violence but because of our cooperation: until very recently, we had evolved into egalitarian beings.[17]

All written history was made possible by the invention of written language, more than four and a half millennia ago. Along with agriculture, this technological leap led to social complexity, an archaeological term for economic specialization and systems of inequality, including hierarchies such as classes or castes of people. Archaeologists debate the rise—and the impetus—of the State, a permanent bureaucracy with territorial control backed by use of force recognized as legitimate. They often assume that a progression of early societies toward accumulation and complexity resulted in a cultural evolution toward states. James Scott, who later published a treatise extolling the virtues of anarchism, questions this value system, arguing that some people might have deliberately run away from the control of a centralized state.[18] Other archaeologists have cautioned against a present-day economic rendering of the motivations behind early state formation.[19] Interestingly these separate state formations occurred roughly around the same time. If we take the stereotypical start of U.S. history as the arrival of the *Mayflower* in 1620, which conveniently skips over more than a hundred years of sugar plantations in the Caribbean and colonies in Spanish-controlled Florida, not to mention the first slave ship to the British colonies a year earlier in Jamestown, Virginia, the transition to agriculture is thirty times as long: if we think of U.S. history as a day, with each generation being roughly equivalent to an hour, this leap into agriculture was a month ago.

Hominids have been around for quite a bit longer than agriculture. New discoveries continue to be made that revise the anthropological timeline, causing scientists to revise our ideas to fit new discoveries. However, using this same time scale of a human generation being an hour long, and four hundred years of U.S. history being a day, the first known hominid for which we have a full skeleton, "Ardi," was walking the savannas in Ethiopia over thirty years ago (4.4 million Earth years).[20] Using this compressed timeline with the *Mayflower* landing a day ago, the recently discovered remains of the first modern human were of a person who lived in present-day Morocco just over two years ago (300,000 Earth years).[21]

It was by no means a foregone conclusion that humans would end up the dominant species on Earth. We had to respond to our environment, to predators, to changes in weather patterns, to natural disasters, and, yes, to each other. We amassed knowledge about survival and also asked questions about where we came from, why, and how to live the "good life"—and what that means in the first place. We created stories, art, language, music, and dance in our free time, and used this creativity to teach the next generation. Until a time machine is ever invented, we will only ever see rare glimpses of these past human lives in the sherds of pottery, stone tools, dwelling spaces, and fragments of human/animal bones. However, since humans began writing things down only in the last couple weeks using this anthropological timeline, we have been very good at telling stories, passing down the heritage of as much human knowledge gained as possible. We gained the abilities to domesticate animals, to shelter ourselves, to tame fire, to cure wounds, to find new sources of water and food. Seeking these necessities, we have walked all corners of the earth.

An anthropological timeline highlights just how recently certain things that we've come to take for granted have become part of the human experience: if right now is midnight in this scale, World War II began just before 8 P.M. The automobile, 6 P.M. The internet, only a little before 11 P.M. The printing press was yesterday afternoon (at least the machine recognized from

Europe . . . in China, woodblocks were first used in 220 CE, or four and a half days ago). Written language itself was only a little more than eleven days ago.

This compressed scale also highlights just how odd this last "day" has been. Global population was relatively stable, around one million, until the Neolithic Revolution, a month ago in this scale. Then it saw a slow rise and again relative stability at 5 million, gradually going up to 7.5 million at 6500 BCE, 12.5 million at 5000 BCE, and 14 million people at 3000 BCE, when Egyptians began a system of writing. The global population rose a little more steadily, to 285 million people, during the time of Jesus Christ and Julius Caesar. Population stagnated as diseases began to spread, like the bubonic plague in Europe and Asia. Estimates of the number of people living in what we now call the Americas in 1492 vary dramatically, from 8 to 112 million. By 1500, the world population was still just over 400 million, rising slowly but steadily. Around 1804, the year Haiti won its independence, the world's population first reached a billion. Then the pace sped up, particularly in the second half of the twentieth century, to a billion new people every twelve years. So to go back to humankind's thirty-year life, the population remained steady until last month, and increased only slowly until today, and exploded this afternoon. What is happening, and why does it matter?

If it isn't already obvious, it is this last bit of our human history that is odd and unsustainable.

So what happened to humanity? And what's the cure? The year 1492 was pivotal; the Spanish Inquisition finally and violently drove out the last of the Muslims from the peninsular nation with the fall of Grenada. It was also the year that King Ferdinand of Spain ordered all Jews out of the country. Triumphant, the Spanish Crown financed the voyage of "discovery" of a Genoan merchant, Christopher Columbus, later that year.

Columbus never set foot on U.S. shores; his ship the *Santa María* was shipwrecked off the coast of present-day Haiti. His presence there triggered the genocide and decimation of the local Indigenous population. Spanish monk Bartolomé de las Casas was so horrified by this Spanish brutality that he petitioned the Crown to stop their abuse of Indigenous people, publishing a couple of books admonishing Spain to enslave Africans instead.[22] Columbus became the viceroy of the Spanish colony of Santo Domingo, renaming the island Hispaniola. Columbus himself was the first to bring enslaved African people to what he called the New World, in 1502, ten years after his first famed voyage. The Catholic Church blessed this "discovery," granting Spain the western portion and Portugal the eastern portion of Hispaniola in a papal bull in 1493, nullifying any rights the local Indigenous peoples had to their land.

The Spanish, at least initially, were primarily interested in gold, not settlements, conquering lands from one end of the hemisphere to the other. French pirates, traders in rawhide, known in the French as *boucaniers* (buccaneers), squatted on the western portion of Hispaniola. With the 1697 Treaty of Ryswick, the French officially took over the territory. Once it officially became a colony of France, the French had different ambitions: they were interested in sugar. Feeding the European desire for sugar, the French, and later the British and other colonial powers, built an institution so brutal that humanity is still reverberating from it today. Fifteen *million* African people were shipped to the Caribbean, to Brazil, and to the U.S. South, not as people but as chattel, real estate. The horrors of the Middle Passage were unimaginable. Fortunately for history's sake some lived to talk about it, like Olaudah Equiano, whose story was retold by Alex Haley and Marcus Rediker, among others.[23] People were packed in ship holds like cattle, chained to one another, stacked on top of one another in wooden "beds," being thrown food and water, unable to leave to vomit or defecate, forced to breathe this stale air. Some committed suicide as an act of resistance. These horrors continued on the sugar plantations, where planters invented all kinds of torture in an attempt to scare slaves into submission. They were so brutal that the French government intervened in the Code Noir of 1685 to delimit precisely the number of lashes an enslaved person could be whipped for particular "offenses." In their cold, capitalist calculation, plantation owners saw that it was cheaper to literally work their slaves to death (the average life expectancy was seven years) than to allow them to live long enough to have children, euphemized as "natural increase."[24]

The colonial planters were often shunned by their more noble peers in metropolitan France and Britain. But the rising bourgeoisie, which eventually revolted against the monarchy, was entirely dependent on slavery and the enormous profits made by it.[25] Financial institutions still around today, like Aetna, MetLife, Lehman Brothers, Wachovia (now Wells Fargo), JPMorgan Chase, and Lloyd's of London made the equivalent of trillions of dollars in today's economy buying and selling the human lives reduced to the status of property, and then insuring the "investment." Following the first-ever U.S. congressional hearing about reparations in June 2019, estimates of their profits ranged from 17 to 51 trillion dollars.[26] Britain's

Industrial Revolution was fed by cotton produced in the U.S. South, and therefore slavery.[27]

Where was the Church in all this? While the Catholic hierarchy was moved to a more "moderate" stance regarding European treatment of Indigenous peoples, it was solidly behind the institution of African chattel slavery. Some invoked a biblical passage about the Children of Ham, burned black because of his sins; others argued that Africans were counterfeits put on Earth by Satan, mocking God's achievement of mankind. Eventually, the Church conceded that Africans are human, but better they were enslaved and Christian, saving their eternal souls, than allowed to live "childlike" and "savage." This was decreed in 1452 with the *Dum Diversas*, the pope's seal of approval on slavery, reaffirmed and detailed three years later in another bull, *Romanus Pontifex*. The demonization of Black culture had begun. This dehumanization was also locked in our brains through use of language: Following this fateful collision of continents, the Spanish word for "black"—*negro*—was first used to describe African-descended people. And the negative connotations of the word "black" as evil or bad multiplied. Eventually this system of capitalism permeated nearly the entirety of the world's peoples and lands through colonialism. Until 1492, Europe wasn't actually the predominant region in the world. As the story goes, Columbus was looking for a shorter voyage to Asia, "naming" the people he encountered in the Caribbean "Indians."

The Spanish Inquisition was fueled by collective anxiety about Muslims. The Crusades, the various waves of European pilgrims and soldiers sent to the "Holy Land" to "rescue" Jerusalem, exposed to Europeans that they were actually behind in science, mathematics, technology, and literature. However, Europeans did transform technologies Marco Polo brought back from his trading visits to China into weaponry. This transformation, combined with collective will and religious zeal, turned Europeans deadly and genocidal. Colonialism required both Bible and sword, and not a small dose of white supremacy. Three entire continents were declared *terra nullius*— empty land. It was Europeans' God-given right, their "Manifest Destiny," to take the "unoccupied" land as theirs, in the system of private property codified in the legal system and backed up by the force of law.

The focus of much of this early competition was the Caribbean. While it might be hard to imagine why the Dutch would prefer Suriname to New York City in today's economy, it speaks volumes about the importance of sugar—and the system of slavery employed to produce it—to the Western

European rivals at that time. The Haitian Revolution, completed in 1804, shifted the balance of power in the New World. People who had been enslaved had succeeded in securing their freedom, forging an independent nation in a sea of slavery. Faced with the prospect of losing Haiti, the "Pearl of the Antilles," France all but gave the middle third of what is now the United States to Thomas Jefferson's emissary, who later laid out the United States' imperialist goals in the 1823 Monroe Doctrine. The 1803 Louisiana Purchase turned the United States from a fledgling seaside nation, threatened by reinvasion from the British, into what was to become the world's superpower. Two things in the way of the ambition of stretching "from sea to shining sea" were an independent Mexico (which had incidentally abolished slavery) and the country's Indigenous peoples, driven off their land by a string of broken promises and savage, racist wars of extermination.

The Haitian Revolution also tipped the balance of British opinion in favor of abolition. Three years after the first free Black republic in the Americas was founded, the British formally abolished the slave trade. This had three major impacts: First, slaveholding planters from Virginia (like eight U.S. presidents) became wealthier by selling enslaved people to the remaining Caribbean colonies, whose plantations still needed labor. Second, Spanish colonies were increasingly turning to sugar production and African slavery. Third, the British found a new coerced labor source after formal emancipation of the peoples they enslaved. A private company, given the blessing of the British Crown, played ever greater roles in territorial governance in the Caribbean. The British East India Company teamed up with the British "West India" Company to bring hundreds of thousands of indentured servants to Jamaica, Trinidad and Tobago, Guyana, and other sugar colonies. The East India Company had perfected the British system of "indirect rule," gradually and systematically rendering India, one of the world's oldest and largest civilizations, dependent on the British economy.

The British, Belgians, Dutch, French, and Portuguese also competed with each other in a competition over Africa (except for Ethiopia, never colonized, and Liberia, settled by former slaves from the United States) and the rest of southern Asia (China and Japan, also empires, were not conquered and did not welcome contact with other nations). As Guyanese historian and political activist Walter Rodney detailed in *How Europe Underdeveloped Africa*, this land scramble changed the course of Africa in the world forever, first through the theft of people in the slave trade, followed by the plunder of natural resources and the systematic destruction of local industries such as textiles.[28] The point of creating colonies is and has always been to bring wealth to the metropole, by any means necessary. The German government, shut out of Africa, hosted a European conference in 1884–5 to formalize land titles and get a piece of the pie for themselves. Frustrated at their continued exclusion, they made an alliance with the Ottoman Empire and started World War I, the War to End All Wars. By focusing on the trigger that started the war, Archduke Ferdinand's assassination, we miss the underlying point of the war: World War I was really a struggle for dominance in colonizing the world's resources. The "Allies"—certainly Great Britain—won the rights to the world's petroleum resources, since the Ottoman Empire, the only Muslim caliphate (led by religious leaders, heirs to Muhammad), had been broken up and was being administered by the British. The colonizers drew up artificial boundaries that left some peoples, such as the Kurds, without a state and set up systems of divide and conquer that masked a strategy of "indirect rule" in places like Palestine, where Muslims and Jews (and Christians) had been peacefully coexisting, and, finally, they set time bombs by grouping warring parties in the same colonial state such as in Rwanda.

Soldiers in World War I saw their shared connections with one another. White soldiers sang a German/English version of "Silent Night" on Christmas Eve 1914, the first year of fighting, as they laid down their arms. Colonized people often found themselves on the front lines, and people who looked like them on the other side. The war radicalized many, causing them to see that they had more in common with one another than with their colonizers, and that they were fighting the wrong enemy—they were not "British" or "French" as their minds had been colonized into believing.

While declaring itself "isolationist," the United States began a colonizing process of its own, wresting colonies from Spain during the 1898 Spanish-American War. Cuba, Puerto Rico, Panama, and the Philippines were among the spoils in this rout. From the earlier Monroe Doctrine came the Roosevelt Corollary: we will invade nations that get in the way of what we declare to be our national interest. The Panama Canal, under U.S. direction, was a boon for shipping, completing Columbus's goal of a global sea route. With Europe's attention on war, the United States invaded Haiti in 1915, followed the next year by the Dominican Republic. Campaigning for vice president in 1920, Franklin Delano Roosevelt bragged about writing Haiti's constitution.

The death toll from World War I was horrifying: between 8.5 and almost 11 million military deaths, 2.25 million civilian deaths from fighting and 6 million from disease, along with 23 million wounded soldiers. Over half a million of the military deaths were soldiers from colonies in Africa and Asia. Bombed-out cities and towns full of shrapnel and dead bodies across the world were in desperate need of reconstruction. Relatively unscathed, the United States pulled back from international affairs, and its unbridled market capitalism spelled out a massive round of consumerism and speculation across the globe. The predictable crash as this reckless, unfettered, unsustainable capitalist consumption reached its limit in 1929 triggered a downward spiral all over the world, including the U.S. Great Depression. Particularly hard hit because of the terms of the armistice after the war, Germany experienced massive unemployment and hyperinflation. Also hard hit were the colonies in Africa, the Caribbean, and Asia as each empire consolidated their resources to rebuild the imperial centers.

Meanwhile, Vladimir Lenin, an exiled lawyer, led a revolution to topple one of Europe's last remaining functional monarchies. Few besides Lenin had considered Russia, a vast nation of mostly peasant farmers, a particularly fertile ground for Marxist ideas, focusing instead on an urban proletariat, the working class. But in October 1917, following the overthrow of the czar earlier that year, a small band of trade unionists seized the moment and took over the legislature. The Soviet Union was born five years later. For their part, many societies in Western Europe gravitated toward democratic socialism. The ideas of British economist John Maynard Keynes took firm root: he thought that raising the floor of how people, at least in the imperial centers, should live would trigger economic growth through spending, government investment, and rising living standards for the working class. In the United States, comfortably wealthy FDR applied Keynesian economics in what he termed the "New Deal."

One country decidedly did not go socialist following the war. With their currency all but worthless, Germans were going hungry, joblessness endemic. With the working class downtrodden, a socialist revolt could have been imagined, as Marx professed. However, it didn't happen that way. Feeding off the hopelessness felt by the German population after the war, and the fear of non-Christians, gays, Roma, and other outsiders, Adolph Hitler, a fiery orator, fanned the flames of hatred. His solution to "Make Germany Great Again" was to scapegoat those who were different. His nationalist vision didn't include gay men or lesbians, "Gypsies," communists, or Jews. Adolf Hitler's hate speech and his single-minded determination for domination and revenge knew no bounds and few parallels. Emboldened and empowered, German bigots turned their fears into violence. Gradually and systematically, Hitler's anti-Semitism, based on a belief in "Aryan" superiority, turned into the "Final Solution," with the internment and mass genocide of six million Jewish people and five million others. Hitler's overcompensating, hypermasculine, racist aggression pulled the European continent and countries all over the world into the Second World War, more devastating than the First: sixty million people perished, two-thirds of whom were civilians. Twenty-five million people were stateless, refugees. This is often described as the world's deadliest war, but this discounts the mass extermination of Indigenous peoples by Europeans in their conquest of the Americas.

Vowing never again, the "Allies" planned for a new world order. While the troop front lines—disproportionately people of color, colonized, and/ or working class—were being killed by the tens of thousands as they advanced through France, the world elites met at the exclusive Bretton Woods resort in the United States, setting up institutions such as the World Bank and International Monetary Fund (IMF). "Development" became the word of the times, based on a familiar evolutionary ranking of societies. Older and more obviously racist terms such as "savage" and "barbarian" were now replaced by "underdeveloped."[29] European society was still imagined as the ideal, and European nations cast as benign father figures, teaching the rest of the world how to "catch up." One difference between colonialism and the postwar period though was that the United States fully stepped into its role as world superpower. And Europe, even more devastated by the Second World War than the First, abandoned the people in its colonies in Asia and Africa, even while they tried to maintain control. Mahatma Gandhi, trained as a lawyer and colonial administrator in Kenya, saw another way forward in his native India. *Hind Swaraj*, home rule, promoted the revival of Indian textiles, starving British colonialism's rent seeking. This, combined with an organized campaign of nonviolent civil disobedience, took their country—Britain's crown jewel—back in 1947. Formal decolonization had begun all over the world. People in Algeria took up arms against France. From 1956 to 1966, thirty-six African nations became independent. Within three years, from 1959 to 1962, the British let go of their colonies in the Caribbean. Sending in troops, France battled to keep Indochina

(Cambodia, Laos, and Vietnam), and eventually the United States took over the fight in the Vietnam War, by conflating the older anticolonial struggle with the newer Cold War fight against communism.

Meanwhile, in the United States, white supremacy was still prevalent. The contradictions between the ideals expressed in the Declaration of Independence and the realities of slavery proved too much for the country to bear. Abraham Lincoln, elected in 1860, took office to a reduced nation. Thirteen slaveholding states, defending "states' rights" (the right to continue slavery), seceded from the Union, thus beginning the bloody American Civil War. Lincoln, who initially wrote that he would have preferred keeping the Union together without freeing a single slave, promised just this in the 1863 Emancipation Proclamation: those slaves *residing in a rebel state* would be free. Northern generals had up until this point been losing, so there was no enforcement ability, and everyone knew it. As a rhetorical gesture, however, it was good foreign policy: Britain, which had sanctimoniously abolished slavery a generation earlier, was forced to side with the northern industrialists, and thousands of people escaped plantations to enlist in the Union Army, willing to die for the chance to end slavery. Thus, the tide turned. One of the terms of General Robert E. Lee's surrender to Ulysses S. Grant was the promise that formerly enslaved laborers would receive forty acres and a mule. Another was that Union troops would be enforcing Reconstruction. Before the rebel states rejoined the Union, the Thirteenth and Fourteenth amendments to the Constitution were ratified. The Thirteenth ended slavery, *except as having been duly convicted of a crime.* The Fourteenth granted citizenship rights to the formerly enslaved. During Reconstruction, public schools were built to educate people who endured slavery for the first time. As African Americans began voting, some also ran for office, like Senator Hiram Revels from Mississippi. Following a contested election in 1876, wherein the Electoral College victor lost the popular vote, southern Democrats negotiated the end of Reconstruction. Segregation was made legal in the 1896 U.S. Supreme Court case *Plessy v. Ferguson.* "Separate but equal" became the law of the land.

The violent reaction to Reconstruction, the Jim Crow period, began. White supremacy's enforcement army included the Ku Klux Klan. Their prime weapon was lynching, a spectacle to terrorize African Americans into knowing their place and to build community ties among whites, drawing the working class into solidarity with the ruling class. A battery of laws aimed at restricting the right to vote provided legal cover and a framework for white supremacy's dehumanization and terrorism of African Americans. Seizing an opportunity for cheap labor provided by this terrorism, northern industrialists and even Black-owned newspapers urged southern Black workers to move to cities like Chicago, Detroit, Cleveland, and New York in what was later called the Great Migration. Capitalists exploited the new mass of African American workers, driving wages down and stoking divisions within the working class along racial lines.

White socialists like Eugene V. Debs, who won 6 percent of the vote in the 1912 presidential election, could have played a unifying role. Unions were becoming stronger since the 1886 Haymarket protest in Chicago on May 1—now recognized outside of the United States and Canada as Labor Day—when they won some important gains such as a minimum wage, age restrictions aimed at curbing child workers, and a weekend. Were it not for their own unacknowledged racism, white trade union leaders could have built a movement that might have unified the working class and also addressed head-on capitalism's racial dimensions, the aftershocks of slavery. Instead, African Americans were left on their own to end the legal segregation of "separate but equal" within the framework of liberal constitutional democracy based on other inequalities.

African American communities built organizations such as the National Association for the Advancement of Colored People (NAACP), founded in 1909. The NAACP began working to systematically chip away at segregation's legal foundations. Dean of historically Black Howard University's School of Law, Charles Houston, led a series of lawsuits, and at his passing, Thurgood Marshall carried the torch, leading up to the Supreme Court's 1954 *Brown v. Board of Education* ruling, striking down public school segregation. The Little Rock NAACP chapter recruited nine brave young souls to enforce desegregation in 1957; they endured people spitting at them, threats of violence, and constant surveillance just to attend school.

The United States had its own internal version of "development" following World War II, including the creation of suburbia and the "middle class." Victorious (white) GIs were granted access to a free college education and a subsidized mortgage through the Federal Housing Administration (FHA). Within a generation, the percentage of U.S. families who owned their homes doubled. Suburbs began to sprawl as people like my parents sought better educational opportunities for their children, because unlike going to war or building the new interstate highway system, the federal government has nothing to do with paying for public schools. This had always been done by local school districts, largely through property taxes. Faced with this federally subsidized "white flight," inner cities, with disproportionately higher percentages of people of color, saw a decline in their property values, tax base, and therefore educational opportunities. Had the GI Bill and FHA loans benefited Black, Latinx, and Native American soldiers who also fought in the war—and not coincidentally in units closer to the front lines with higher casualties—the middle class and suburbs would have been a diverse group, and the urban core would not have suffered such a dramatic blow. Regardless, with the rest of the world rebuilding after World War II as well, or rapidly decolonizing, the U.S. economy experienced a rising tide of growth that lifted all boats, albeit definitely some much higher than others.

This changed as global capitalist strategies shifted in the 1980s, especially with formal decolonization. Business owners saw new opportunities to invest overseas. Regulations were much looser, and either there was no urban proletariat, or they were prevented from organizing. The newly independent states' debt obligations were high, as colonial investments turned into loans. Many former colonies discovered that their natural resources had already been plundered.

Minimum wages in the United States are as much as forty times greater than in places like Mexico, Haiti, Jamaica, India, China, or the Philippines, so profit-seeking companies left the United States for cheaper labor markets elsewhere. With some of the white working class going to college and moving to the suburbs, communities of color left in the inner cities were devastated by the deindustrialization that followed. Growing up in a first-ring suburb of one of the largest Rust Belt cities, I was told to fear Chicago and its residents because of the social issues brought by endemic unemployment.

During the Cold War, the United States and its allies put some funds into Third World (nonaligned in the Cold War, a term that has since come to mean lower than poor) countries in an effort to win new allies and prevent the massive poverty and hopelessness that are fertile grounds for communist or socialist revolutions. Trillions of dollars were spent on "development." But with the fall of the Berlin Wall in 1989, and the end of the Soviet Union two years later, all bets were off. Triumphant, capitalism was presented as the only game in town, emblematized by Thatcher's quote at the beginning of this chapter: "There is no alternative."

"Globalization" became the name of the game. University of Chicago economist Milton Friedman had at this point trained dozens of "Chicago Boys" and placed them in international institutions such as the World Bank and IMF, or they returned to run their own country's ministries of finance or economy. Friedman's economic revolution was aimed at purifying capitalism from government interference, from Keynesian or "New Deal" social welfare. This new form of capitalism, called neoliberalism, was field tested following a CIA-backed coup in Chile on September 11, 1973. IMF technocrats believed that only military dictatorships would be able to impose the necessary "shock therapy" to people who had grown accustomed to benefits like pensions, minimum wages, basic social safety nets, and so on. U.S. foreign policy in Latin America was a perfect test case for this economic warfare on the world's working classes. The World Bank and IMF, which controlled the debt of these Latin American countries, seized these opportunities for cutting services as cost-saving measures. But the "softer" form of capitalism, development, had to be capitalism's public face. President George H. W. Bush ran on a platform of making the United States a "kinder, gentler nation." However, once the Berlin Wall and the Soviet Union fell, he began talking about a "new world order."

With no viable alternative, and therefore no need to maintain appearances, global capitalism reared its ugly head. Global inequality has skyrocketed following the end of the Cold War. In 1980, U.S. CEOs on average made 42 times more than the rank-and-file workers.[30] By 2014, this amount had shot up almost tenfold to 373 times.[31] By 2000, the richest 1 percent of the world's people owned 40 percent of global wealth, with the richest 10 percent owning 85 percent. In 2014, the world's richest eighty-five people owned as much wealth as half of the world's population, three and a half *billion* people. By January 2017, this club had shrunk to a mere eight people: all men, all but one white, and two from the United States.[32]

Seeing the Forest and the Trees

I realize this is a lot of ground to cover in just a few pages. Libraries are full of the details, but retelling this brief human history helps shine light on a few things. First, contemporary neoliberal capitalism is *not* the only option for a viable global economy, although it may feel like it now—this political and economic system is very recent in species terms. However, this very recent addition to the way humans live it is destructive and unsustainable, undoing hundreds of millennia of our evolution wherein we survived because of egalitarian structures. Also seeing this "world history" as a day in humanity's thirty-year life highlights how global capitalism is directly connected to—and connects—issues that on the surface may feel isolated. The next several chapters detail three of these issues. Racism was built into the very foundations of this global economic order, to which we turn in chapter 2. Zooming out also helps clarify what Lilla Watson and others have said, that our destinies and collective well-being and liberation are already intertwined.

Anthropological research shows that, inevitably, all empires eventually fall. There is something new this time around though: this transnational capitalist empire controls almost the whole planet's resources. Change, therefore, must come from within this system. Citizens of the empire, "in the belly of the beast," have a special responsibility to make this change. And given that these resources are rapidly being used up, we need to act now. For alternative models for how our species can adapt and continue to survive, we can look to humanity's 99 percent—not just of the world's current population, but the 99 percent of the time that humans have lived before empires, before slavery, before colonialism, before capitalism.

Unbounding Liberation

Anthropology, in its unique, if overambitious and often colonialist, self-named mandate can help tap into this wisdom. In addition to seeing with humanity's deep history, using an anthropological imagination draws on research from all corners of the globe, allowing us to see how the species-wide crisis of the twenty-first-century neoliberal empire is being lived, understood, and confronted by real living beings. We can also use our anthropological imagination to understand how urgent current issues, usually presented in isolation, are already deeply connected, as manifestations of the global capitalist order that was built on colonialism, native genocide, forced migration, and slavery. While there are several urgent issues, and they seem to be constantly multiplying, this book discusses three: white supremacy, climate change, and migration.

Working together requires humility. It also requires opening up our minds to other possibilities for organizing human society. An anthropological imagination helps us take the first step to

- Believe in the interconnectedness of specific local struggles for justice, and to see the underlying root causes of oppression, to defend our shared humanity.
- Understand that capitalism is not just an economic system; it's also a political and moral system.
- Imagine alternative ways of organizing human society.
- See how out of sync global capitalism is with humanity's several-million-year history.
- Understand that as a very recent addition within humanity's life span, global capitalism was built on Indigenous genocide, settler colonialism, and slavery, supported by patriarchy. And as such, capitalism and white supremacy have an intimate relationship.
- Identify particular struggles as confronting local manifestations of this global system.
- See that specificities—people's lives, experiences, analyses, and activism—are essential. We need to start from the bottom up, unraveling the loose threads where we are.

Humanity can't prevent our own extinction as long as racism or white supremacy continues to divide us. It is to this that we turn in the next chapter.

2

Dismantling White
Supremacy

We realize that the liberation of all
oppressed peoples necessitates the
destruction of the political-economic
systems of capitalism and imperialism
as well as patriarchy. . . . We are not
convinced, however, that a socialist
revolution that is not also a feminist and
anti-racist revolution will guarantee our
liberation.

The year 2016 was pivotal not only for the United States but also for the
world.

U.S. voters came close to electing a socialist as president. Instead, we
elected a white supremacist.

While many lessons are still being learned from this fateful election, one
of the most important was offered to those who would listen almost forty

years before: the quote that began the chapter was part of the 1977 *Combahee River Collective Statement*. As the *CRC Statement* opens, "We are a collective of Black feminists who have been meeting together since 1974." The *CRC* Statement also launched the concept of "identity politics," which has since been distorted and maligned to stand in for seemingly everything that's wrong with progressive politics and movements. Predictably pundits cited identity politics when explaining Democrat Hillary Clinton's Electoral College loss to Republican Donald Trump.[1]

Looking at the 2016 election with an anthropological imagination helps reveal that not *less* but *more* attention to issues of racism and white supremacy could have helped the Democrats in 2016.

Following the lead of scholars and activists, someone with an anthropological imagination defends the importance of the specificity of struggles and movement demands and the necessity of having and promoting a transformative, liberatory identity politics. An anthropological imagination helps one not only highlight the strategic alliances created in a principled, identity-conscious solidarity politics, but also acknowledge that racism and white supremacy are injustices created by the capitalist world economy. As such, dismantling racism is and should be at the heart of all struggles for humanity's liberation.

Having an anthropological imagination helps us to pluralize what it means to be human, noting that identities—*all* identities—are socially constructed. Further, having an anthropological imagination allows us to call into question the colonial, racial processes behind the category "human," which is exclusionary by design, as Sylvia Wynter argued.[2] Afro-pessimists such as interdisciplinary scholar Frank B. Wilderson III argue that humanity and Blackness are irreconcilable, an antagonism.[3] Anthropologists Jonathan Rosa and Vanessa Díaz argue that race constitutes all identities, grounding them in particular states of being, what they call "raciontologies."[4]

As detailed later in chapter 5, anthropology has a long way to go, but as scholars in a discipline focusing on humanity, anthropologists *should* be able to repoliticize and defend an inclusive notion of what it means to be human. An anthropological imagination gives us the potential to humanize particular identities that have been marginalized, shut out, discriminated against, or targeted. Human liberation—and as the next chapter reveals, human *survival*—requires supporting politics informed by these particular identities.

While an anthropological imagination can help us identify specific connections between various local injustices and help construct the scaffolding of solidarity politics, it also underscores the point powerfully articulated by the Combahee River Collective, succinctly stated by #BlackLivesMatter cofounder Alicia Garza, "When Black people get free, everybody gets free." Dismantling the institutional racism that devalues Black lives will make visible and start to unravel other forms of oppression that are intertwined with it, such as climate change and xenophobia, discussed in the next two chapters. Pulling at this loose thread of racism requires action at all levels at once, from the global capitalist economy to the police state it actively supports and grows alongside it to the ways in which our own lives are complicit.

Trump: Chickens Coming Home to Roost

The presidential election of November 2016 was a wake-up call to many white people. Despite losing the popular vote by almost 3 million (2,868,691 to be exact, per the official count), Republican Donald J. Trump won the Electoral College, sweeping the swing states of Florida, Ohio, Michigan, Pennsylvania, and Wisconsin. Particularly jarring for white liberals, exit polls reported that 53 percent of white women voted for the man who openly bragged about assaulting women and who had been accused of sexual harassment by fourteen women.[5] A Pew Research Center study later reported the percentage of white women voting for Trump as 47 percent, still a plurality, to 45 percent for Clinton.[6]

Many white liberal pundits' first reaction to Clinton losing was denial; then came accusations of Russian meddling in the election.[7] Another instinct from many white liberal commentators was to point fingers at the white working class, which according to conventional wisdom should have carried the four Rust Belt swing states for the Democrats. Typically positioned as pro-union, Democrats counted on payback for Obama's bailout of General Motors and the auto industry. Losing Michigan, just as Michael Moore had predicted, particularly stung, with a margin of 10,704 votes, 0.2 percent.[8]

To this point, *Atlantic* columnist Ta-Nehisi Coates didn't mince words: "From the beer track to the wine track, from soccer moms to NASCAR dads, Trump's performance among whites was dominant."[9] Trump led every white age group and income group: younger voters (eighteen to twenty-nine) by 4 percent, thirty- to forty-four-year-olds by 17 percent, forty-five- to sixty-five-year-olds by 28 percent, and 19 percent of white people sixty-five and older. Trump's biggest supporters among white people were those classified as "middle income," people who earned from $50,000 to $100,000 per year, with a 28 percent lead over Clinton, compared to 20 percent of voters who earned less and 14 percent of voters who earned more.[10] Coates drew parallels between the eight years of the Obama presidency and the eight years of Reconstruction following the Civil War: just like white southern politicians and vigilante groups who heaped revenge on newly empowered African Americans following the contested 1876 election, "Trump has made the negation of Obama's legacy the foundation of his own."[11]

As uncomfortable as it may be for some to acknowledge, the 2016 presidential election was about race, as Obama's were before: he received 43 percent of white votes in 2008, and 39 percent of white voters cast their ballot for Obama in 2012, 54 percent less than Black voters.[12] A key difference between Obama's victories and the outcome of the 2016 election was in voter turnout. In 2008, Obama surprised pundits by bringing three million new voters to the polls, messing up pollsters' predictions of "likely" voters. In 2016, many white people, particularly those at lower educational levels (quickly glossed as the "working class"), were also not counted as "likely" voters but turned out for Trump. In Obama's case, community organizing made a difference. Trump's "off-script" rants, in which he promised to shake up the system, and his thinly veiled racism also brought his base out to vote, surprising many in the United States with truths they had been all too willing to forget, ignore, or erase.

The Politics of Identity

The 2016 presidential election brought the phrase "identity politics" to the forefront. Several political commentators in the media blamed identity politics for Clinton's Electoral College loss. First articulated by the Combahee River Collective, identity politics was originally posed as a challenge to binary, "either/or" thinking. As asserted in the 1977 *CRC* Statement, "We believe that the most profound and potentially most radical politics come directly out of our own identity, as opposed to working to end somebody else's oppression." Barbara Smith, member of the collective and coauthor of the *CRC* Statement, recalled to Keeanga-Yamahtta Taylor, "What we were saying is that we have a right as people who are not just female, who are not solely Black, who are not just lesbians, who are not just working class, or workers—that we are people who embody all of these identities, and we have a right to build and define political theory and practice based upon that reality. That was all we were trying to say."[13] True, the term—like all others—gained additional meanings as more people used it. However, Smith, who also cofounded Kitchen Table Press, panned critics of identity politics' laziness: "And so it's almost as if by embracing one's identity, that you give up on any sort of hope or notion that there is such a thing as solidarity . . . that sounds like an excuse to me."[14]

Identity politics has long been a target, not only of the right but of self-named progressives who argue that the left has been steadily losing ground since the heady 1960s. But scapegoating community organizations, social movement and political leaders, and intellectuals for refusing to sit at the back of the bus while demanding some ill-defined "unity" has created more division in the country. Turning "identity politics" into "political correctness" has played into the hands of those who want to turn back the clock on civil rights gains. Using the term "identity politics" pejoratively frames whiteness and maleness as being outside of "identities," and therefore universal. Cofounder of Black Youth Project 100 Charlene Carruthers scolds commentators for "fail[ing] to fully acknowledge . . . how whiteness, maleness, and working-class and upper-class status—all identities—played major roles in the election's outcome."[15] She argues that "identity politics in the United States is as old as the nation's founding."[16] The original U.S. Constitution specifies that only white males—"of good moral character"—could become citizens and have the right to vote. They must also own property, pushing out working-class and poor whites. Coates concludes that "all politics is identity politics."[17]

If anything, the Democrats lost the White House in 2016 because they didn't pay *enough* attention to identity politics, taking Black and Latinx voters for granted. As Taylor pointed out, while 94 percent of Black women voted for Clinton, fewer of them showed up to the polls than in 2012. As she reported, "The overall turnout for Black voters declined for the first time in a presidential election in twenty years, falling to 59 percent from its historic high of 66 percent in 2012."[18]

Florida is a special case in point. After the 2010 earthquake, the Clintons were very influential in Haiti. Bill Clinton was appointed the UN special envoy and cochair of the Interim Haiti Reconstruction Commission, while Hillary Clinton was U.S. secretary of state. The Clintons were involved in no-bid contracts for shoddy homes, high-end tourism, an apparel factory outside of Port-au-Prince, and gold prospecting.[19] The Republican candidate seized upon his opponent's weakness, trumping up the charges of corruption and making the U.S. and UN failures in Haiti a campaign issue. Adding insult to injury, several of my Haitian colleagues in the Miami area noted that Clinton had almost no ground game there: no staffers or volunteers knocking on doors, no lawn signs visible. Worse, Clinton never showed up in Little Haiti, allowing herself to be upstaged by Trump, who made a particular point to visit, bringing several handpicked Haitian leaders from outside Florida to stage a photo op. Many of Florida's almost half a million Haitian residents just stayed at home during the election, handing the Sunshine State and its twenty-nine electoral votes to Trump.

Talking heads often pin the blame for her loss on Clinton herself, whose public persona was famously "repackaged" depending on the audience. One comment she made at a fundraiser in New York City dismissing half of Trump's supporters as a "basket of deplorables" went viral. The right has long had it in for Clinton since even before her husband was elected. To them, as an ambitious, intelligent woman who considered herself as talented as her husband and who kept inserting herself into the national conversation, she represented a threat to patriarchal society and family. The right had a field day with her citing "an African proverb" that "it takes a village to raise a child."[20] She made other comments as First Lady that also resurfaced in 2016. Defending Bill Clinton's "three strikes" policy, which resulted in an exponential increase in the population locked away in prison, particularly African American and Latinx people, Hillary Clinton called Black men in urban communities "superpredators," using a term coined by right-wing political scientist John J. DiIulio.[21] However, Clinton also endured incredible sexism from the media and much of the electorate in the coverage of her performance as a candidate. Scapegoating Clinton—who, it bears repeating, won nearly three million more votes than Trump—is a deflection. The Democrats, as the party in power, were the ones who oversaw increasing inequality and greater poverty among the working classes of all races.

And if the Democrats needed another lesson in the potential of identity politics, the Latinx community handed them the House of Representatives in 2018 because of the real and imminent threat posed by Trump's immigration policy (detailed in chapter 4). The midterm elections were marked by a partial "blue wave," with forty-one congressional seats going

Democratic, though they lost seats in the Senate. Political scientist Ricardo Ramirez argued that the Latinx vote played a crucial role in several close races. A Pew analysis cited at least nine districts with at least 10 percent of Latinx voters that went "blue."[22] While the Democrats touted that their investment of $30 million in Spanish-language ads resulted in a record 174 percent turnout increase, Ramirez cautions that this represented a small fraction of the DNC's overall ad budget, less than 1.5 percent.[23]

Still, some commentators want to believe Trump's election was not about race or to somehow make Trump exceptional. As Jonathan Rosa and Yarimar Bonilla argue, this move "delinks present-day racism from colonial histories of power, disavows U.S. settler colonialism, and silences critiques of global coloniality."[24]

Make America Hate Again

Trump's personal history matters. While he often claims not to have a racist bone in his body, Donald J. Trump's real estate empire, inherited from his father, was built on racism. In 1973, the U.S. Department of Housing and Urban Development (HUD) sued the Trump Management Company for violating the 1968 Fair Housing Act, based on systematic evidence of racial discrimination. The Trumps fought the case for two years, even attempting to bully HUD with a $100 million countersuit for false information, which was thrown out of court. Coming to the Trumps' rescue was right-wing power broker and attorney Roy Cohn (of the McCarthy Red Scare), whose strategy of bluster and counterattack has since become Trump's trademark.[25]

An antiestablishment mood in the country was decidedly rising. In addition to his wealth boosting his chances, Trump got free press coverage because of his headline- (and other-) grabbing antics and larger-than-life persona. He rose to the top of a very crowded conservative field of Republican contenders, including Tea Party darlings Ted Cruz and Marco Rubio, because of his race baiting and stumping about building a wall between the United States and Mexico. Trump's brazen and unpredictable tweets merely put racism out in the open, in defiance of the "dog-whistle" politics that had been articulated in 1981 by Republican strategist Lee Atwater as the "Southern Strategy."[26] As Atwater explained, "By 1968 you can't say 'n____'— that hurts you, backfires.... Now, you're talking about cutting taxes, and all these things you're talking about are totally economic things and a byproduct of them is, blacks get hurt worse than whites."[27] Keeanga-Yamahtta Taylor argued, "The Southern strategy was contingent on two assumptions: that the Democratic Party would implode across the South, and that Republicans could appeal to the racism and resentments of white workers, whom they presumed were chafing at what Blacks were gaining through protest."[28] Until Trump's election, while I had heard the words "white supremacy" only spoken by my Black studies colleagues, that didn't mean it wasn't there. Far from it.

On the evening of June 17, 2015, twenty-one-year-old Dylann Roof attended a prayer meeting and Bible study at Mother Emanuel African Methodist Episcopal (AME) Church in Charleston, South Carolina. After a disagreement on scripture, Roof waited until people closed their eyes in prayer to open fire. He first turned his handgun on eighty-seven-year-old Susie Jackson. Her nephew Tywanza Sanders confronted Roof and leapt in front of Jackson, taking the first bullet. Roof's hate killed nine people, including the senior pastor, Clementa Pinckney, also a state senator. Roof also killed Cynthia Marie Graham Hurd, Ethel Lee Lance, Depayne Middleton-Doctor, Daniel L. Simmons, Sharonda Coleman-Singleton, and Myra Thompson. Three people survived, pretending to be dead. One survivor told local NAACP president Dot Scott that Roof intended to spare one to be a witness since he planned to shoot himself, failing to do so only because he ran out of bullets. While calling himself a "sociopath" in his defense, his white supremacy was deliberate and premeditated. Roof published his white nationalist beliefs in a manifesto weeks before the shooting, and the AME Church was not chosen at random. It is the oldest Black church south of Baltimore, long serving as a gathering place for civil rights activism. Indeed, Pinckney had called for legislation mandating that police wear body cameras after Charleston police shot and killed unarmed Walter Scott, on the anniversary of MLK Jr.'s assassination, barely two months prior. Roof's motivations leave little to interpretation, and they reproduce familiar, specific stereotypes. Writing from jail, he said, "I would like to make it crystal clear, I do not regret what I did. I am not sorry. I have not shed a tear for the innocent people I killed."[29] On January 19, 2017, the day before Trump took office, Roof received the death penalty.

This act of terrorism rekindled a long-standing debate in the South about whether continuing to fly the Confederate battle flag and to honor other monuments to the Confederacy condoned white nationalism. Within a week, retailers said they would stop selling the Confederate flag, and on

July 9 the South Carolina Senate voted to take down the flag, reaching the two-thirds majority required by the state constitution.

White nationalists met these actions with increasing violence. A breaking point came on August 12, 2017, seven months into Trump's presidency. On February 6, the city council of Charlottesville, Virginia, home to Thomas Jefferson's plantation and the University of Virginia (UVA), had narrowly voted to take down its statue of Confederate general Robert E. Lee. Richard B. Spencer, a Neo-Nazi and "alt-right" activist who openly embraced the title "white supremacist," led a May 2017 rally to protest the statue's removal, to be repeated on July 8 by another rally held by the Ku Klux Klan. Other white nationalist groups joined in, organizing a "Unite the Right" gathering for August 12. Carrying torches, reminiscent of the most terrorizing mob violence in the Jim Crow South, a group of about 250 white nationalists jumped the gun, gathering at around 8:45 the night before. Around 30 counterprotesters, mostly UVA students, confronted the white nationalists near the statue around 9 P.M. The white nationalists shouted, "White lives matter!" and made monkey noises, in the most vulgar tradition of racial slurs. Police arrived, and the crowds disbursed.

The following day saw even greater confrontation. Scheduled to begin at noon, the white nationalist rally began early, by 8:00 A.M. Since Virginia is an "open carry" state, many of the protesters carried guns. At least one carried a sign identifying Roof as a national hero. Community members, including civil rights organizations and Black Lives Matter activists, joined the UVA students in counterprotest. The racially mixed counterprotesters sang spirituals and joined arms, reminiscent of civil rights demonstrations. The *Atlanta Journal-Constitution*'s Debbie Lord reported, "To the chants of 'our blood, our soil,' a group of church leaders responded by singing, 'This little light of mine, I'm gonna let it shine.'"[30] Lord reported that an armed militia, dressed in camouflage, also appeared. Police were in the area but did not engage; the police chief explained it was because they were not dressed in riot gear. At around 11:00 A.M. white nationalists took their shields and sticks and moved into the park, attacking counterprotesters. At 11:22 the police declared the assembly unlawful, and the crowds began to disburse. Unite the Right demonstrators began to reassemble in another park a mile from the center of town. Governor Terry McAuliffe declared a state of emergency at 11:52. At 1:42 P.M. a car driven by white nationalist James Alex Fields sped into a group of counterprotesters, killing thirty-two-year-old Heather Heyer and injuring nineteen others. Around 5 P.M. a state patrol helicopter crashed, killing the two officers on board, Jay Cullen and Berke Bates.

The Robert E. Lee statue remains standing. In February 2018, a judge ordered the black shroud that the city council voted to cover the monument to come off, backed up by a federal ruling in February 2019.

In a news conference on Tuesday, August 15, three days after the violence, Trump said, "I think there is blame on both sides. . . . Many of those people were there to protest the taking down of the statue of Robert E. Lee. So this week, it is Robert E. Lee. I noticed that Stonewall Jackson is coming down. I wonder, is it George Washington next week? And is it Thomas Jefferson the week after? You know, you really do have to ask yourself, where does it stop?"[31]

Trump's question *where does it stop?* would be better posed to the rising tide in white supremacist violence. Far from being a clear condemnation of the events in Virginia, Trump's equivocation on the issue emboldened hate groups. On October 27, 2018, capping seventy-two hours of three hate crimes across the country, a man named Robert Bowers stormed the Tree of Life synagogue in Pittsburgh and killed eleven worshippers. Like Roof, Bowers made no secret of his bigotry, posting anti-Semitic manifestos online. Fueling this hate and inspiring copycats is a host of right-wing (or alt-right) online social media platforms like Gab.[32] The Anti-Defamation League documented a growing community online of "Saint Roof" fans.[33]

White supremacy—and its violence—is not contained by national borders. On March 15, 2019, in Christchurch, New Zealand, Australian Brenton Tarrant entered two masjids (their proper name—"mosques" was initially a racist slang, referring to mosquitos) while people were in prayer, shooting and killing forty-two people in El Noor and seven in Linwood. One died in the hospital. Tarrant praised both Roof and Trump in his "manifesto" later made unavailable by Facebook.[34] Despite this, Trump again denied that white nationalism was on the rise, just as he did after the Charlottesville incident.[35] By contrast, New Zealand prime minister Jacinda Ardern condemned the attacks as "terrorism" and was unequivocal in her rejection of racism and Islamophobia. Within six days of the massacre, New Zealand banned the sale of semiautomatic weapons and passed stricter screening for people wishing to buy guns.[36]

If this isn't a wave of white supremacist violence, what is?

Like "identity politics," the phrase "white supremacy" has gained a specific meaning in the media that makes it too easy to pigeonhole. This meaning limits the phrase's use to violent fringe actors like Roof, Bowers, and Tarrant. However, focusing only on the spectacle of groups quickly rejected as "fringe" (or "bad apples") serves to normalize—and hide—the many ways in which white supremacy benefits even "good" white people who have at least one POC friend. It allows for multibillion-dollar companies like Uber, Facebook, Airbnb, and PayPal that regularly discriminate against POC to engage in surface-level virtue signaling, visibly displaying their righteous outrage at these outsized expressions of hate, all the while successfully appealing to white liberals who might otherwise investigate the racial disparities within social network platforms (maybe even including their own networks) or in the sharing economy.

Using an anthropological imagination helps us see that white supremacy is more than just isolated killers like Roof or bigots like those in Unite the Right. It is a set of institutional power relationships and systems of beliefs that maintain global capitalism's racial order to benefit a subset of individuals socially constructed as white, backed up by state power.

State Violence

Individual people with racist beliefs are not acting alone or in a vacuum. Violence against people of color, and particularly Black bodies, is sanctioned by the state. In too many instances, this violence is committed by the state and its agents, betraying their persistent devaluation of Black lives.

In response, the #BlackLivesMatter movement is shedding light on, and working to end, police violence, including the regular killing of Black men, women, and trans people. Alicia Garza and her colleagues Patrisse Khan-Cullors and Opal Tometi created the movement after George Zimmerman, a state-sanctioned neighborhood watch person, was found not guilty of killing Trayvon Martin, a seventeen-year-old African American boy walking to the store. Zimmerman shot and killed Martin on February 26, 2012, in Sanford, Florida, a suburb of Orlando. On July 13, 2013, an all-female jury that included one woman of color found Zimmerman not guilty of second-degree murder. Zimmerman's fiancée had received a restraining order against him prior to the shooting, and six months before the trial his cousin accused him of molesting her.[37] Zimmerman had also made forty-five unsubstantiated calls about "suspicious black males" to the authorities. Martin had no criminal record. How could someone like Zimmerman get away with murder? Zimmerman's attorney fueled, deployed, and preyed upon racist stereotypes of Black male youth, whose presence is apparently "suspicious" in the suburbs.

Martin was by far not the first nor the last person of color to be killed by those in power in the United States. Thirteen-year-old Emmett Till was lynched on August 28, 1955. Till's "offense" was allegedly catcalling a white woman. Sixty-two years later, this woman, Carolyn Bryant, confessed to falsely accusing Till. Till's mother decided upon an open-casket funeral in her hometown of Chicago, where Emmett was born. The images of the brutalized boy shocked the conscience of the nation and energized Black communities to ramp up the struggle for civil rights.

On March 3, 1991, after a traffic stop on the highway, Rodney King was pulled out of his car and beaten by four Los Angeles police officers for fifteen minutes while a dozen other officers watched and commented. While King was certainly not the only victim of police brutality during that time period, his beating was caught on videotape. The trial of the accused cops was moved out of the county to the conservative, white-majority suburb of Simi Valley, California, with nine white jurors, one mixed race, one Latinx, and one Asian. On April 29, 1992, the verdict came in, with all four officers cleared of wrongdoing despite the video evidence. Judge Stanley Weisberg announced that a verdict had been reached two hours before he said what the verdict was, giving law enforcement time to prepare. The acquittal triggered an immediate response from many within South Central Los Angeles, who had suffered years of police repression, disinvestment, and racialized poverty. Called "riots" by corporate media, the Los Angeles Uprising that lasted six days resulted in sixty-three deaths, including two people identified as Asian, fourteen white, nineteen Latinx, and twenty-eight Black.[38] Some commentators were surprised about the verdict and the city's militaristic response to the community's anger because LA's long-standing mayor, Tom Bradley, was African American. However, before becoming mayor in 1973, Bradley had been a police officer.

On August 9, 1997, NYPD officers arrested Haitian immigrant Abner Louima outside of a Brooklyn nightclub. After handcuffing him, the officers pulled Louima's pants down to below his knees and dragged him into the bathroom at the police station, where Justin Volpe took a broken broomstick handle and sodomized Louima. Like Rodney King, Louima lived to testify. In this rare occurrence, two officers involved were sentenced to prison in a 1999 federal trial.

Not everyone was so "lucky." On February 4, 1999, a twenty-three-year-old immigrant from Guinea, Amadou Diallo, was shot forty-one times by NYC police. On November 25, 2006, Sean Bell, who was also twenty-three years old, was killed outside a nightclub in Jamaica, Queens, after a bachelor party, the night before his wedding. Five police officers shot fifty rounds of ammunition at him. The officers were acquitted in 2008.

In April 2013, as the trial of Zimmerman was happening, the Malcolm X Grassroots Movement published a report, "Operation Ghetto Storm."[39] It contained a statistic that has since gone viral, that in 2012 state-sanctioned individuals killed 313 Black people, or one every twenty-eight hours.

Increased police violence is a direct result of the War on Drugs. Following the very close 1968 presidential election, in which white nationalist governor George Wallace split the Democratic vote, Republican Richard Nixon played on white people's racial fears, criminalizing communities of color by declaring a War on Drugs. Statistics are highly politicized, but it is clear that the War on Drugs has failed to lower use and addiction rates.[40] Some estimates show increases; scare tactics backfired as claims proved to be false. Others point to a flat line from 1970 to 2015 of about one percent of the population that is addicted. Stories in 2010, as the War on Drugs turned forty, from across the political spectrum (right wing to center, what passes for left in U.S. media), Fox News to CNN, panned it as a failure, a waste of a trillion dollars of taxpayer money.

The War on Drugs, however, did succeed at attacking civil rights gains at home and provided military aid for right-wing human rights abusers across Latin America. As a result of the War on Drugs, the United States now has the highest rates of incarceration of any society, including those the U.S. media and politicians like to portray as the worst offenders of human rights, 693 per 100,000 people, five times the global average.[41] And this is most definitely racialized: 2,207 out of 100,000—just over 2 percent—of African Americans are incarcerated, a rate almost six times higher than that of whites, at 380 per 100,000, and over twice the figure for the Latinx population at 966.[42] Laws targeted the "crack epidemic" with mandatory minimum sentencing: people in possession of crack—disproportionately Black—had 100 times longer sentences than people (mostly white) in possession of powder cocaine, until 2010, when this was reduced to 18 to 1.[43] Michelle Alexander calls this the *New Jim Crow*, since convicted felons are stripped of their right to vote in all but two states (Maine and Vermont, not coincidentally both with large white-majority populations).[44] According to the Justice Department, as of 2013 there were 2.2 million people in federal or state prisons or county jails, and an additional 4.75 million on parole, for a total population of 6,899,000 people in the criminal justice system or "prison-industrial complex," greater than the margin of victory of all but ten presidential elections to date.[45]

On August 9, 2014, the community had decided enough was enough—their response was a product of both slow, steady, at times invisible organizing and a generation of young, social-media-savvy Black communities seeing a nearly endless stream of state-sponsored violence. The movement was ready, with necessary civic infrastructure such as having a social media architecture, community organizing strategy, and network in place.

The trigger was immediate: unarmed eighteen-year-old Michael Brown was fatally shot in the back by white police officer Darren Wilson in Ferguson, Missouri. Wilson had driven by Brown and his friend, demanding they walk on the sidewalk instead of the street. When they refused, an altercation started, and Brown was shot multiple times. Black Lives Matter cofounder Khan-Cullors recalled a different reception toward Brown's death than in suburban Sanford, Florida, following Trayvon Martin's murder: the community in and around Ferguson rose up to defend Brown, embracing him, honoring him in radio broadcasts and in the streets.[46] The police and mainstream media wasted no time sullying Brown's reputation in an effort to exonerate the police. However, as Barbara Ransby wrote, "Brown did not have to be a church-going, law-abiding, proper-speaking embodiment of respectability in order for his life to matter, neighbors insisted. And they insisted loudly."[47]

Activist rapper Tef Poe said, "This ain't your grandparents' civil rights movement."[48] Activist groups who responded in Ferguson were diverse, from the queer-led Millennial Activists United to the long-standing Organization for Black Struggle. They saw connections between their struggle and events in Gaza, Palestine, which was being shelled that summer. Not only were parallels of struggle apparent, with hundreds of Palestinians—including children in hospitals—killed by Israeli rockets, but the same Israeli military contractors were arming the militarized police response in Ferguson and elsewhere. Three weeks after Brown's murder, Khan-Cullors teamed up with Darnell Moore to organize Freedom Rides to support local activists. Khan-Cullors was heartened by the community's embrace of the activists, including the offer of housing for out-of-town organizers by

St. John's United Church of Christ. Rev. Starsky D. Wilson did not flinch at welcoming the BLM organizers, who were openly queer and feminist. St. Louis native Rev. Ofasgyefo Uruhu Sekou said, "I take my marching orders from 23-year old queer women."[49]

The Ferguson Uprising forced the hand of a reluctant president Obama, who seemed at pains to avoid the topic of race in his speeches, and to present himself and the nation as "post-racial." At the height of mobilizing, #BlackLivesMatter was tweeted a hundred thousand times a day, and 40 percent of U.S. Americans supported what they took to be the aims of the movement.[50] At a speech to the July 14, 2015, annual meeting of the NAACP, Obama argued for a comprehensive overhaul of the criminal justice system: "Mass incarceration makes our country worse off, and we need to do something about it. . . . Around 1 million fathers are behind bars. What is that doing to our communities?" Keeanga-Yamahtta Taylor argued, "This transformation in Obama's rhetoric is welcome, but none of it would be possible without the rebellions in Ferguson and Baltimore or the dogged movement building that has happened in between."[51] Following a stumbling performance by candidates Martin O'Malley and Bernie Sanders at a July 2015 Netroots Nation conference and a direct action from #BlackLivesMatter protestors, all major contenders for the Democratic nomination for the 2016 election had to say the phrase "Black lives matter." In an October 2015 debate candidates were asked, "Black lives matter or all lives matter?" Candidates lined up offering single-line answers. More important to activists, though, were proposals for action and policy.

Black Lives Matter didn't just spring up from nowhere: it is a product of seasoned organizers of this generation. A dual major in anthropology and sociology, Alicia Garza went on to become a tenants' organizer in Oakland after graduation, foiling governor Jerry Brown's plans for gentrification while he was mayor. Khan-Cullors gained experience with the Strategy Center in Los Angeles, which mobilizes communities of color, blending revolutionary ideas with concrete struggles, like creating the Bus Riders Union. Raised in Phoenix, Black and immigrant, Opal Tometi used her University of Arizona master's degree in communication to build BLM's social media architecture, later becoming executive director of the Black Alliance for Just Immigration.

The BLM movement is deliberately intersectional, documented by Garza's "A Herstory of the #BlackLivesMatter Movement."[52] Garza writes,

"Black Lives Matter affirms the lives of Black queer and trans folks, disabled folks, Black-undocumented folks, folks with records, women and all Black lives along the gender spectrum. It centers those that have been marginalized within Black liberation movements."[53]

In addition to principles of inclusion, the movement is also intersectional out of necessity: It is not just Black men who get killed by the police. State-sanctioned violence has not spared women and trans people of color. For example, Fannie Lou Hamer and four other African American women were arrested in Montgomery, Alabama, on June 9, 1963. Once they were in jail, the white male police officers stripped the women naked and slapped them. Hamer shared her story at the 1964 Democratic National Convention. Knowing they wouldn't have fair representation in the Democratic Party structure of the Deep South, Hamer and others created the Mississippi Freedom Democratic Party, of which Hamer was a delegate. Hamer's courage empowered her to detail this state violence, but she wasn't the first or the last to be targeted. Since plantation slavery Black women have been singled out for violence, actions that were coded into the law and continue to the present.[54]

"Say Her Name: Resisting Police Brutality against Black Women" is a report for the African American Policy Forum coauthored by Kimberlé Williams Crenshaw and Andrea J. Ritchie, from INCITE! Women of Color against Violence.[55] It was published in May 2015, two months before twenty-eight-year-old Sandra Bland was stopped in her car for failing to signal a lane change, arrested, and thrown in jail. She was found dead in her cell three days later, July 13, 2015. Bland was moving to take a new job at Prairie View A&M, her alma mater, in Waller County, Texas. Bland had a vlog and was active in the Movement for Black Lives, and so her death—officially dismissed as suicide—gained visibility. And there are many, many others. Between 1980 and 2014 the number of women in jail or prison increased by 700 percent.[56] In Atlanta, for example, Black women are 6.4 times more likely than white women to be arrested, and Black girls 19 times more likely than white girls.[57]

Transwomen are particularly vulnerable: 38 percent of Black transgender people who encountered the police reported harassment, 14 percent physical assault, and 8 percent sexual assault.[58] In "Killed Outright or Left to Die," Matt Richardson demonstrates that trans people face additional harassment within law enforcement. Richardson cited a 2014 National

Coalition of Anti-Violence Programs report: "In 2013, 72 percent of all anti-queer homicides were of transwomen and 66.6 percent were of trans-women of color, primarily Black women."[59] Because of her trans identity, Duanna Johnson of Memphis was shut out of social services. Police pursued her for alleged prostitution even though there was no client. When Johnson attempted to defend herself, police officer James Swain held her down while officer Bridges McRae pepper-sprayed her and beat her with handcuffs around his knuckles while hurling homophobic and transphobic slurs. Like the Rodney King beating, this was caught on video.[60] Unlike King, Johnson was found dead several days later. Her death, like Sandra Bland's, remains a mystery.

As this brief discussion illustrates, the Black Lives Matter movement was founded to be explicitly intersectional, drawing inspiration from the Combahee River Collective and other Black feminist movements and thinkers. It puts a human face to statistics, defending and reclaiming the value of human lives. The movement calls into question specific processes that devalue Black lives in particular, beginning with the state.

Structuring the Violence

Alicia Garza's "Herstory" details several forms of state violence, beginning with Black poverty:

> It is an acknowledgement Black poverty and genocide is state violence. It is an acknowledgment that 1 million Black people are locked in cages in this country–one half of all people in prisons or jails–is an act of state violence. It is an acknowledgment that Black women continue to bear the burden of a relentless assault on our children and our families and that assault is an act of state violence. Black queer and trans folks bearing a unique burden in a hetero-patriarchal society that disposes of us like garbage and simultaneously fetishizes us and profits off of us is state violence; the fact that 500,000 Black people in the US are undocumented immigrants and relegated to the shadows is state violence; the fact that Black girls are used as negotiating chips during times of conflict and war is state violence; Black folks living with disabilities and different abilities bear the burden of state-sponsored Darwinian experiments that attempt to squeeze us into boxes of normality

defined by White supremacy is state violence. And the fact that the lives of Black people—not ALL people—exist within these conditions is consequence of state violence.[61]

Anthropologist Faye Harrison used Gernot Köhler's concept of "structural violence" to detail the ways in which neoliberal globalization and associated policies such as structural adjustment, and development projects such as "free trade zones," result in death in Jamaica.[62] Harrison noted how structural violence particularly harms low-income Jamaican women. In a later text, anthropologist Paul Farmer built on Johan Galtung's use of the same term to analyze the deadly grip of international, and particularly U.S., policy toward Haiti.[63] State violence *is* structural violence.

Institutional racism—a term coined by Black Power activist Stokely Carmichael (later named Kwame Ture) and a colleague—impacts not only Black lives but Black *bodies*.[64] Anthropologist Orisanmi Burton writes, "Not only does inhabiting a Black body increase the likelihood that someone will die from direct (state) violence, it also mediates processes of 'slow death.' Race impacts the quality of air we breathe; the levels of toxins we are exposed to; the quality of food we have access to; and the likelihood that we will develop chronic diseases such as asthma, diabetes, heart disease, cancers, and HIV."[65] The pollution of the water system in the impoverished, Black-majority city of Flint, Michigan, is an example of environmental racism perpetrated by the state. African Americans are more than 1.5 times less likely than "non-Hispanic whites" (the official federal term) to have health insurance, and this disparity grows over the life cycle.[66] This means, among other things, that African Americans are twice as likely as European Americans to die as infants.[67] In other words, as Burton demonstrates, race has biological impacts.[68] Given all this—institutional power and its reproduction of inequalities—one does not have to intend to be racist to act in a way that is racist, doing harm, reproducing structures of racial inequality. Sociologist Eduardo Bonilla-Silva described this as "racism without racists."[69]

Given the real and significant achievements of the long civil rights movement and the end to legal segregation, many people, supported by the messages fed to them by corporate media and politicians, believe the United States to be color blind or postracial. Racism is supposedly a thing of the past—meaning that talking about race at all is racist. But having an anthropological imagination reminds us that the past lives in the present.

Making History

Since police brutality and racial profiling are obviously not new phenomena, why did the BLM movement arise when it did, following the acquittal of Trayvon Martin's murderer, going viral after Michael Brown's death? Anthropologist Aimee Cox argues that far from the limelight, people's everyday "choreographies of survival" lay the groundwork for more visible protest.[70] In addition to the organizing genius and deliberate, careful message of inclusion by young intersectional feminist leaders, Black Lives Matter struck a chord because it offered an analysis of the current moment that spoke to a generation of disaffected, neglected, marginalized African Americans.[71]

Activists with Black Lives Matter came of age after 9/11, radicalized not only by the War on Terror's racial profiling but also by Hurricane Katrina and what it laid bare.[72] On August 29, 2005, almost exactly 50 years to the day after Emmett Till's murder, Hurricane Katrina reached the shores of the U.S. Gulf Coast. Milwaukee Movement for Black Lives organizer M. Adams wrote that Katrina played an important role in the movement: "It in some ways laid the ground to articulate the state's negligence as violent—and it helped folk question what the function of what a government/state is."[73]

By 2005, the so-called Global War on Terror was in full force, with two active wars in Iraq and Afghanistan. The U.S. administration and corporate media framed the military deployments as a direct response to the attacks on the World Trade Center and Pentagon on September 11, 2001. Given the shock and horror that was felt by Americans on being attacked in their own country after being sheltered from the turbulence happening elsewhere in the world for so long (including violence caused by U.S. military and foreign policy), patriotism was strictly enforced. Anyone who dared to question the links between the 9/11 attacks and the specific targets in Afghanistan and Iraq were vilified as "anti-American." Few elected officials had the courage to oppose the wars, even after 1,335 reported combat deaths of U.S. troops by the end of 2004 in Iraq alone. Less often reported, the U.S. war killed an estimated 182,272 to 204,575 Iraqi civilians.[74]

The financial support for the wars included $7 billion in a no-bid contract for multinational petrochemical logistics corporation Halliburton, with Vice President Dick Cheney still on the board, and $3 billion for engineering contractor Bechtel, with Secretary of State Donald Rumsfeld on the payroll. Incidentally the same politically connected firms,

Halliburton and Bechtel, received no-bid contracts for the post-hurricane recovery effort.

Katrina's heavy rains destroyed the levee system that protected the city of New Orleans, walled on two sides by water: Lake Pontchartrain on the north and the Mississippi River on the south. The resulting scenes of disaster, broadcast the world over, were horrific and gripping: cars and houses washed away in a brown torrent that destroyed thousands of homes. Images of despair and depression mingled with many residents' anger and frustration at the Federal Emergency Management Agency (FEMA) for ignoring clear warning signs of the strength of the impending storm, for cutting the budget of the Army Corps of Engineers, for the government's slow and inadequate response, and for their seemingly inhumane disregard for protecting lives and livelihoods by instituting effective preventive and response measures.

The callous response of the federal government, with its resources focused on wars in the Middle East, exposed the deadly toll of institutional racism. Even though at least 1,833 people died as a direct result of Hurricane Katrina, Bush decided to remain on vacation. An official investigation from the state of Louisiana found that most people killed were African American despite being a third of the population.[75] Race and racism played a role in determining who was able to evacuate, who was stranded, where people were sent, whether they were allowed to return, and whether their neighborhoods were rebuilt or gentrified. Racism and Bush's callousness were so obvious that people in Haiti openly talked about it, some who had previously refused to believe that the United States wasn't the "land of opportunity" promoted by Hollywood. The most iconic statement about the situation was made on a live telethon. Kanye West moved off script, making his cohost Mike Myers uncomfortable. Myers's face betrayed the shock some white people felt during West's mic drop: "George Bush does not care about Black people."

A scant four-hour drive away from New Orleans is the small town of Jena, home to approximately three thousand people. On December 3, 2006, fifteen months after Katrina, while many people were still displaced, a Black student asked his principal if he and other Black classmates could sit under a tree in the schoolyard. The answer came the following morning: three nooses were hung on the tree.

Also that day, six Black students were charged with second-degree attempted murder of a white student, beaten and sent to the hospital. One of the "Jena Six" was seventeen-year-old Bryant Purvis, who published his story in 2015.[76] The Jena Six were tried as adults, with an all-white jury. Purvis, who maintains his innocence, recalls how he was bullied into accepting a plea deal, despite no evidence connecting him with the beating. Being one of the Jena Six followed Purvis and the others around the rest of their lives.

This is the America of those who rose up in Ferguson and beyond. As Khan-Cullors explains, "We are a forgotten generation. Worse, we are a generation that has been written off. We've been written off by the drug war. We've been written off by the war on gangs. We've been written off by mass incarceration and criminalization. We've been written off by broken public schools and we've been written off by gentrification that keeps us out of the very neighborhoods we've helped build."[77] Having grown up in a world with Black bodies dying from poverty, dying from state neglect, or dying as soldiers fighting (and killing) those racialized as "terrorist" (including children and non-soldiers), people were ready to hear the message and do something about it. Using our anthropological imagination helps us point to the larger structural forces creating this "forgotten generation."

Racism in the Rust Belt

Ferguson, Missouri—about two-thirds African American—was hollowed out by the economic "restructuring" that laid off hundreds of thousands of people working blue-collar jobs. The endless growth machine of capitalism, always in search of greater profits, found workers in other countries willing to accept a fraction of the wages paid to U.S. American laborers. So a generation of workers became expendable. As Manning Marable argues, the Black working class and working poor were particularly worse off.[78]

The first-ring suburb of Ferguson grew as African Americans who wanted a piece of the American Dream moved out of St. Louis, purchasing homes. As the manufacturing base that employed these workers rusted out, the communities became poorer. St. Louis has been steadily hemorrhaging people: its population is just over one-third of what it was in the 1930 census. The lack of jobs and economic base for the town has also meant that Ferguson's municipal government—and particularly the police—increased revenue by ramping up enforcement and slapping fines on the local population, which aggravated the hostile climate and poor relationship between law enforcement and the community.

Ferguson is not alone. The largest of the Rust Belt cities, Chicago also had a difficult time reinventing itself when a generation of workers—of all races and ethnicities—was rendered irrelevant by the changing economic marketplace since the 1980s, thrown out by capitalism's profit motive and search for ever lower wages overseas. The population of the entire metropolitan area—not just the city itself—remains in decline. On the one hand, Chicago is often presented as *the* segregated city, the archetypical "urban laboratory." Chicago is also singled out for being violent. A perennial target of Trump's tweets, Spike Lee also dubbed the Windy City "Chi-raq," the title of one of his movies. On the other hand, Chicago has also been a gathering place for activists and an incubator of social justice. The city is home to traditions of community organizing from Saul Alinsky to the Midwest Academy to Black Youth Project 100 (BYP100).[79] Charlene Carruthers, cofounder of BYP100, has argued, "If we drew a map of the creation story of the Black radical tradition, Chicago and its people would appear at nearly every critical point in time."[80]

Chicago is a tale of two cities: one hollowed out by outsourcing and downsizing as global capitalism deindustrialized the United States, and one that is experiencing a rapid pace of gentrification. Outsourcing and gentrification are really two sides of the same process of racial capitalism. Contemporary violence and poverty are direct outcomes of generations of disinvestment and deliberate racial animosity fomented among so-called white ethnics—the much-vaunted working-class heroes of union lore. White Citizens Councils used informal scare tactics to keep families of color from moving into their neighborhood. Lorraine Hansberry's play *A Raisin in the Sun*, not coincidentally set in Chicago, details one Black family's resistance to this.[81] Individual scare tactics were backed up by lenders' refusal to grant mortgages to families living within high-poverty areas because they were deemed "high risk." This practice, called redlining, also included the denial of insurance and other services to people of color. A generation of active struggle against formal housing segregation by activists led to modest victories. Redlining and other racial discrimination in the housing market were officially banned in 1968 with the passing of the Fair Housing Act, the last plank in President Johnson's "Great Society" and a blow to one of the last remaining vestiges of formal segregation.

Neighborhoods that were redlined are still stunted from the disinvestment, even fifty years after housing discrimination was banned. A 2018 report from the National Community Reinvestment Coalition found that three out of four neighborhoods deemed "hazardous" by federal agencies in the 1930s are still struggling economically, with higher rates of endemic poverty and racial segregation.[82] Progressive journalists like Studs Terkel and Alex Kotlowitz documented the impacts of segregation and urban disinvestment following the restructuring of the economy, heralding the loss of living-wage blue-collar jobs in Chicago's African American community.[83] Chicago has the highest Black unemployment rate of the five largest cities in the United States.[84] Another important consequence of redlining is the erosion of financial support for public education, which is usually based on local property taxes (chapter 5 will offer greater detail). Redlining kept Black families out of better neighborhoods where they might have been able to get a better education for their children. Compounding this, in 2013 Chicago mayor Rahm Emanuel closed fifty neighborhood schools, ostensibly to save money, predictably on the South Side and West Side (predominantly Black and Latinx, respectively).[85] There is also ongoing conflict with the teachers unions. In 2000, 40 percent of Chicago Public Schools teachers were Black. In 2015, that percentage was down to 23 percent.[86]

Capital interests have now found new uses for Rust Belt cities like Chicago.[87] Chicago's hollowed out inner city has become "prime real estate" as urban developers displace low-income communities of color through gentrification, particularly on the city's North Side and West Side. Using sociologist William Julius Wilson's analysis, Bill Clinton's Department of Housing and Urban Development (HUD) argued that areas of "concentrated poverty" caused most urban ills like unemployment, drug use, and crime.[88] The most notorious area of concentrated poverty in Chicago was Cabrini-Green, a large public housing complex near downtown profiled in many media accounts because of its high crime rates and other social problems. Unlike the Dearborn homes along the Dan Ryan Expressway in Chicago's South Side, which remain standing today, Cabrini-Green was close to the city center, a short distance away from North Michigan Avenue's Magnificent Mile—in other words, it was hard to imagine a more "prime" real estate. Following the demolition of the public housing complex, median sales prices for single-unit homes in that same area soared from $138,000 to $700,000; and while seven thousand fewer African Americans lived in the area in 1990 compared to the 1980 census, the neighborhood gained four thousand more non-Hispanic whites.[89]

Investing in gentrification peaked in the 1990s and early 2000s.[90] Millennials discovered the advantages of living in the urban core—walkable neighborhoods, renovated historic buildings, and a dense concentration of retail establishments like coffee shops, art galleries, and trendy clothing stores. Wealthy, heavily white majority suburbs—created by federally sub-sidized "white flight"—used their clout to resist integration. Smaller, low-income, first-ring suburbs like Ferguson became places where African American communities established roots. However, towns like Ferguson, nearby East St. Louis, and Chicago Ridge are still among the poorest in the nation.

As is usually the case, things collapsed when capitalism based on the idea of boundless growth finally reached a limit. It is not just coincidence that the Great Recession was triggered by a collapse in the subprime housing market bubble and that Black and Latinx communities were disproportion-ately impacted. As Keeanga-Yamahtta Taylor notes, "Since Obama came into office, Black median income has fallen by 10.9 percent to $33,500, com-pared to a 3.6 percent drop for whites, leaving their median income at $58,000."[91] For this reason, Barbara Ransby argued that "BLM is a *class* struggle informed by, grounded in, and bolstered by Black feminist politics."[92]

The contradictions of global capitalism created the gangrene of poverty and massive inequality in the Rust Belt that destroyed inner-city commu-nities of color. The response of the police state—state violence—serves to divert our attention from the failures of capitalism. Rather than address the problems of inequality and disinvestment, the response from the police state was to lock up communities, taking license to kill the urban poor and dis-possessed. Ruth Wilson Gilmore and Craig Gilmore called this "profound austerity and the iron fist necessary to impose it."[93] In addition, the police established boundaries within which they declared people fit to die, keep-ing the violence bred by this system contained in racially segregated neighborhoods.

Using our anthropological imagination we can see that institutional rac-ism and state violence are results of shifts within the global capitalist econ-omy, what Cedric Robinson termed "racial capitalism." And, in fact, it goes much deeper—this economy has been five hundred years in the making.

Capitalism and Slavery

The particular struggles of the post-Ferguson movement are shaped by the contemporary socioeconomic conditions of neoliberal capitalism as well as institutional racism.

An anthropological imagination takes the analysis a step further. While human beings have sorted people into "in-groups" and "out-groups" since as long as there have been different societies, what groups people use and what we do to "outsiders" have varied over humanity's four-million-year life. "Race" as we understand the term today is a recent creation in species terms. It is at the very least an outcome of capitalism, if not a coproduction. Capitalism was built upon foundations of Indigenous dispossession and genocide and enslavement of African people. An entire apparatus of thought and belief was built to justify these patently inhumane acts of theft and murder to enable the profit accumulation of their assailants.

While there are obviously somatic—physical/body—differences between individuals, how they are classified into races is a result of colonial contact.[94] There is significant variation within what is considered a racial group. Which somatic differences are chosen as significant by whom and how they are used to order society, granting differential access to privilege and resources, are not biological but social—in other words, race is a social construct.

As a social construct, race also has particular origins. As Janis Hutchinson, Oliver Cox, Cedric Robinson, and others have argued, while people living within societies in "antiquity" noticed somatic differences, those differences did not translate into "racial" groups.[95] In ancient Egypt, people from different cultural or "ethnic" groups cycled through positions of power and prestige. In other words, culture groups were not permanently ranked within a hierarchy, "racial" or otherwise. As Robinson argued, racial thinking was a product of European society. Robinson defined racialism as "the legitimation and corroboration of social organization as natural by reference to the 'racial' components of its elements."[96] Analyzing the relationship between the Irish and British peoples, Robinson argued that racialism was employed by ruling classes to drive a wedge between poorer working classes and serfs who could have otherwise have identified common class interests.

Driving the Wedge

Racism and white supremacy are deliberate coproductions of settler society, which elites deploy to justify massive murder, genocide, and forced removal. The Americas were founded on African slavery and Indigenous extermination. Following the expropriation of Indigenous peoples' lands, plantation slavery involved the forced removal and murder of 15.4 million people from Africa.[97] Slavery reduced human beings to the status of property: chattel or "real estate" that could be bought, sold, owned, insured, whipped, raped, or killed at the whim of the master. Chattel slavery is dehumanization in its basest form.

In order to get away with it, people directly involved in the bloody business of African slavery needed to concoct a belief system so powerful that it would be not only learned but internalized for generations. As discussed in the previous chapter, the Catholic Church sanctified the slave trade in 1452 in *Dum Diversas* and again 1455 in *Romanus Pontifex*.

The creation of white privilege and a distinct white identity, and the idea of white supremacy—what Hutchinson calls the "meshing of race and class"—had its U.S. origins following a moment of interracial solidarity.[98] In the 1670s, colonial Virginia was expanding, in direct violation of treaties they entered into with neighboring Native American nations such as the Pamunkey. Indigenous groups pushed back, and the friction understandably upset the fragile peace. Nathaniel Bacon, a wealthy émigré from England, publicly quarreled with his distant cousin, William Berkeley, governor of the colony of Virginia, who had called for a return to peace talks with the Native Americans rather than war. Bacon and a group of other planters who wanted to expand their holdings were in favor of just attacking the Pamunkey, who were led by a woman named Cockacoekse, who white settlers called a queen.[99]

In 1676, Bacon published a list of grievances against Governor Berkeley, who was also, like all of Virginia's colonial rulers, a wealthy landowner. This open defiance inspired many people, particularly poor folks. White former indentured servants and enslaved Africans raised arms against Berkeley's rule. On September 19, three to five hundred people chased Berkeley out of Jamestown and set fire to the colonial capital. This incident, a rare occasion of Black and white unity, became known as Bacon's Rebellion.

Bacon's Rebellion was short-lived though, as Bacon himself died of dysentery a month later. However, the ruling planter class learned their lesson. As Michelle Alexander argued, "The events in Jamestown were alarming to the planter elite, who were deeply fearful of the multiracial alliance of [indentured servants] and slaves."[100] From that point forward, they did away with white indentured servitude and deepened their dependence on African slavery. Political and economic policies systematically drove a wedge between poor whites and African Americans, wooing the former by creating a white identity and privilege that solidified their dependence on the ruling class of white landowners to keep what little privilege they had.

And what a powerful identity it was.

Whiteness is a worldview, internalized at an early age as a member of society.[101] Growing up white in a society built on white supremacy, one learns to *become* white, and it feels natural. This whiteness, which is fundamentally a racist identity, is invisible to those of us who possess it. We need to unlearn it. Unfortunately the way most of us unlearn involves injuring people of color in the process as we thrash about. The fear of being labeled "racist" stems from a host of privileges, and a Judeo-Christian moral understanding that focuses on individual intentions (whether or not we *mean* to be racist). Leaving "intentions" aside, we profit from the privilege being white affords us. Whiteness as identity and oppression is systematic, sitting atop other so-called Western beliefs such as individualism and universalism. This rhetorically leaves white people off the hook, while simultaneously extracting unpaid, certainly unacknowledged, and often unappreciated labor from people of color to "educate" us on racism.

But white supremacy—or, if you like, white privilege, color blindness, and a white identity—is toxic, even to those of us who have benefited from it. As Ta-Nehisi Coates concludes, "White people are, in some profound way, trapped; it took generations to make them white, and it will take more to unmake them."[102] Many Marxists have argued that racism keeps white workers from advancing their self-interest as workers, disrupting their solidarity with other workers, who may be POC, by spinning false consciousness, so that these white working-class people identify more with rich white people like their bosses than with their fellow workers.

In this way, capitalism profits off of racism. In an 1866 letter to François Lafargue, later republished in *Capital*, Karl Marx wrote, "Labor cannot emancipate itself in the white skin where in the black it is branded." From W. E. B. Du Bois to Claudia Jones, from C. L. R. James to Oliver Cox, radical Black Marxist intellectuals in the United States and the Caribbean understood the central importance of dismantling racism in order to overcome class or income inequality. Claude McKay spoke at the Fourth World Congress in 1922: "The Negro stood at the fulcrum of class struggle; there could be no successful working-class movement without black workers at the center."[103] Race and racism still play a central role in dividing the working or otherwise oppressed classes.[104]

Another example of how white privilege works against white people's interest is the frontal assault on civil liberties that took place during the War on Terror. The U.S. political establishment and mainstream (read: white) social movements largely remained silent during the War on Drugs that targeted particularly Black communities, laying the groundwork for the law-and-order "by any means necessary" police state. Once empowered, this police state grew and further encroached on our constitutional rights. In 1995, Congress voted down three to one the exact text of the Fourth Amendment to the Constitution protecting against illegal search and seizure, proposed by Representative Melvin Watt (D-NC) as an amendment to a bill. Following 9/11, the police state began searching emails and cell phone calls without a warrant, as whistleblower Edward Snowden exposed. In other words, people defined as white allow for social policies and policing practice that dehumanize African Americans at our own peril.

As long as white society is still trading on our animosities, our fears, and the established racial order, no one is safe. No one.

Having an anthropological imagination can help us see the material ways that white supremacy harms even white folks. In so doing it helps inspire solidarity and identify shared interests. But this solidarity requires that those of us who are white identify the particular ways in which our bodies, and our individual lived experience, both are structured by and reproduce the social order. Seeing is the first step to disrupting and dismantling privilege.

Racism beyond Borders

In addition to dismantling privilege, it is necessary to see the global connections in order to understand and combat the specificities of anti-Black racism in the United States. In an 1964 interview for *Monthly Review*, Malcolm X argued for internationalizing the struggle: "Now, as a civil rights movement, it remains within the confines of American domestic policy and no African independent nations can open up their mouths on American domestic affairs, whereas if they expanded the civil rights movement to a human rights movement they would be able to take the case of the Negro to the United Nations."[105] In a "Letter from Cairo," he also wrote about the ways that African Americans' welfare and standing in society were intimately tied to the status of Africa within the world system.[106] Specific campaigns for justice in Harlem, where he lived, and decolonization in Africa were merely different battlegrounds in the common struggle for justice. As Charlene Carruthers noted, "The struggle for Black liberation has always been global."[107]

In addition to acknowledging the tactical advantages of a coalitional approach espoused by a later Malcolm X, developing an anthropological imagination highlights the ways that white supremacy traverses national boundaries, shifting form according to context.[108] Colonialism and imperialism use white supremacy to sort the world's people into vastly unequal groups. And as a discourse, race and racism travel globally, shaping people's life chances and access to resources.

The Shifting Color Line

In his 1903 *The Souls of Black Folk*, W. E. B. Du Bois famously predicted that "the problem of the twentieth century is the problem of the color line."[109] As a product of global capitalism, the color line—dividing those with access to resources and power from those without—is also international. However, "race" and "racism" as social constructs operate differently in different societies. For example, researchers of and from the Caribbean point out the ways that the European plantation system there shaped postcolonial race in the area. The "one drop rule" in the United States is a holdover from British colonial policy; someone with "one drop" of African blood was considered "Black." An exception was Louisiana's Creole identity. Claimed and colonized by the French, Louisiana was briefly taken over by the Spanish in 1763 and held under their rule until 1800. Rape on any plantation was systematic, reinforcing white planters' power and control. However, in France and, by extension, French territories, the Code Noir (Black Code) of 1685 outlined the rights of inheritance and slaves' status as property. French colonial society had thirty-three racial classifications, going back seven generations. Predictably, the classifications got more fine-grained the closer they got to white: someone who was 1/128th African ancestry (a single great-, great-, great-, great-, great-grandparent) was still not white. As another example, Spanish conquistadores also forced themselves onto Indigenous women in their new colonies. Racial mixing is known throughout Latin America as *mestizaje*.[110] These various racial categorizations were demonstrated and emphasized in different ways across the colonies in the New World. In its version of a "melting pot" ideology, Mexican independence leaders such as Father Hidalgo declared Mexico a "mestizo nation." Brazil is often self-proclaimed as a "racial democracy," however Brazil's actually-existing social hierarchies and treatment of Black Brazilians betray this ideology. Similar to the effect of Trump's election in the United States, the lurch toward fascism with the 2018 election of ultra-right-wing Jair Bolsonaro looks less "exceptional" when seen through the eyes of Black Brazilians, as Keisha-Khan Perry shows.[111]

Outside of the Americas, widely understood as being built on plantation slavery, scholars tend to ignore race as a social category shaping inequality within nations.[112] One exception to this is South Africa, colonized by the Netherlands but taken over by the British and ruled by a white settler minority. South Africa was infamous for its system of apartheid—formal segregation—that lasted from 1948 until 1994. While apartheid is often portrayed as a strictly national issue, Tiffany Willoughby-Herard details the role that transnational circuits of philanthropy played in creating the apartheid regime, funded with large and targeted investments from the Carnegie Corporation.[113] Beyond the visibility of the formal system of racial inequality in South Africa, British colonial administrations perfected what they called "indirect rule" in their colonies. Chosen elect from the home populations—racialized as closer to white, such as the Brahmins in India—were granted privileges they maintained during postcolonial times, following formal independence. For example, Jemima Pierre documents the persistence of segregation in Ghana despite leaders' embrace of Pan-African ideology.[114] Going further, she discusses the ways that international development reproduces white supremacy, grounded in local racial hierarchies, though Wilderson cautions that white supremacy cannot stand in for anti-Blackness.[115]

Perhaps concerned about the potential for overuse of the term, or perhaps because it implicates us, many white people recoil at the term "white supremacy."[116] One tactic to deflect from the term is to point to instances of ethnic strife between nonwhite peoples such as the 1994 genocide in Rwanda, where extremist Hutu people massacred Tutsi, Twa, and Hutu people who allied with the latter groups. Missing from this defense is acknowledgment of the ways that the Belgian colonial government systematically stoked these ethnic divisions in the first place, creating essential categories and classifying Tutsis as closer to white.[117] The genocide was a result of a complex of factors that included a violent retribution against the intermediaries Belgian colonial leaders chose to benefit and prop up. In a postcolonial context, people who can be called "proxy whites" often inherit positions as enforcers of white supremacy, sometimes literally, as Aisha Beliso-De Jesús demonstrates in her ethnography of police recruits.[118]

One of the most effective strategies to maintain the racial order is for colonized people themselves to become tools of their own oppression. Frantz Fanon, a scholar from Martinique, then a French Caribbean colony, analyzed the ways in which colonialism and its value systems (white supremacy, anti-Blackness) are internalized, in his words, "epidermalized" (within the skin).[119] Kiri Davis's documentary *A Girl Like Me* offers a sad example, depicting young African American girls projecting racist understandings onto black dolls as "bad" or "ugly."[120]

These local systems of racial hierarchies, internal and otherwise, are not created in a vacuum. Formal decolonization usually followed wealth extraction by the imperial body and resulted in massive debt. Having an anthropological imagination can help us see the ways local, culturally specific forms of racism intersect with global forms of inequality, or "global apartheid."[121]

Global Apartheid

Racism facilitates what is commonly called "globalization."[122] Slavery wove together the economies, societies, government structures, and people of four continents. The global economy sorts peoples and nations according to a colonial blueprint, with resources plundered from what Vijay Prashad called "Darker Nations."[123] Given this unequal access to resources, disproportionately flowing to white-majority colonial and imperial centers, Faye V. Harrison uses Salih Booker and William Minter's term "global apartheid" to describe globalization. Deliberately recalling South Africa, Booker and Minter define global apartheid as "an institutional system of minority rule whose attributes include: differential access to basic human rights; wealth and power structured by race and place; [and] structural racism, embedded in global economic processes, political institutions and cultural assumptions."[124] The United States, Canada, the United Kingdom, Germany, France, and Italy—six of the ten largest economies in the world—have a combined population of just over 640 million, or around 8 percent of the world's population.[125] But at over 35 trillion dollars, they control almost 40 percent of global wealth.[126] These countries, which, with the exception of Canada, were all colonial or imperial powers at one point, also wield most of the political power in the world. Half have permanent seats on the United

Nations Security Council. The United States alone has military bases in more than seventy countries.

In his 1915 essay "African Roots of War," Du Bois argued that World War I was a conflict over the colonial scramble for Africa. And still, as Harrison notes, most international relations scholars ignore race and racism in their analyses of how the war affected the continent.[127] Slavery and colonialism set in motion processes of inequality and underdevelopment that continue to this day. As Walter Rodney wrote, slavery created a massive drain on the productive economy of Africa, and the "exchange" of "Western" goods such as textiles and weaponry devastated local production.[128]

White supremacy was maintained in the colonies through colonial administrations and imperial policy, exemplified by the phrase "white man's burden." Not just slavery and the economic system that it built—capitalism—but the colonial world order depended on racial inequality. And so a powerful belief system was created about different "races" of people, some meant for leadership and some for servitude, for servility, for slavery.[129] Racism was given a booster shot during the time of empire. "Natives" found in Africa, Asia, and the Caribbean were rendered grotesque, marketed as a curiosity, like Saartjie (Sara) Baartman, literally shipped around like a circus animal, and billed as the "Hottentot Venus."[130]

This profoundly racist social order was—and is—woven into the DNA of so-called Western civilization. Given the invisibility of white privilege, it might be difficult for white folks in white-majority nations to see the racial elements of this order. However, Black Marxist intellectuals saw the fascism and the explicitly racist Holocaust of World War II not as some sort of isolated, exceptional, sudden turn, but as the logical outcome of a Western civilization built on colonialism and African slavery.[131]

Just like the radical Black intellectuals in the 1930s, whose marginalized position in society allowed them to see capitalism and so-called liberal democracy clearly, today's activists see Donald Trump's presidency and the rise of white nationalist violence that he's unleashed not as an aberration but as part and parcel of the exclusions and white supremacist ideology sewn into the fabric of white settler colonialist capitalist society. Rosa and Bonilla connect this activist insight to the anthropological imagination: "The framing of Trump as an exception to, rather than an indictment of, liberal democracy presents this moment as one of recuperation and rescue rather than of reimagination."[132] Burton argues, "Theorizing the political and epistemic dimensions of Blackness can . . . help us see that #BlackLivesMatter is not only a demand for police reform or a disavowal of Black dehumanization; it is fundamentally a critique of capitalist modernity."

As I finish this chapter, I am in Haiti. The country is gripped by protests demanding government accountability regarding funds from PetroCaribe, a regional cooperation led by Venezuela. Demonstrations also centered on deteriorating living conditions triggered by massive inflation. Activists called for the formation of a new state and the reconfiguration of Haiti's relationship with the outside world. Tellingly, many colleagues here in Haiti are also critical of capitalist modernity: *sistèm kapitalis la rive nan bout li.* The capitalist system has reached its limit.

What's next?

I use the concept anthropological *imagination* deliberately, inspired by Robin Kelley's *Freedom Dreams* and other works.[133] Before we can dismantle white supremacy, we need to be able to imagine alternatives. As Carruthers notes, "Our collective imaginations must burst open in order to believe that liberation is possible."[134]

The challenge remains—how to support movement actors' focus on and specificity of local issues while not just issuing a "lazy parallels of unity" in Garza's words. Taylor articulates a key element within an anthropological imagination: "Solidarity did not mean subsuming your struggles to help someone else; it was intended to strengthen the political commitments from other groups by getting them to recognize how the different struggles were related to each other and connected under capitalism. It called for greater awareness and understanding, not less."[135] Carruthers argues that we need to begin solidarity activism not with "selflessness" but with seeing our self-interest: "Identifying self-interest is essential because it allows individuals to work not simply as allies but as *accomplices* in our collective liberation."[136]

An anthropological imagination offers us a tool in this process of identifying how our self-interest can align with others and the common struggle for justice and liberation. Specifically,

- An anthropological imagination helps us defend the importance of specificity in our struggles and the necessity of supporting marginalized identity politics.
- An anthropological imagination not only helps us highlight the strategic alliances we can form in a principled, identity-affirming solidarity politics, but also shows us that racism and white supremacy are core injustices created by the capitalist world economy.

- Racism or white supremacy is the fulcrum on which other inequalities rest. In effect, humanity learned this mass dehumanization on enslaved Black bodies and murdered Indigenous bodies.
- As such, dismantling racism is and should be at the heart of all struggles for humanity's liberation.
- While particular struggles are connected, it's also necessary to look at their specificities and begin in the local context of struggle.
- While humans have always been sorted into in-groups and out-groups, race and racism are products of global capitalism, particularly its genesis in plantation slavery.
- Dismantling structural racism and white supremacy entails a radical overhaul of the historical systems of oppression that marginalize others. We need to pay attention to how our lives and cultures are complicit in these systems.
- A world without white supremacy allows for solidarity between peoples, greater equality of opportunity, and equitable distribution of resources.
- Repressive state violence is called upon and legitimated to maintain the current obscene and criminal inequality.
- Subsequent movements, like the gay liberation movement, adopted the language, concepts, tactics, and strategies of the civil rights movement, just like tactics and strategies of the abolition movement were adopted by the (first wave) feminist movement. So, truly, the liberation of Black people provides tools for the liberation of humanity as a whole.

White supremacy colors all other human activity, acting in tandem with other systems of oppression. In the process of devaluing Black lives and polluting the environments of Black communities, racial capitalism thus hastens the destruction of the whole earth. Racism keeps our species divided, all the while rendering many people more vulnerable to one of the most existential crises our species has ever faced.

3

Climate Justice versus the Anthropocene

An important biological species is at risk of extinction because of the rapid and progressive liquidation of its natural living conditions: humankind.

One might think these words were spoken by the activist group Extinction Rebellion, which has transformed the landscape since their founding in London on October 31, 2018, or Greta Thunberg, the young Swedish climate activist who has become the media's face of this issue, including nabbing *Time* magazine's 2019 Person of the Year. However, these words were uttered over twenty-five years ago, on June 12, 1992—as I was graduating high school—at the United Nations Earth Summit in Rio de Janeiro, Brazil. This conference was a defining moment in human history, when representatives from the world's governments first got together to grapple with the problem of climate change.

The author of these remarks went on to name the culprit of anthropogenic (human-created) climate change: capitalism and overconsumption. He was one of 108 heads of state, a representative of one of the 172 governments in attendance.

These words are even more prophetic today. It is not exaggeration, rhetorical flourish, or hyperbole to say that *Homo sapiens sapiens*, our species, is at risk of extinction. When we use our anthropological imagination, we can see that the decisions we make and the actions we take in this next quarter century to address global climate change may well determine the fate of the human race. Looking from a species point of view, particularly using the anthropological timeline provided in chapter 1, we can clearly see the impact of the past few hundred years, the "last day" in humanity's thirty-year life. Indeed, our species' closest relatives, apes, are already facing extinction on a massive scale, as their habitats are being irrevocably altered and destroyed.[1]

Why were these words unheeded? Undoubtedly in no small part it was the messenger, Cuba's Fidel Castro Ruz, who led one of the world's only remaining socialist revolutions and was long a nemesis to the United States and the capitalist world order. The message itself was also hard to hear, and still is: global climate change is a direct outcome of global capitalism, five hundred years in the making. The primary drivers of global climate change are the current global economic order and the racism inherent in it.

It is also possible that several other aspects render climate change a challenging issue to organize around. One is scale: it is overwhelming to grasp the magnitude and impact of climate change. Another is timeline: it seems impossible for activists and scientists to convey a sense of urgency, particularly for the large subset of the global population that has grown accustomed to instant gratification, and the even larger group of us trained by our media outlets to respond only to cataclysmic images of immediate disasters. Incremental climate change provides very limited photo ops.

Related to this is that people have difficulty imagining a core constituency for climate change: we are not used to thinking of issues that impact the entire human race. That said, climate change is most definitely *not* a one-size-fits-all issue: it impacts particular communities differently. Local realties and the expressed priorities of local movements can be quite different from place to place, especially now that the issue has to compete for bandwidth with waves of right-wing "populist" nationalism popping up in ever more countries.

The very aspects that make climate change a challenging issue to organize around—scale, timeline, constituency, the need to track back and forth between local and global, and the identification of the interconnectedness of apparently disparate issues—are the core of what an anthropological imagination can provide.

Unfortunately, discussing climate "change" doesn't go far enough. The climate crisis is the deadly outcome of racial capitalism and white supremacy. While activists and governments from the Global North point the finger at India and China for scaling up their economies, humanity would need four Earths if all seven billion people on the planet consumed like the average U.S. American. Herein lies a major, less often discussed "Inconvenient Truth." Given the massive inequalities in opportunity and capital, and the brutality of how the "West" became dominant in the first place discussed in the previous chapter, it is no coincidence that communities with higher climate vulnerability are disproportionally those of people of color or within the Global South.

For all these reasons, our anthropological imagination helps us see that the conversation needs to be about climate *justice*, not just climate change. Unfortunately, the media and political parties tend to flatten this issue. The first-ever presidential forum on environmental *justice* was held in November 2019, at a historically Black college and university (HBCU), South Carolina State. It was almost completely ignored by the media.

Pondering our extinction as a species is admittedly uncomfortable. My students used to call me a "Debbie Downer." My response to them is that I believe not only that must we do something about the problems we face but that we, in fact, can. We need to be fighting *for* something. An anthropological imagination offers this generation of humanity tools to do right by our ancestors and our children, and also the earth itself and the life supported by it. This chapter offers a few tools for concerned people to hopefully imagine and articulate solutions. If there is a silver lining to the climate crisis, preventing our pending extinction offers a real opportunity for people to work in solidarity and to identify a shared self-interest: humanity. That's why we as a species—even those of us with privilege—need to dismantle white supremacy.

First, we need to do the work.

Setting the 'Cene: Climate Change as an Issue

One challenge within climate change activism involves its status as an "issue" in community organizing language. Issues are beyond simply "problems" and should contain potential solutions. An issue must have a core constituency, a group of people (individuals and/or communities) directly impacted by it. It should also have a clear "target" or "decisionmaker," a real person (or elected body) who can act to fix the issue. There are many types of community organizing, from labor unions to civil rights groups. Radical labor activist Saul Alinsky formalized some of the "best practices" and principles from his organizing experience in his book *Rules for Radicals*.[2] The Midwest Academy, a training school for organizers across the progressive movement, offers an approach that embraces civil rights leaders, organizations, and their methods. The Midwest Academy formalized lessons in a specific user-friendly manual for training organizers, which unlike Alinsky's book focused more on strategies rather than tactics.[3] Rinku Sen, an Indian American author and activist, was director of the racial justice organization Race Forward and publisher of Colorlines.com. She voices the concerns of many folks stuck on the margins of a least-common-denominator approach in her organizing handbook commissioned by the Ms. Foundation, *Stir It Up: Lessons in Community Organizing*.[4] Too often, a single-issue least-common-denominator approach flattens complexity and diversity in the name of building a "winnable" issue. Looking for "what-we-have-in-common" tends to reproduce priorities of white, cisgendered men. True, issues like a living wage or universal health care might well be important to many communities, but the ways in which the issues are defined and framed often take away from the specificity of people's identity and very real priorities that keep, say, transgender youth or Indigenous people from being able to access formal wage labor in the first place. And women of color and/or immigrant women have issues as "workers" that go far beyond wage theft or even the wage gap; intersectional gender oppressions operate to keep them particularly vulnerable as workers. Safety is thus a "working-class" issue. Also, a "people's organization" includes those behind bars. For these reasons, as the previous chapter discussed, we need a politics that begins by respecting the specificity of struggles and, as Charlene Carruthers argued, brings your full self to the table. Even, and especially, for an issue as complex as climate change.

Advocating for climate action—much more so than addressing local educational injustices at the school board level or passing a citywide ordinance such as for living wages, bathroom safety, or antidiscrimination—is decidedly complex and fraught with daunting challenges, so much so that it can be dispiriting or disempowering. A core challenge to discussing climate change is to fully grasp the scale and the severity of the problem without losing sight of the specificity of how it triggers local impacts and what needs to be done. One key stumbling point within climate activism is how to convey a sense of urgency. For example, very few of us are able to visit glaciers, and those who do tend to be already predisposed to support nature and public resources. And there's never a critical mass of people who are fired up, even if somehow our pictures of a disappearing glacier over the years go viral on social media.[5] Calling it "slow violence" like Rob Nixon does is an attempt to discuss human costs and urgency.[6] Earth scientists talk about the "tipping point" when melting polar ice caps will change ocean currents, speeding up the current warming trend. The movie *The Day After Tomorrow* offers a particularly vivid dystopian interpretation of what could happen, a sudden-onset Ice Age.

In 2000, the dawn of the new millennium, Nobel Prize–winning chemist Paul Crutzen and colleague Eugene Stoermer coined the term "Anthropocene" to depict the seriousness of industrial capitalism's output of carbon dioxide and its setting into motion irreversible changes to the global climate.[7] The term "Anthropocene" has been gaining traction of late. Building on "anthropogenic" (caused by humans), it declares us to be in a new geological epoch, one dominated by human action, replacing the Holocene, which began at the end of the last Ice Age 11,700 years ago. In 2008, the Royal Geological Institute voted to consider officially adopting the term, and in 2019, the Anthropocene Working Group formally voted to adopt it. Both terms—anthropogenic and Anthropocene—in their attempt to show the influence of human actions on nature also reproduce a dichotomy that defines Western thinking, separating mind from body, and human from animals. But at the least it is an acknowledgment from natural scientists that human beings are a part of the world's ecosystem, and that social sciences need to be incorporated into natural sciences. This recognition of the role of humans in shaping our climate also calls upon anthropologists, ostensibly those studying the human race, to do something to address it.

However, the term "Anthropocene" is problematic. It focuses too much on humans, whereas we know that our actions cannot be isolated from nonhumans.[8] Also problematic is the gloss over *which* "humans" created this particular problem. Aiming at greater specificity when defining the era,

Jason Moore proposed "Capitalocene," and critical Black studies scholars such as Katherine McKittrick center plantations in their analyses.[9] For example, Janae Davis and colleagues propose "a radical awareness of the plantation's role in producing global environmental change."[10]

Indigenous scholars argued that the Anthropocene also normalizes colonialism and the mass violence and genocide perpetrated against Indigenous peoples by settler societies, and that dating the Anthropocene must begin with Indigenous epistemologies (systems of knowledge) and thus place the "golden spike" when we shifted eras at the height of colonization and Indigenous genocide.[11] Whether intentionally or subconsciously by settler scientists, the most commonly proposed timeline of some as-yet-undefined "future" of the apocalypse erases the experience of many Indigenous peoples. For many Indigenous peoples, contemporary climate change is merely an extension of ongoing violent processes of settler colonialism, where white outsiders pushed Indigenous communities off their land and radically altered and polluted that land to apocalyptic proportions.[12] Guilt-ridden white saviors, as depicted in the movies *The Last of the Mohicans*, *Dances with Wolves*, and *Avatar*, often resort to trapping Indigenous peoples in what Michel-Rolph Trouillot called the "savage slot," romanticizing them as "noble savages" or naturally good environmental stewards.[13] Calling Indigenous peoples "Holocene survivors" offers a racist sleight of hand that serves to erase Indigenous peoples who have been forced to survive and adapt to this hostile takeover of their land and environment.[14]

Indeed, many of the first cultural casualties to contemporary climate change are Indigenous communities forced to relocate as their lands are swallowed up by the sea or melting away with the permafrost, like in Isle de Jean Charles in Louisiana or Shishmaref and Kivalina in Alaska. To many Indigenous leaders, this is their third removal; the first being geographic removal from their ancestral land, formalized by the Indian Removal Act of 1830 and the ensuing "Trail of Tears," followed by the wars of extermination two generations later. The second removal was the ethnocide triggered by the forced reeducation of Indigenous children in English within Christian boarding schools, resulting in family separation and cultural brainwashing of those children away from their traditions and communities.

An anthropological imagination helps us identify specific connections between real people facing real issues, rather than lumping all of humanity together.

Impacts of Climate Change

Using our anthropological imagination can also help us identify issues that are directly related to climate change that may otherwise be missed in a single-issue lens. Anthropologists have long attempted to identify the human dimensions of climate change.[15] Starting with people's current realities and lived experience, we can identify common roots and common cause, pointing out similarities of issues some groups have been facing for a while and the larger issue of climate change. Climate change increases the intensity of events we consider "natural" such as wildfires, flooding, and hurricanes. Being able to see the linkages between already-occurring realities and underlying structural causes is a first step in solidarity.

Wildfires

I first drafted this chapter in Northern California in July 2018, at the height of the wildfire season. Just outside the main western entrance to Yosemite National Park, the Ferguson Fire, spanning almost a hundred thousand acres, had started two weeks before. The first night, it looked like the northern lights, long eerie streaks of green coming down the mountain. We were about sixty miles, as the wind blows, from the blaze, and the smoke was still visible through the pine trees. Even overhead at noon, the sun was a yellowish-orange, the colors of creation below an eerily muted hue. At the time, there were simultaneously four major wildfires burning. One closer to us started later, and one over three times the size of the Ferguson Fire was burning north of Santa Rosa, California, in Mendocino. Over a hundred thousand residents of Santa Rosa had to be evacuated because of last year's fires. This year, they relived their trauma as ash began visibly piling up on parked cars. In Redding, on the northern edge of California's Central Valley, firefighters hadn't yet begun to contain an even larger inferno, the Carr Fire. This same community fought another raging forest fire last year as well. And yet some residents, including elected officials, continued to disbelieve there is a link between the increasing ferocity of the flames and a warming climate, which in this part of the world also spells out greater droughts.[16] Worse, the U.S. secretary of the interior pinned the blame of California's worst wildfire season on record on "environmental terrorists."[17] Then, in November 2018, wildfires again overcame Northern California.

While climate activists can continue to finger wag until we choke from the fumes, people's resistance to accepting the reality of climate change, call it denialism, is bound up in what anthropologists call a "worldview" (our understanding of how the world is). In this internet age, when we are bombarded by terabytes of data on seemingly (but only seemingly!) everything, on top of a proliferation of screen time, we process this information through our preexisting worldview. Linguistic and psychological anthropologists have long pointed out that these frames or cultural models are learned.[18] Cognitively, we make sense of the world, imagining coherence. If new information comes our way that doesn't fit our conception, an all-too-common response is to reject or suppress it. This tendency is being Trumped up by the administration's insistence that "fake news" and "alternative facts" are circulating and that people should not believe what they see and hear.

Particular resistance by people to any analysis of the connection between burning fossil fuels and a warming and increasingly unpredictable climate is fed by propaganda put out by the fossil fuel industry to muddy the waters and advance the industry's agenda. In the 1980s, Big Oil's scientists discovered a connection between levels of carbon dioxide in the atmosphere and mean global temperatures. Since then, these particular companies have invested over a half billion dollars in junk science, spin, alternative readings of their own facts, and the bullying of scientists, obviously with their own bottom line—and profits to shareholders—in mind.[19] Why people buy their story is another matter.

The results of anthropological research would advise not another bombardment of facts, of which we have plenty, or a pundit shouting match, but respectful engagement with climate deniers and the careful, deliberate construction of new narratives that also serve the need for coherence. Given the ambitious and even colonialist global reach of our research, anthropologists have fanned out all over the globe to begin identifying patterns or commonalities within human societies. And given our declared respect for local knowledge, many anthropologists have experience engaging with local ontologies (the belief system of how the universe functions) and juxtaposing structural perspectives—the interaction between the emic (insider) and etic (outsider). When it comes to climate change, one's anthropological imagination should be inspired by the experiences, struggles, and wisdom of communities for whom climate change is already an increasingly deadly reality. Today.

A kernel in the otherwise conservative worldview expressed by NorCal climate change deniers might be a useful place to start to grow an anthropological imagination. California's wildfires are seemingly out of control because water resources have been deliberately taken from the mountains and given to large farmers and corporate agribusiness as well as ever expanding cities. Much of California's natural landscape was originally desert. It is always striking to see the impact of irrigation on this landscape—you can see where it stops as an abrupt line dividing green crops from the tan or brown brush. Not only is the land supporting more than thirty-nine million Californians, these specific developments have pushed the land way past its carrying capacity. Central Valley agribusiness produces almost half of the vegetables and more than two-thirds of the nuts and fruits consumed in the United States.

Finally, Southern California was built with the automobile in mind, with freeways paving over the existing mass transit system. As a result, and because of its unique topography, Los Angeles became a city suffering under its own generated smog. Combined with the sprawl that justified the cars, and the clogged concrete arteries of the highway systems, the suburban car culture of Los Angeles, fed by Hollywood's images of perfect family life, led to individual household decisions to buck natural landscapes for perfectly manicured Kentucky bluegrass lawns, that need a lot of watering to stay alive in this new ecosystem. So rather than railing at "the system" or "the government" for stealing water resources, we could be more specific and actually open space for identifying common cause, pointing out that these problems are part of a common pattern in capitalist development, particularly that fueled by colonialism.

Under Water: Climate Change and Displacement

If out-of-control fires weren't enough, entire societies are currently at risk of flooding. Indigenous peoples are disproportionately impacted. Entire Inupiat (Alaska Native) villages like Shishmaref and Kivalina and a hundred others are threatened with displacement as the permafrost where their homes, schools, and other institutions are built thaws beneath them.[20] As foragers (what anthropologists used to call "hunter/gatherers" and what is known locally as "the sacred act of subsistence"), these communities depend on the land, which, for as long as their ancestors can remember, included the permafrost, for their survival. So relocation is not an easy task for them, even if everyone agreed that this was the best course of action. Exacerbating the injustice is that the Inupiat did almost nothing to contribute to anthropogenic climate change. A further injustice is that the federal government paved the way for white settlers in that same area, including offering these outsiders annual oil dividends.

Indeed, state governments allow the fossil fuel giants a lot of leeway when it comes to the law. This is typified by the government regulators' lenient and at times almost apologetic treatment of Exxon following the spill of 260,000 barrels of crude oil into 11,000 square miles of ocean and beach, as the *Exxon Valdez* tanker crashed ashore on March 24, 1989.[21] Photos of tarred baby seals shocked the conscience of many within the "lower forty-eight" states, fanning the flames of an emerging environmental movement. The environmental damage done by the *Valdez* is still noticeable thirty years later.

Like Alaska's, Louisiana's economy is also dominated by the fossil fuel industry, so oil corporations also operate there with immunity thanks to friendly state regulators who often look the other way. On April 20, 2010, 4.9 million barrels of oil were spilled into the Gulf of Mexico, almost twenty times more oil than from the *Exxon Valdez*.[22]

Long before Louisiana was a French colony, and still today, Indigenous groups called the area home. During the waves of U.S. expansion and forced removal of Indigenous peoples in the mid-nineteenth century, the Biloxi-Chitimacha-Choctaw peoples resettled to the bayous of southern Louisiana.[23] They adapted to fishing and harvesting clams. Like the glaciers and the permafrost in the Arctic, the islands in the Mississippi River Delta have been steadily disappearing over the past two generations. In addition to erosion as the sea levels rise, the bayou islands are casualties of oil companies' dredging and drilling. Like the people from Shishmaref and Kivalina in Alaska, the Isle de Jean Charles band of Biloxi-Chitimacha-Choctaw peoples are climate change survivors, or "climate refugees." Bob Gough, secretary for the Intertribal Council on Utility Policy, calls them pioneers and scouts, paving the way for others.[24] Under the leadership of Chief Albert Naquin, the tribe received a $48 million award from a National Disaster Resilience Competition funded by the U.S. Department of Housing and Urban Development (HUD) and the Rockefeller Foundation in January 2016. Despite winning such a substantial award, they face obstacles at every turn. Because of this plan to relocate, moved forward by the state of Louisiana in 2019 without input from the tribe, the community has no assistance in the meantime to repair damage to their existing homes and utility services. For just the relocation of Indigenous populations in the United States alone, climate change has a steep price tag. And this assumes suitable land can be found. The Isle de Jean Charles band hasn't been able to relocate yet because every two years in southern Louisiana, an area the size of Washington, D.C., is lost to the rising waters.[25]

Making Connections Elsewhere

Even the U.S. military has already conducted research on climate-change-induced migration. In their worldview, the potential migration of tens of millions of people presents a threat against which to prepare. In addition to overall temperatures, local weather patterns and particularly rainfall are also changing. Climate change is increasing desertification in areas like Northern California that are experiencing longer and more severe drought conditions combined with hotter temperatures. The massive fires in the Amazon and Australia in 2019 are a deadly reminder that the devastation is not contained by the U.S. border.

Climate change does not respect nor recognize national boundaries, but people are forced to. When a people's traditional farming or grazing land becomes a desert, the community risks starvation as their means for survival and livelihood dries up. Rather than face starvation, many people, particularly "pastoralists"—those whose primary livelihood strategy is tending livestock—follow their animals to new sources of water and vegetation. Some wander into contested territory or cross enemy lines. Still others who prefer not to starve to death are specifically vulnerable and targeted for recruitment into transnational networks of armed insurgents.

One such place where these dynamics are occurring is Syria, which exploded with violence in 2011.[26] Some commentators choose to see these issues as "terrorism," others as a proxy war between the United States and Russia. Still others claim the conflict is about religion. Whatever the analysis of the cause, a clear outcome of the increased violence is a massive flow of people fleeing the area, seeking asylum. Our anthropological imagination helps us to see this Syrian conflict and the resulting "refugee crisis" (we'll get to that in the next chapter) as in part an outcome of climate change, a harbinger of more to come if we as humanity fail to act.

Again, patterns are clear. The Rwandan crisis discussed in the previous chapter can be cast in a racist postcolonial light, or it can be seen in part as a conflict over dwindling freshwater reserves. Boko Haram, a group that deploys terrorism in western Africa, is being fueled by the impact of climate change on Lake Chad.[27] This analysis is definitely not to replace a complex local issue with a one-size-fits-all theory, but an anthropological imagination helps us recognize and understand pressures from a global scale, offering a holistic approach that brings non-climate-related challenges into conversation with the effects of climate change. Importantly it also helps disentangle some of the motivations of this often-maligned group whose religious identity is often used as synonymous with "terrorist."

These particular groups can continue to be maligned and Orientalized, fanning the flames of ultra-right-wing nationalism.[28] Or we can remember that the people living in these communities are human. An anthropological imagination helps us rehumanize these communities and identify planetary issues that are changing the rules of the game, encouraging massive migration and resistance. Rather than see groups as "terrorists," an anthropological imagination helps us offer another, more human approach and suggests peaceful long-term alternatives to U.S. military counterinsurgency. It is within our power to address this underlying motivation, and it offers common cause between "them" and "us," what postcolonial theorist Dipesh Chakrabarty called "species thinking."[29] Recast in this less xenophobic and Islamophobic, more humanist frame, our anthropological imagination helps us see the Syrian conflict as an early warning sign for climate change's destruction of people's livelihoods. Estimates of the number of future climate change refugees range as high as one billion by 2050, with the most frequently cited estimate coming from the United Nations at two hundred million.[30] It is hard to define "climate refugees."[31] However, we can point to how many people flee extreme weather events or disasters as a start; the Norway Refugee Council estimates twenty-six million per year.[32] In 2016, thirty-one million people were displaced by a disaster.[33]

Climate Change, Disasters, and Haiti

Syria is just one particularly vivid example of displacement. In Haiti, where I've worked for nineteen years, climate change is already wreaking havoc on the peasant economy. Farmers like Jean Baptiste, a local leader with the peasants' organization Union of Small Peasants of Small River, who have been able to survive on the margins, growing corn, pigeon peas, and hot peppers on land he inherited from his family, are increasingly struggling as weather patterns change. Climate change has altered the average rainfall in the area. Before Hurricane Matthew in 2016, the Organization for the Rehabilitation of the Environment in Camp-Perrin, Haiti, had documented a steady decrease in rainfall over the previous twenty years, each year with less rain than the previous. Now in addition to droughts, the region is subjected to severe flash floods that wash away the seedlings, the season's crops. Jean Baptiste says, "You don't know what to do. You can't plan ahead. There's no security at all. You never know when to plant, and if you do, if you will have a harvest."

Fortunately for Jean Baptiste, Camp-Perrin has a canal that dates back to colonial times, the *only one* of its kind. As Haiti was a sugar colony, it never would have occurred to French planters or the government to invest in food production. Self-sufficiency was, and is, never the point for colonies: in fact, it's the opposite. Benith and other members of her organization, Alliance for Progress in the Sixth Section, barely twenty kilometers away from Camp-Perrin, are not so lucky. Absent irrigation canals, Benith has no recourse to care for her crops other than prayer. She does pray, every day.

Prayer couldn't stop Hurricane Matthew, which made landfall on Haiti from October 4 to 6, 2016. As a category 4 (130–156 mph) storm, Matthew was the most powerful direct hit to Haiti in over sixty years.[34]

Matthew was destined to be a forgotten disaster, striking just a month before the pivotal U.S. presidential election, but also in the shadow of the earthquake that struck Haiti on January 12, 2010, which was still impacting the country. The $16 billion response to the earthquake failed to live up to Bill Clinton's promise of "Building Back Better." In many ways the aid itself was dangerous. Haitian filmmaker Raoul Peck called it "Fatal Assistance," and I called it "humanitarian aftershocks."[35] The international response to Matthew represented just 2 percent of the aid given following the earthquake.

The official national death toll for Hurricane Matthew in Haiti was 546, with 438 injuries, but this number never accounted for those who passed in the following days.[36] Over 80 percent of buildings were destroyed in the South and Grand'Anse provinces, as were roads, communication infrastructure, and the entire season's crops.[37] Worse, fruit-bearing trees like mangos, coconuts, and breadfruit were laid barren as the heavy winds and rain, which appeared to fall sideways, ripped the leaves off.

The official response was slow, complicated by processes of economic and governmental centralization that began under the 1915 U.S. Occupation and accelerated with neoliberal economic policies imposed by the U.S. government and multilateral agencies such as the World Bank and IMF that make getting relief to the provinces much more difficult.[38]

Paradoxically, because of its isolation—before the past few years the trip on the national highway took twelve hours—the Grand'Anse has noticeably more trees than other provinces. But this is changing. Commentators from all across the Grand'Anse have commented on the connection between fixing the national road and an uptick in charcoal production. Across the country, cutting trees for charcoal production has rendered Haiti much more vulnerable to extreme weather events. The photos of the deep brown deluge during Matthew testify to the topsoil being washed away, which could have been otherwise protected by tree roots.

Grassroots organizations in Torbeck, in the South provinces, within twenty kilometers of the provincial capital, are doing what they can to rebuild after the storm. Lafrisilien Peasants Association's leader Jean Molin said, "The government never once came and checked on us." Rachelle Moïse, of the Oscar Romero "Small Church" community, critiqued "paternalistic" foreign agencies for "failing to address our needs with their top-down, predetermined aid."

The increasing destructiveness of hurricanes is a particularly vivid and violent manifestation of climate change. However, climate change isn't the entirety of the problem. "Slow violence" and "structural violence" are terms that attempt to make this point.[39] Within six years, Haiti shot up from seventh to third most vulnerable country to climate change.[40] The order of magnitude of death and destruction in Haiti is a direct result of deliberate capitalist and white supremacist action by powerful outsiders over a very long period of time. In short, this is what capitalism—and its associate white supremacy—looks like.

"Hurricane Alley"

Haiti's island neighbors share a similar fate, since the Caribbean basin is sometimes called "hurricane alley." The Caribbean has long been used by colonial capitalist powers for exploitation, beginning in the violent reign of King Sugar. History may be repeating itself in the birthplace of capitalism. The 2017 hurricane season was one of the most devastating on record, with the second most powerful storm ever recorded. Not coincidentally that storm followed three record-breaking years of global high temperatures.

Weeks before Hurricane Katrina, Kerry Emanuel and colleagues published a report in *Nature* documenting the connection between rising sea temperatures and the intensity of tropical cyclones.[41] NASA climatologist James Hansen came to similar conclusions in his own long-term research.[42] Other recent research has backed this up in various places, including within the Caribbean.[43] The fundamental unfairness as descendants of slaves are now disproportionately killed by the impacts of climate change amounts to what Melissa Checker has called "Eco-Apartheid."[44] Mimi Sheller terms this "islanding effect"—that climate change is part of the same processes of colonial dispossession.[45]

Puerto Rico is a perfect example of these colonial legacies of injustice. Puerto Rican scholar/activists see Hurricane Maria in 2017 as a continuation of another disaster, 2016's PROMESA (Spanish for "promise"), the federal government "bailout" package, extracting further foreign control over and ownership of the island and pushing people off their land. The economic strictures of PROMESA set the stage for Maria, crippling Puerto Rico's recovery. In May 2018, eight months after Hurricane Maria, a million people in Puerto Rico, about a third of the population, were still without power. At the end of that month, a Harvard study estimated the death toll in the U.S. commonwealth to be 4,645.[46] Citing this figure, which exposes the U.S. government's lamentable official toll of 64 dead, many Puerto Ricans and their allies question the federal government's indifference and disregard of people's suffering in the colony.[47] To many, the prolonged, snail's-pace recovery and the suppression of the death toll show the federal government's wanton disregard for human life. To put it quickly, colonialism kills.

Cuba, Haiti's Photo Negative

Fifty miles across the sea from Haiti is Cuba, the largest island in the Caribbean. Haiti is Cuba's nearest neighbor. The same Taino Indigenous people as in Haiti first settled the eastern portion of Cuba as well. However, Cuba was among the last holdouts in the Caribbean to abolish slavery, in 1886. Abolitionists like Antonio Maceo and José Martí became leaders in the struggle for Cuban independence. Explicitly anti-imperialist, Martí's vision of "our America" is an early articulation of regional solidarity.

Cuba's hard-won independence was quickly undermined by U.S. imperialist interests in the island following the Spanish-American War, with the sinking of the *U.S.S. Maine* serving as pretext for a quick rout of Spanish forces by U.S. troops. Under U.S. tutelage, client regimes, including that of right-wing dictator Fulgencio Batista, quickly built a tourist industry, playing on the fact that Key West was a mere ninety miles away from Havana. During this neocolonial period, export-oriented agribusiness was also developed, a model of the "banana republic." Finally, with a small band of guerrillas, Fidel Castro waged an armed struggle, and on January 1, 1959, the Cuban Revolution was declared victorious.

The United States feared having a Soviet-backed country so close to its own shores, so the first five years of the new socialist republic in Cuba were marked by intense U.S. counterrevolutionary terrorism. The most infamous incidents were the assault on Playa Girón, the Bay of Pigs invasion, and, in October 1962, the "crisis Octubre," the Cuban Missile Crisis, when the clock almost struck midnight on mutual nuclear annihilation. According to the Cuban government (the Monumento Denuncia), the U.S.-CIA intervention to attempt to topple the Castro regime resulted in 3,476 assassinations. The economic blockade that the United States set up during that time and has maintained ever since has cost Cuba $1 trillion through 2014.

However, the Revolutionary Armed Forces had a new enemy the following October that killed more people in two days than any battle and laid waste to most of the battlefields of the Cuban Revolution. From October 4 to 6, 1963, Hurricane Flora meandered through the eastern mountains of Cuba, killing 1,126. Castro personally led a convoy of several army tanks, almost having been killed himself twice en route.[48] The conquest of the storm included forty-seven daily flights from Havana to the Oriente (East) province; 40,000 people were evacuated. Castro's statement, "more powerful than hurricanes is man's feeling of solidarity," became the battle cry of two new institutions, the National Meteorological Institute, created on October 12, 1965, and the Civil Defense, created on July 11, 1966, with the goal of "avoiding the loss of a single life."[49] Civil Defense coordinates the mandatory evacuation orders, sets up emergency shelters, distributes emergency food rations, and publishes a guide for families.

This hands-on centralized approach has saved many lives in subsequent storms. The United Nations has used Cuba's disaster risk reduction program as a model for other nations to follow. In 2004, Oxfam published a report distilling Cuba's formula.[50] Between 1996 and 2002, six major hurricanes struck the island. In that period, only 16 people died in Cuba, compared to 649 for its island neighbors. Sadly, the contrast with Haiti is far too instructive. The Oxfam report was published just before a tropical storm killed 3,007 people in Haiti.

On Friday, September 8, and Saturday, September 9, 2017, as Houston was still reeling from Hurricane Harvey, and weeks before Hurricane Maria laid waste to the deliberately undercapitalized U.S. colony of Puerto Rico, Hurricane Irma blew all along Cuba's north coast. Civil Defense evacuated 1,863,589 people before the hurricane. Within three weeks, according to official reports, 99.9 percent of electricity was restored. Many people shared, in detail, and with a mixture of sadness, indignation, and shame, that ten people perished from Irma. Eight of the ten had disobeyed Civil Defense orders.

South-South Solidarity

In April 2017, five months before Irma, the Ministry of Science, Information, and Environment (CITMA in the original Spanish) announced one of the most ambitious plans yet produced anywhere to confront climate change. Called "Tarea Vida"—life's homework or tasks—the Environmental Agency called for a multipronged adaptation approach to climate change in the short-term, long-term, and very long-term (from 2050 to 2100) scales. In addition to shoring up the country's Civil Defense and the Meteorological Institute, the plan includes a moratorium on construction in vulnerable coastal areas, measures to restore natural buffers such as mangroves to prevent erosion, and research into varieties of crops that are resistant to flooding and salination. It's obviously too soon to evaluate the program. However, even thinking about the very long-term timeline, through the end of the century, and attempting to pose solutions contrasts sharply with the very short-term rhythm of the quarterly shareholders' report or making policies to impact the Dow Jones Industrial Average.

The Cuban government is also involved in regional cooperative organizations such as the Organization for Caribbean States, with twenty-five member states and seven associate members. Disaster Risk Reduction is one of the five priorities of the partnership. The organization encourages exchange of scientists, policy planners, disaster responders, and governance specialists among its members. Most notable for Cuba are the country's medical brigades: as of 2017, over fifty thousand Cuban doctors have worked in seventy countries. In November 2018, when Brazil's newly elected right-wing president expelled over eight thousand Cuban doctors, there were an estimated twenty thousand total working outside of Cuba. In the Caribbean alone, as of 2017, over five thousand Caribbean students graduated from a Cuban university. Cuban response teams, not just medical, but civil defense and electricity brigades, offer direct material aid as well as capacity building to other countries following disasters. The United States refused Cuba's offer of assistance in 2005 following Hurricane Katrina, and again in 2017 following Maria.

In Havana in June 2016, during its sixth summit, the Organization for Caribbean States approved a Program to Confront Climate Change. In March 2017, also in Havana, a conference, Cooperation of Caribbean States followed this up to reinforce the cooperation of member states for protection of the Caribbean. Seven projects were approved, with four having a direct impact on the climate, mitigation of the effects, protection of wetlands and coral, and responding to invasive species. The other three reinforced transportation between the island nations.

This forward thinking from one of the world's most vulnerable regions to climate change is based on regional collaboration and unity. Importantly, this South-South partnership does not depend on, nor did the impetus derive from, the capitalist world system. We need to be thinking outside the box if our species is to survive. And we need to act. Now.

Thinking Anthropologically, Acting Anthropologically: Solutions

A common slogan identified with the 1970s U.S. environmentalist movement is to "think globally, act locally." It's an attempt to remind people that our consumer choices matter, like millions of individual polyps forming a great barrier reef.[51] However, this message can reproduce top-down, single-issue thinking. Instead, it is always important to address the problem globally and locally simultaneously. It is becoming increasingly clear that the status quo isn't cutting it. While buying consumer products labeled "green" might make us feel better, the pace of global warming is only increasing. Capitalist solutions like carbon offsets or cap-and-trade deals not only amount to "paying someone else to go on a diet" but also encourage human rights violations, *all* of which is on Indigenous homeland.[52]

Many people within consumer capitalist societies like the United States are trained from an early age to think that we can make a difference only as individuals, by buying our way into the new world. It reflects a powerful worldview that the capitalist system will fix itself. True, every dollar—or euro or pound or yen—we spend is a vote for the world we live in. But let's be clear: we don't all have the same number of votes. Collective solutions engaging structures of power, involving social movements, are necessary as well. Having an anthropological imagination helps us shift our focus by thinking locally as well as globally, acting globally as well as locally. Importantly, it helps us weave connections between issues that are often spun as separate, like UN climate talks, divestment, and direct action, particularly around preventing pipelines. Importantly, an anthropological imagination helps us widen our analytical lens to see and support issues of justice, not just as an afterthought or slogan.

United Nations Climate Treaties

The 1992 Earth Summit got the ball rolling, creating the United Nations Framework Convention on Climate Change, which 197 countries have ratified. Three years later, in 1995, the UN held a conference in Kyoto, Japan, and the resulting Kyoto Protocol, ratified two years later, was the first set of international emission targets. The UN's climate work is done in two parallel tracks, the permanent bureaucracy—secretariat—and the member states. Within the former is the UN Intergovernmental Panel on Climate Change (IPCC), which commissions Assessment Reports every five years. As I write this, the last one was in 2013, the Fifth Assessment Report. According to the IPCC website, "It is categorical in its conclusion: climate change is real and human activities are the main cause."[53] Member states meet annually at the Conference of the Parties (COP).

The most significant commitment was made at the twenty-first COP, in 2015, held in Paris, and resulted in the Paris Agreement, ratified by 175 governments the following Earth Day, April 22, 2016. The 2015 Paris Agreement represented a sea change in the often-glacial pace of diplomacy, bowing to pressure and momentum by member states and the UN itself, as well as NGOs.

The core of the Paris Agreement is the goal to keep global temperature rise to "well below" two degrees Celsius above preindustrial levels. This is done by member states' "Nationally Determined Contributions" to specific plans of action to limit the emission of greenhouse gas. The agreement is essentially a culture of accountability and (hopefully) peer pressure. Assisting countries in making the changes they voluntarily committed to, the Paris Agreement outlines mechanisms for funding, technology transfer, and capacity building. Every five years, parties to the agreement will take stock of progress. For the first time in UN climate policy, inequality was specifically mentioned, with mechanisms for richer countries to send $100 billion a year to poorer countries to help them build capacity to respond. The word "justice" appears a couple times, but the language stops short of "reparations."

As argued in the previous chapter, an anthropological imagination should help us understand the importance of reparations. We need to see the processes of uneven global development as part of the long, five-hundred-year march of global capitalism; we need to understand that in fact the United States and Western Europe's wealth is directly connected to the deliberate and at times violent and racist extraction of resources from Indigenous peoples and enslaved Africans, followed by formal colonization and now "development" of their land. Reparations is the only framework strong enough to muster the real action and necessary sacrifices. Allusions to the Manhattan Project or the Marshall Plan attempted to inspire the scale-up necessary for global collective will and political commitment.[54] But both plans arise from an ascendant, prosperous U.S. empire, which was waging the Cold War, and as such their usefulness is also limited. And generations of damage do, in fact, need to be repaired.

In addition to illuminating the moral imperative for why we must act and showing how justice is a way to restore bonds of humanity, an anthropological imagination helps us identify specific ways that local issues, refracted as singular particular events, are directly connected to one another. Climate activist groups and leaders of UN member nations caught in the crosshairs of climate change, such as the Maldives, indeed pushed for stronger language in the Paris Agreement.

Fueling Climate Change: Investment and Divestment

Divestment, or the act of selling off business interests or investments, is gaining steam. This tactic was successfully used by the African National Congress—and their solidarity partners in several countries—to help take down the apartheid regime in South Africa, and since 2013 mainstream churches such as the United Church of Christ have divested fossil fuel companies from their investment portfolios. On Earth Day 2018, Caritas, the Catholic Church's international NGO, and thirty other Catholic agencies announced at least a partial divestment from fossil fuels.[55] University students, who face the consequences of our failure to act, often lead the charge for divestment of fossil fuels from their university's endowment. When students at Harvard pushed for divestment, shutting down classes in March 2017, their actions made international news, as Harvard's endowment was valued then at $37.1 billion. In February 2020, when the faculty overwhelmingly voted in support of divestment, the endowment was valued at $40 billion. The tide may be changing. Even the Rockefeller Family Foundation, inheritors of John Rockefeller's fortune from Standard Oil, divested from fossil fuels in 2016, following the Rockefeller Brothers Fund's 2014 pledge. Even the government of Norway, whose wealth was never from colonialism or slavery but from its oil reserves, began divesting its trillion-dollar sovereign wealth fund in November 2017. It adds up: as of August 2018, 902 institutions have pledged to divest, representing $6.2 trillion.[56]

Our anthropological imagination can also help us address the root causes of our warming climate. The capitalist addiction to oil and other fossil fuels in the first place has led to untenably fragile marriages of convenience within the oil-producing world, most notably the countries of the Arabian Peninsula, which produce a third of all oil annually and contain over 43 percent of the world's proven oil reserves.[57] Before the invention of the automobile and airplane, crude oil was used for little more than kerosene lamps. The British Empire used not only the victory of the Allies following World War I but also the isolationist stance—if not the practice—of the United States to administer the breakup of the Ottoman Empire themselves and thus control its oil reserves. Breaking countries into administrative divisions for the convenience of the colonizer created time bombs, as different ethnic groups were lumped together or divided arbitrarily. With Western Europe devastated following the even more destructive World War II, the United States stepped into its current role as standard bearer of the "Western world" or "the free world." In other words, U.S. empire took the reins from the British, who over the following generation gave up administration of nearly all of their colonies.

With the construction of highways and the increasing electrification of cities, consumption of fossil fuels increased beginning in the 1950s. And so U.S. empire found itself increasingly jockeying for access to cheap oil.

Instead of engaging in formal colonialism and just taking over the government of these countries, the United States used international institutions, headquartered in Washington, D.C., like the IMF and the World Bank, to do the dirty work. Massive fluctuations in global oil prices in the 1980s triggered immense Third World debt, and these international institutions imposed "shock therapy," forcing these governments to abruptly change their spending, cutting programs and opening up the country for privatization.

The oil-rich Arabian Peninsula was an unlikely coconspirator with the United States. Since the very beginning, when the Prophet Muhammad revised Judeo-Christian orthodoxy, European elites used religious differences to carry out campaigns of conquest in the Middle East with impunity, even raising tens of thousands of conscripts in the Crusades, when Christian armies descended on the Middle East to "save" the Holy Land from the "infidel." Economically, technologically, and militarily, the Muslim world outpaced feudal Europe, yet their countries were never given respect in international negotiations with European powers. Centuries later, these historical tensions were enflamed again when the United States got involved in the region with its support for Israel, a country created out of the wreckage of World War II, displacing the Palestinian people.

The United States allied themselves with the Royal House of Saud, in Saudi Arabia, offering them technological and military support in exchange for a seemingly unlimited supply of oil. This long-standing relationship allows the Saudi royal family to deny clear human rights violations that might otherwise be investigated more thoroughly were it not for the Saudis' close relationship with the United States, their provision of oil to the open market, their $646.4 billion gross domestic product, and their share of the U.S. national debt.[58] However, the October 2018 murder of *Washington Post* columnist Jamal Khashoggi got the world's attention. Despite evidence connecting his murder to the Saudi Crown, the Trump administration accepted the Saudis' denial that they were responsible.

The United States made similar alliances with the Shah of Iran, the Taliban in Afghanistan, and even Saddam Hussein in Iraq when each declared allegiance to the United States against the Soviet Union. These deals were meant to help the United States win the Cold War and to keep the oil flowing. However, the Iranian Revolution of 1979 cut off a large supply of oil. And after he invaded Kuwait in 1990, the secular regime of Saddam Hussein became the United States' public enemy number one, a role conveniently reprised after the flimsiest of evidence following the September 11, 2001, attacks on the World Trade Center and the Pentagon. The target couldn't be further from the mark: the group responsible for the attacks, then called al-Qaeda, was headquartered in Saudi Arabia, explicitly challenging the secular regime. The Taliban also found itself the "bad guy" to the United States after 9/11, their abuses of women's rights suddenly an urgent issue.[59] The United States wasted no time invading Afghanistan after the 9/11 attacks, on October 7, 2001, and U.S. troops are still there as I write this chapter seventeen years later. The war in Afghanistan is the longest in U.S. history aside from the wars of extermination and territorial expansion against Native America, and everyone is losing.

All this is to say that our anthropological imagination can help us highlight connections between issues of climate change and others like the War on Terror. Absent the end of empire itself, kicking capitalism's carbon habit might also go further as a longer-term, peaceful alternative to the mobilization and Islamophobic nationalism building up to war against the enemy du jour, short-term friends who may in a few years become the next target.

Drawing a Line in the Tar Sands: Keystone XL

Capitalism requires local spaces, whether for factories, stores, farms, or mines. This particularly pertains to oil: fields are used for drilling and other lands for refineries. Connecting these spaces, oil needs to be moved across communities, and sometimes across national borders. One such project for moving oil was a pipeline called the Keystone XL, or the Tar Sands pipeline, because it processed oil from "sands"—crude bitumen—from a field north of Fort McMurray, Alberta, Canada. Keystone XL was designed to pump 800,000 barrels a day to Nebraska, in the United States, where it would then get pumped to refineries on the U.S. Gulf Coast. The plans for Keystone XL began in 2008 by the TransCanada Corporation. Almost immediately, climate activist groups like 350.org, also founded in 2008, put up a fight, building its network in opposition to Keystone XL.

And it was—and is—a long fight. On their website, 350.org reported 750 local actions, including several lawsuits and vigils in front of the Obama White House. With hundreds of media stories, several petitions with tens of thousands of signatures, and the support of several Native American nations, the fight against the Keystone XL made a media splash.

Eventually these high-profile Keystone XL protests forced the hand of a reluctant President Obama, who had several times spoken of the importance of clean energy. On November 6, 2015, well after the last midterm elections and as the 2016 presidential race was already in full swing, Obama accepted Secretary of State John Kerry's recommendation that the pipeline was not in the interest of national security. It was later approved by the Nebraska Supreme Court in August 2019, but as of February 2020 it appears that investors may be backing off. It is still very much a live issue as this book goes to press.

Water Is Life: Resistance to DAPL

The Dakota Access Pipeline (DAPL), also called the Bakken Pipeline since it begins in the Bakken oil field in North Dakota, is another one of these oil pipelines. This pipeline pumps 500,000 barrels of oil daily from western North Dakota to southern Illinois, over 1,100 miles. Energy Transfer Partners began constructing the $3.6 billion pipeline in 2016.

As with many energy infrastructure projects, financing for DAPL came from a range of investment banks, most visibly Wells Fargo. The construction of DAPL met with resistance from several Native American nations whose land and waters lay along the pipeline, the path of which threatened sacred Native American sites. Several tribal governments appealed to the U.S. Army Corps of Engineers to conduct a full environmental impact statement, a process legally required for the easement necessary to allow the pipeline to cross the Missouri River. The Army Corps of Engineers was involved because they had been officially granted stewardship of the Missouri following the Flood Control Act of 1944, after which they built five dams. These violated the 1851 and 1868 Fort Laramie treaties with the Greater Sioux Nation, which granted the Indigenous people rights to the country's widest river.[60] Not willing to pin all their hopes on a legal outcome with the federal government that had consistently, time and again, broken promises, Indigenous water protectors also staged direct action, converging on the Standing Rock Indian Reservation that straddles North and South Dakota, invoking the principle of *Mni Wiconi*, translated as "water is life." Sacred Stone Camp sprung up just outside both the reservation and the construction site below the river to house as many as four thousand protestors.

Nick Estes, cofounder of Red Nation and American studies faculty at the University of New Mexico, has published several analyses of DAPL.[61] In addition to being a citizen of the Lower Brule Sioux Tribe, Estes was an active participant in the #NoDAPL protests. Estes argued that DAPL was an extension of the wars of extermination, which peaked in the 1870s through the 1890s. And he added that water protectors were nothing new, as seven Sioux Nations had been flooded by the Army Corps of Engineers' dams, four of which were placed on reservation lands. Over 600,000 acres of Native land were taken via eminent domain, and these sovereign nations lost over 300,000 acres of rich-soil bottom lands.[62]

Estes also highlights Standing Rock's legacy. Following the 1973 Wounded Knee Occupation, in which over two hundred American Indian Movement members and supporters took control of the site of an 1890 U.S. government massacre of over two hundred Indigenous people, Standing Rock convened ninety Indigenous nations, laying the groundwork for the international movement that secured the UN's 2007 Declaration of the Rights of Indigenous Peoples. Like in the 1970s, in 2016 Standing Rock and the camps, like Sacred Stone, Oceti Sakowin, and Red Warrior, were gathering places for non-Indigenous and Indigenous people from over two hundred Native nations from all over the world.[63]

Native peoples joined their sisters and brothers in Standing Rock in solidarity to stand up for sovereignty, justice, land rights, and humanity. Estes writes, "Every act on our part to recover and reclaim our lives and land and to resist elimination is an attempt to recuperate that lost humanity— humanity this settler state refuses and denies even to its own."[64] From Standing Rock, Amy Goodman broadcast her daily radio show, *Democracy Now!*, on September 3, 2016. The video, which showed dogs attacking protesters, went viral. After this, more mainstream environmental groups joined the effort. Non-Natives came from Minneapolis and were educated about the historical legacies and continuities of Indigenous disempowerment and colonial violence. Sacred Stone had living and teaching spaces expressly designed for non-Native allies or accomplices. Less than a week following *Democracy Now!*'s attack footage, the Seattle City Council passed a resolution opposing DAPL. Protests ramped up when lame-duck North Dakota governor Jack Dalrymple, already tapped to join the Trump team, ordered an evacuation of protestors on November 28. Within the week, faced with a groundswell of pressure, on December 4, 2016, the Army Corps of Engineers suspended construction of the pipeline until the completion of the environmental impact assessment.

It was a victory not only for the fight against climate change but also for Indigenous people's long-standing fight for sovereignty and rights to their land and water. As Estes said, "The oils themselves personify capitalism because they solidify settler states' control over Indigenous lands."

But the pause in construction was only that, a pause. Indigenous activists and those in solidarity called for divestment of Energy Transfer Partners' financing.

On January 24, 2017, within four days of taking office, President Trump lifted the restriction on the pipeline's construction. And on February 7, 2017, just as the Army authorized construction on the pipeline, the Seattle City Council—following Indigenous activist mobilization—voted unanimously to cut ties with Wells Fargo because of its role in financing DAPL. Several websites by Indigenous groups include strategies and how-to guides for divestment campaigns, such as at mazaskatalks.org and lastrealindians .com.[65] Following Seattle, the cities of Raleigh, Los Angeles, and even San Francisco, where the financial behemoth Wells Fargo is headquartered, joined suit.[66] Public employee retirement fund CalPERS also divested, citing opposition to DAPL.

This is only the briefest of discussions of the issue. The journal *Cultural Anthropology* published a forum co-curated by Dhillon and Estes during the height of the mobilization.[67] There are other resources by Winona LaDuke and Kyle Whyte, Estes's *Our Past Is the Future* and Jaskiran Dhillon and Nick Estes's volume *#NoDAPL and Mni Wiconi*, an article by Edwin López, and a crowd-sourced online syllabus project, similar to that compiled by Black Lives Matter activists.[68]

Construction on the pipeline was completed in April 2017, with the first oil pumped in May. In mid-August 2018, during a meeting with Energy Secretary Rick Perry, Energy Transfer Partners hinted at an expansion.

A Tale of Two Pipelines

Why would it take mainstream (read: majority white) climate change groups so long to take on #DAPL as an issue, when they were at the fore against Keystone XL? The reason Obama finally settled on was nationalism: while Keystone XL might have been good for Canada, it was not good for the United States. However, it might also be that Indigenous people and their issues are valued less than those of settler society. As the previous chapter demonstrated, this differential value attached to human life is demonstrated repeatedly, in the sentencing for crimes against a white person versus a person of color; in settlements awarded in class-action environmental lawsuits brought in white communities as opposed to those of POC neighborhoods; and in the amount of airtime and therefore philanthropic dollars donated following a disaster. Corporate and even "alternative" media sources often resort to distancing language, making it seem like the issue is happening to people who are "not us," preventing viewer/reader identification with the impacted community. Language also distances the people themselves. They appear distant, less than fully human.

Radical empathy requires humanizing accounts of tragedy, so that regardless of the language people speak, the clothes they wear, their family structures, or the gods they worship (or not), their human loss is felt just as deeply as that of people who look and think like us, whoever that us is. And let's be real—that "us" has for quite some time been white, middle class, ablebodied, heterosexual, cisgendered, and Christian. Media outlets, like history textbooks, have been dominated by this small subset, the beneficiaries of brutal acts of genocide and forced removal. Even if we successfully decolonize our understanding of what it means to be human, provincializing white identities enough to care equally about the suffering of Indigenous peoples, NGOs involved in climate change have not easily identified this as an issue.

Supporting Local Communities' Struggles for Justice

In the struggle to defend humanity from climate change, a stronger, self-enforced international regulatory framework is not enough. Turning off the financial spigot for dirty energy is not even enough. As with all human systems, capitalism's addiction to fossil fuels also requires local spaces—local environments, local communities, local people—to consent to being polluted by extraction for the enrichment of the world's largest corporations. True, many are lured to support these gambits with prospects of jobs or meager financial compensation, but even if they wanted to say no, it would be hard.[69] These communities are not able to have their NIMBY (not in my backyard) politics stick: in the United States they are either poor whites or more typically urban communities of color or Native American reservations. Colonies like Puerto Rico and the Marshall Islands are legally shut out of saying no to having their environments destroyed by corporations in pursuit of profits. In the Global South, this dirty capitalism is often steamrolled by Structural Adjustment Programs put in place by "Economic Hit Men" sent by the World Bank or IMF, who give corporations virtually unfettered rights to operate in countries crippled by debts inherited by postcolonial regimes in return for minor investments in the country and jobs for their populace.[70] As with all of humanity's struggles, the carbon war is being waged on local battlefields. The struggle for climate justice was already being fought at Standing Rock long before *Democracy Now!*'s coverage finally brought mainstream climate activist organizations into the fight.

Climate activist groups might at first be forgiven for their sluggishness. They were doing what NGOs do: institutionalize issues. Being entities created within so-called Western democratic states that offer tax benefits for donors, NGOs must work against the inequities structured into the system, which includes a zero-sum logic. And the Standing Rock tribal government and the Sacred Stone Camp did not at first prioritize the words "climate change." The community at Standing Rock was initially defending treaty rights, protesting the pollution of their sacred water as well as other sacred sites on land. Activists from over two hundred Indigenous nations came to the camp in no small part because of the need for constant vigilance regarding the defense of Native sovereignty granted through treaties with a foreign government, the United States.

Communities engaged in an active local struggle for justice cannot always be expected to translate these struggles into issues of global relevance. An anthropological imagination can help us do this work. Local struggles for justice may well emphasize a different set of priorities or even use different language that reflects a different worldview. For example, a fuller translation of *Mni Wiconi* is not just water is life, but "water is alive"—a moral agent, a family member, with whom the living have a reciprocal obligation.[71]

One of the oldest tricks rulers employ is to divide and conquer the population. However, exploited communities have more in common with one another than with their oppressors. The same corporations that have laid off workers in manufacturing centers across the Rust Belt are driving wages down in Mexico, the Caribbean, and Asia. Noted in chapter 1, the idea that we are all more alike than different is expressed in the Lakota term *Mitakuye Oyasin*, often translated as "we are all related" or "all our relations."[72]

This doesn't mean that settler colonialists can assume the right to speak on behalf of Indigenous protestors or appropriate (some use the word "colonize") Indigenous issues for their own benefit. Far from it. Engaging in solidarity *does* require introspection, self-critique, and being open to critique from others. It does not mean turning Indigenous or other local communities into educators for outside allies. We need to own our privilege and educate ourselves first. Having an anthropological imagination can help us establish solidarity with targeted communities and not indulge in "do-gooderism." Acting as accomplices with local activists on a particular struggle, in this case keeping dirty oil in the ground in a particular place, helps us unravel the systems of inhumanity these activists face in this situation while defending the overall survival of the human race by safeguarding a global commons, our planet's atmosphere.

Justice and Solidarity

Having an anthropological imagination encourages complex thinking: rather than framing an issue within a single "either/or" understanding, it encourages us to see issues as "both/and." An anthropological imagination also helps us point out the multiplicity of scales included in each issue. The stakes of each issue are always global and local at once: each and every time the struggle is lost, precedent is set, rendering injustices easier in the next time and place, and the next time and place, and the next. By contrast, successfully saying NO to more pollution and atmospheric-warming carbon offers tools and momentum, a blueprint, for other communities to follow. And in so doing, local solidarity activism can illuminate particular global connections: Who are the investors, and which media outlets and politicians are on their payroll? How do particular histories of white settler violence call upon, and reinforce, white supremacy?

White, middle-class professionals may be able to afford to be explicitly environmentalist, choosing single-issue politics. For some people, the issue chose them: colonized people in the Marshall Islands or Vieques, Puerto Rico, did not get to choose whether the federal government used their lands for nuclear testing.[73] The same can be said of Prairie Island, Leech Lake, and many other Native American reservations.[74]

In other words, climate activism must always be about climate justice.

And having an anthropological imagination helps us see that "justice" is more than just a slogan, an add-on. If marginalized communities were chosen by coal and oil corporations to include the route of a pipeline or to have a refinery built in their territory, then climate activists should not only follow the lead from these communities, however the issue is understood and defined locally, but also offer support to locally identified priorities. Activism must also directly engage the structures that make these communities targets for dirty capitalism in the first place. In other words, we need to work to respect Indigenous peoples' treaty rights and sovereignty, create real living-wage job opportunities within urban communities of color, and end the disempowerment of millions of disproportionately Black and Latinx people by mandatory sentencing minimums.

Stemming the Rising Tide

Silicon Valley and the tech industry and its many networks such as TED put out the hope that technology can solve this issue, just as it can solve inequality. At least when I was an organizer, a common response—that is to say, dismissal—to demands for specificity and what is often maligned as identity politics was some variant of the phrase "a rising tide lifts all boats." However, the main problem is the rising tide itself: capitalism and its promotion of endless consumption. We need to use our anthropological imagination to identify other ways of living the "good life." An *archaeological* imagination provides other models.

Tech-friendly approaches attempt incremental changes while keeping the virtual economy powered on. A "carbon tax" was proposed in six countries as of 2018, including oil-rich Canada and Norway, forcing companies to pay for the damage they caused by burning fossil fuels and using the tax resources to fund alternative local energy projects.

One possible alternative a carbon tax can fund is solar power. The solar power industry offers jobs that can't be outsourced, as installation is always done locally. Every house could potentially produce solar power. However, this makes big power companies' concentration of wealth more difficult. So they are attempting to block people's access to solar energy systems by paying off local governments to create zoning ordinances that forbid the installation of solar panels.

True, we could keep looking for new power sources. *The Matrix* offers a particularly chilling solution, just as *Soylent Green* did for the hunger crisis. But *The Matrix* isn't that far off. Fossil fuels are merely the mainlining of the drug, feeding our addiction to acquisition and consumption. Oil was not the first black liquid to fuel the global capitalist system and its appetite for consumption. That was molasses, boiled sugar cane juice, sometimes poured onto slaves as punishment: capitalism's first fuel was the blood of fifteen million people ripped from Africa and enslaved in the so-called New World.

Given the inequalities just noted, and the brutality of how the "West" became dominant in the first place, the conversation of climate change activists needs to be about climate *justice*, not just climate change. The hypocrisy shown by advanced capitalist societies and large corporations regarding the production of greenhouse gases is only one element. Climate justice explicitly confronts basic inequalities: the world's biggest polluters are not those most acutely affected by climate change. The big polluters are also the biggest winners in this economic system. It is no coincidence that communities with higher climate vulnerability are disproportionally people of color or within the Global South who are already economically and politically disenfranchised.

While it might bring us some comfort to define empowerment as "lifting" low-income communities up so they can consume goods and services like the middle class, the demands of justice and equity mean instead that middle classes must consume *less*. This is even more important considering that capitalism operates on lands that have been colonized already.

More radical (which simply means getting at the root) solutions were proposed by a group of Indigenous scholar-activists and compiled by Waziyatawin and Yellow Bird.[75] Their book, *For Indigenous Minds Only*, offers several approaches to free the mind and body from colonialism and also prepare for the collapse of the carbon economy and hence the settler world system dependent on it. We know this new world is coming; coal and oil are finite resources, and although some people are going to extraordinary lengths, like fracking and mining tar sands, to squeeze the last drops from inside the earth, eventually there will be nothing left for them to take. The contributors to *For Indigenous Minds Only* argue for a return to, and protection of, sacred ancestral land.

This is most definitely *not* the same as the survivalism increasingly depicted in pop culture dystopias. From *Survivor* to the seemingly endless fascination with the "zombie apocalypse," the message seems to be clear: rugged individual, save thyself. Kill or be killed.

The reality is that there are now over seven billion human lives on this planet, and this number will only increase. It is irresponsible to retreat into survivalist mode, trying to revive a foraging way of life and living "off the grid." There just isn't enough land to sustain the hunting and gathering necessary to fill that many stomachs. At best this scenario is blind to this fact. This dream of a survivalist retreat requires a certain level of privilege to imagine it. Worse, it reproduces a genocidal, settler logic: whose land will (white) folks learn to live off of?

The human race needs forward-thinking solutions, not a retreat into settler, genocidal fantasies. Anthropological research has shown that indeed necessity is often the mother of invention. Facing the limitations of our resources offers us an opportunity to rethink our priorities and fix, once and for all, our unequal system of distribution. We have the capacity to feed eleven billion people, and that's without assuming a change in diet. Changing to a vegan diet would not only be more equitable, but is also one of the best ways to cool the planet, even if more foundational changes to agribusiness are not made. A global consciousness that takes seriously the possibility that we will not be around if we don't make major changes—species thinking or using an anthropological imagination—could be useful in actually coming together, to take seriously the belief that we are all connected. We need to make inequalities and hunger in a world of plenty part of the old regime, when we thought the sky was our limit. Unfortunately, we have been polluting that sky. We need to look for alternative energy sources, but we also need to ask why we want more in the first place. Are we as a species happier under capitalism? Working longer hours, accumulating more stuff, investing ever greater resources in guarding that stuff? Creating massive prisons and increasing state violence rather than fixing the structural inequalities?

Our anthropological imagination helps us loosen the vise of consumption so we can see alternatives. Anthropological research has uncovered a plethora of other models. Bhutan, in the Himalayas, sandwiched between the world's two most populous nations, is the only country in the world that is "carbon negative," pulling more carbon dioxide from the atmosphere than it emits. The country also scores the highest on the "Gross National Happiness" index, a term coined by Bhutan's King Jigme Singye Wangchuck in 1972 and developed into a philosophy of holistic development enshrined in their 2008 constitution.[76]

These models aren't some New Age romanticizing of poor folks who have to make do with less, putting them forward as more "spiritual" or "salt of the earth." As discussed in chapter 1, the !Kung San (also called the Dobe Ju'Hoase), in the Kalahari Desert in southern Africa spent only twenty hours a week on survival, which leaves plenty of time for other things like leisure, enjoying time with family and building community.[77] Feminists correctly pointed out the gender bias in this research.[78] And we must always remember that the !Kung were placed in reservations by European colonial governments. Even with these obvious shortcomings in the anthropological record, the !Kung offer lessons in sustainability desperately needed now.

Even societies with what anthropologists call rank inequality, with differences in status and prestige, managed to figure out ways of channeling status consciousness into distributing rather than accumulating things like the "potlatch" from First Nations in the Pacific Northwest.[79] These ceremonies were highly public displays of leaders' power and prestige by giving goods to neighboring communities. The archaeological record is also full of examples of societies resisting incorporation into larger empires. The Maya "collapse" is usually reported on by Spanish conquistadores to justify their plunder: they're gone, and/or they were also empires, so what's the big deal? All across the Yucatán and Guatemala, millions of descendants beg to differ: their linguistic diversity and their many livelihoods offer a different reading. While they practiced sustainable swidden agriculture, the "collapse" was more likely folks' decision to abandon cities, scale down, and live more sustainably.[80] We too can decide to reduce our footprint.

Given advances in technology, archaeologists have increasingly more precise carbon dating, zooming into the past, being able to pinpoint when an artifact was created or settlement used to within a decade. A more complex picture emerges, a more precise snapshot of a given space and its occupants: How long was a site occupied? How was the site used? When during the year was it habited? Humans have faced climate change in the past, such as during El Niño events, as well as longer periods such as the Ice Age (the last of which ended 13,700 years ago) that literally bridged the Americas and the so-called Old World in what is now the Bering Strait. Those who survived must have been doing something right, evolutionarily speaking. Every human alive is a descendent of these survivors. Evidence shows that societies that were flexible, able to adapt to change, have been able to survive. Importantly, human societies with high degrees of *cooperation* did well. And, in truth, being on the move has been one of the surest adaptation and survival strategies we've come up with. Settler colonialism has cut this strategy off by imposing borders: as species migrate, humans, particularly Indigenous communities, can no longer migrate with them. One of the most memorable scenes from the movie *The Day After Tomorrow* depicted hordes of people trying to cross *south* at the U.S.-Mexico border. If migration is our only hope, that reproduces the same genocidal logic of settler colonialism, unless we leave the earth like in the movie *Interstellar* or the Netflix series *Lost in Space*. And in those stories, we're explicitly colonizers. The term itself is reclaimed and positive. The film *Elysium* presents a more complex tale, focusing on those left behind.[81]

Our anthropological imagination offers us the tools needed to face head on the changes in store. Our anthropological imagination respects our different local realities and understandings while seeing the global scale, "species thinking"—seeing the forest *and* the trees. While respecting and tapping into local knowledge, including what Dan Wildcat calls "indigenuity," our anthropological imagination helps us identify a politics of solidarity, something to fight *for*.[82]

So to recap what using our anthropological imagination offers to our understanding of climate change,

- Within an anthropological timeline, which began millions of years ago, we can see that this contemporary climate change is real and significant.
- Truly and without exaggeration we can acknowledge that our species itself is at risk of annihilation.
- It becomes clear that contemporary climate change is a human-created phenomenon.
- But it is not some distant dystopian future—climate change is already happening *now* to many in tropical coastal areas, not to mention it has been happening *for several hundred years* as Indigenous populations were murdered, taken from their land, and forced to assimilate into settler society, their climate already irrevocably destroyed.
- We can see that the roots of climate change are anchored within the global economic order and the racism inherent to it, needed to justify the widescale murder, theft, forced removal, and enslavement necessary to make it run.
- Therefore, we know that climate change is always about *justice*, since societies most at risk of losing their lands and resources are usually the survivors of colonialism and slavery.
- We can tell the struggle is always local and always global and that localized struggles tend to have different languages, different terms

of the debate, and different and multiple strategic foci besides the ones that we may think are important.

- We understand that we need to learn lessons about adaptation on a massive scale and that our flexibility, cooperation, and diversity have helped us to survive.
- Anthropological evidence can identify societies that have rejected hypercompetition and short-term gain and have adapted, resisted, and survived.

The rules of the game set up by the global capitalist class blind us to alternative ways of living, and with a combination of fear and cultural programming we are made to think that we need to literally buy into the system to survive and that this competitive, shortsighted, violent approach is a reflection of human nature.[83] It's not. While we have the capacity for violence and destruction, we also have the capacity for love and creativity. Our anthropological imagination can help us identify moments in human history and contemporary examples that encouraged these greater capacities. And hopefully our anthropological imagination can help us come together, identifying common cause and mustering the will to make the necessary changes if we are to survive.

Finally, an anthropological imagination helps us identify the fact that since migration has historically been one of humanity's most successful responses to climate change, one major step required for our survival is a radical rethinking of borders.

4

Humanity on the Move

Justice and Migration

> Migration is an expression of the
> human aspiration for dignity, safety,
> and a better future. It is part of the
> social fabric, part of our very make-up
> as a human family.

At first glance, threats to migration and immigrants may not seem to be an existential threat to humanity's survival. But not only is migration directly connected to our species' survival, it is one of the most divisive political issues in the United States, Europe, and rising powers like India, the lynchpin in a rising tide of nationalism and racism. It is thus particularly striking that the statement opening this chapter, which hails an inclusive humanity, was uttered by then-secretary-general of the United Nations, Ban Ki-moon, in 2013.[1] While the UN did make progress on climate change in 2015, policies regarding migration are another story.

Rising xenophobia is certainly evident in the United States. President Trump ended 2018 with a government shutdown, bullying Congress into accepting his proposal to spend $5 billion extending and reinforcing the wall along the U.S. border with Mexico. Predictably the people most hurt by the shutdown—in addition to the workers kept at home—were those who received life-sustaining, necessary services from the government. Long-term investments in infrastructure, knowledge, and science were also put on hold. Government shutdowns are a favorite tool of the Republican Party, which professes not to support "big government." This shutdown also played to Trump's base since campaigning on his ability to build the wall between the United States and Mexico catapulted him to the top of a very crowded candidate field during the presidential election in 2016. The government shutdown also competed for airtime with the tragedy of two children from Guatemala who died in U.S. custody in December 2018, seven-year-old Jakelin Caal Maquin and eight-year-old Felipe Alonzo-Gomez. This was an all too fitting end to a year marked by Trump's repeated attacks on immigrant children and families.

The centerpiece of Trump's politics of hate, the family separation policy, marked a new low in the country's treatment of migrants. Even high-ranking members of Trump's party and family publicly broke with the president. People came out of the woodwork to express support for immigrant communities. Millions of people marched, carried signs, chanted, sang 1960s protest songs, or posted multilingual signs welcoming neighbors, an affirmation of humanity. Unfortunately, much of this support came with partisan strings—or blinders. Many not directly affected were apparently ignorant of the record-breaking number of deportations by Trump's Democratic predecessor, President Obama, or that the legislation authorizing the militarization of the border and starting up the deportation machine was signed by Democrat Bill Clinton during his reelection year.

This chapter offers people who pledged support for immigrant communities the necessary tools to deepen their understanding of migration. Our anthropological imagination is critical if compassion and empathy and support for humanity are not to become fodder for partisan positioning. More importantly, our anthropological imagination gives us a useful blueprint for building an effective resistance in order to actually put an end to the dehumanization of migrants, helping us identify specific structural roots. A holistic perspective, seeing the common threads in these quite urgent threats to humanity, is a necessary step to get us off this cycle of lurching from one pressing issue to the next, always on the defensive. It weaves them together to promote a solidarity politics, giving us something to fight for, particularly since we now need the more privileged of humanity to act boldly in accompaniment and as accomplice with those most marginalized and targeted.

While an anthropological imagination begins with and helps us value the specificity of struggles, it also helps us explore parallels and common themes among various causes. It helps us put a human face on an issue such as migration and helps us point out the connections that we already have with one another. As Jason de León reminds us, "[Migrants] pick your fruit, detail your cars, and process your meat."[2] The ways that the U.S.-Mexico border was strategically used by Trump on the campaign trail and the ways in which this emphasis targeted individual bodies tend to limit people's understanding of migration. That is why a coalitional / solidarity politics is useful, particularly now. Big talk and increasingly terrifying action against targeted immigrant groups require a proactive, rehumanizing response.

And our anthropological imagination allows us to see the parallels between the very particular, complex, and increasingly terrifying situation along the U.S.-Mexico border and other crises in other parts of the globe.[3] In addition to these ways that a holistic perspective is useful, our anthropological imagination helps us sharpen the focus on the global capitalist system, and the state apparatus itself, highlighting the circuits of inequality and uneven development that drive migration.[4] And as mentioned in the previous chapter, our anthropological imagination also reminds us that humanity has always been on the move. It was one of our earliest adaptations and survival techniques. And finally, our anthropological imagination helps us refocus the discussion on people's humanity.[5] Behind every statistic in the news is a human story. Activist groups are calling upon nontargeted people to be not only allies to those dealing with migration and immigration challenges but also *accomplices*. Our anthropological imagination helps us absorb all this and outline the contours of a coalitional/solidarity politics.

Building Bridges between Particular Local Struggles

It was a Friday, a sunny eighty degrees the first day of June 2018, in Cortland, Illinois. The forecast called for a nice weekend. There had been more rain than previous summers, and the corn and soybeans were both doing well. Nothing seemed out of the ordinary. Cortland's population had quadrupled since the 1990s, leveling off following the Great Recession in 2008 at over four thousand. Like small towns all across the United States, Cortland struggled to rebuild following the 2008 subprime mortgage bubble and the lagging recession that followed. One business that managed to stay afloat was Alfredo's Iron Works, employing skilled blacksmiths who worked on, among other things, public art outside of the local university's alumni center.

Cortland sits outside of DeKalb, a regional agribusiness hub, home to Northern Illinois University. Like that of many college towns, DeKalb's economy waxes and wanes with the tide of student enrollment, unfortunately currently on a downward trend. Illinois had been without a state budget for over two years at that point, and the county's largest employer definitely felt the pinch. It was also summer for the university, and it showed, as many local businesses were relatively empty.

But June 1, 2018, was no ordinary day in Cortland.

Hundreds of texts, tweets, and Facebook instant messages were swirling around the community, triggering panic. U.S. Immigration and Customs Enforcement (ICE) officials had been sighted in the area. ICE was running active campaigns in thirty-seven local communities in Illinois, including a raid the previous week in the city of St. Charles, a half hour's drive from Cortland. With most students gone, including the activists of Dream Action NIU, a group organized by undocumented students, the task of responding to these urgent messages and verifying their contents so as not to induce panic fell to a couple of individuals from a group called Welcoming Western Counties, a community organization mostly of undocumented allies. This community coalition had successfully lobbied DeKalb's new mayor that March to sign a Welcoming Proclamation, which pledged among other things to not actively pursue deportation actions.

The rumors about the ICE raid proved true: eight blacksmiths at Alfredo's Iron Works were arrested by ICE and sent to an undisclosed location. When questioned, the county sheriff's office confirmed they had established a perimeter around the building for ICE officers. Several other area businesses, including Mexican restaurants, closed their doors, their employees in mortal terror.

After two weeks, with no information surfacing about the eight people brought into ICE custody, U.S. representative Bill Foster from nearby Naperville wrote to ICE, demanding answers. There were none, and those people were disappeared, literally erased from the public eye. Two of the eight ironsmiths in Cortland jailed by ICE were deported. Working with attorneys from the Illinois Coalition of Immigrant and Refugee Rights and the American Civil Liberties Union, community members from Welcoming Western Counties were able to obtain the successful release of the six others. In addition to having to pay several thousand dollars in court costs and other legal fees, the families of all eight were traumatized. This trauma is shared by many people across the United States.

"Zero Tolerance"

The Cortland ICE raid was only one of many examples of communities being ripped apart as an orchestrated campaign of state-sponsored terror spread throughout the country. On April 6, 2018, U.S. attorney general Jeff Sessions declared that his department would be enforcing a "zero-tolerance policy" against undocumented people like the Cortland blacksmiths. While illegal entry had been a federal misdemeanor and reentry a federal felony since 1929, previous administrations had prioritized deporting individuals with a criminal record. Sessions's goal was 100 percent criminal prosecution of illegal entry—even of people seeking asylum from countries where their lives were in danger, and even though asylum seeking is authorized under U.S. law—on the idea that a "get tough" attitude and stiffer sentencing would deter people from trying to enter the United States unlawfully.[6] Yet the vast majority of undocumented residents arrive legally.

The zero-tolerance policy led to the separation of migrant children from their parents, echoes of how in an earlier period Indigenous children were ripped away from their parents and forcibly assimilated into white American society. Within two months, thousands of children, some of whom were in diapers, were locked up in detention centers. The Department of Homeland Security (DHS) reported 2,432 children separated from their parents, a likely underestimate. Images of frightened, crying children left alone in detention centers shocked the world, as did the stories that came out of child suicides, a hunger strike, and the hospitalization that was required for injuries sustained while in detention. Surely this wasn't the United States of America, the land of the free! Wasn't this the nation of immigrants?

Disgust with the policy reached a fever pitch following Father's Day weekend, June 17. The following day, the editorial page of Rupert Murdoch's *New York Post*, usually emphatically pro-Trump, declared, "It's not just that this looks terrible in the eyes of the world. It *is* terrible."[7] Objectors included Speaker of the House Paul Ryan, White House advisor Kellyanne Conway, and even Melania Trump.

Faced with pressure even from those in his own camp, Trump relented, signing an executive order on June 20 ending the policy of family separation. In its place he ordered a policy of family detention. Children caught entering the United States outside of the legal channels would still be put in jail, but they would be with their parents. With the most draconian policy rescinded, there was still the matter of family reunification for those children who had initially been taken from their parents. A court-ordered deadline of July 26 passed, and 711 children were still separated from their parents.[8]

As of September 2018, 12,800 children were being detained, a number five times greater than the previous year. The *New York Times* reported that following this deadline at the end of July, within a span of a few weeks, 1,600 children were transported in the middle of a night, "under the cover of darkness," to a sprawling Texas tent city in the desert along the border near El Paso.[9] The tent camps are supposedly temporary, a stopgap measure, but there is no end to this practice in sight at the time of this writing. The number of children, their length of stay, and the fact that there is nowhere else to put them all highlight the fact that the system crashed, overwhelmed by the Trump administration's zeal. Transporting the children at night was purportedly meant to minimize the risk of them running away, but it also conveniently kept this traffic in children hidden, away from the public and media spotlight. Also away from the spotlight, a November 2018 *ProPublica* report documented that the Trump administration had quietly resumed family separation.[10] A special issue of the journal *Cultural Anthropology* delves into this issue.[11]

Killing the Dream

There are an estimated 11 million undocumented people in the United States, almost two-thirds of whom have been in the United States for at least a decade.[12] Of this population, there were an estimated 1.1 million minors in 2010 and 4.4 million people under thirty.[13] Undocumented and legal immigrant youth who migrated before the age of twelve are called the 1.5 generation.[14] Many of these 1.5-generation immigrants speak English as their first language, having been socialized in the United States since they were quite small. Many are also DACA eligible. DACA stands for Deferred Action for Childhood Arrivals, an executive order signed by President Obama on June 15, 2012, during his reelection year. DACA directed DHS to delay deportation action against people who came to the United States as children, some as babies. But in order to be safe from deportation because of this program, undocumented immigrants had to register with the government. The decision to apply for DACA protection is fraught for these young people, as receiving the benefits comes with the risk of targeting their parents for deportation action, as well as themselves if the Trump administration succeeds at ending it. As of September 2017, just under 700,000 people were registered with U.S. Citizenship and Immigration Services (USCIS).

DACA was initially intended as a Band-Aid to allow Congress time to work out a new, more comprehensive solution to the immigration system. The term "DREAMers" refers to the DREAM Act, the Development, Relief, and Education of Alien Minors Act, bipartisan legislation first proposed in 2001 by Democratic senator Dick Durbin and Republican senator Orrin Hatch. If passed, the DREAM Act would order DHS to cancel deportation orders for anyone who came to the United States as a child and would conditionally provide a legal pathway toward citizenship. However, as of this writing, the DREAM Act seems permanently stalled. In the meantime, as of October 2018, nine states have their own legislation allowing 1.5-generation students to register for public universities and pay tuition the same as "native-born" residents of the state. Still, this is only a patchwork solution to a national problem, exacerbated by racism and the inability of Congress to pass any meaningful legislation on immigration.

Public comments in support of DACA sometimes use the language of fault and blame, arguing that since these young people came to the United States as children, they did not choose to enter the United States and therefore should not be penalized for their parents' choices. However, by extension this discourse blames their parents, whom many undocumented students call "the original DREAMers," for bringing their children to the United States in search of a better life.[15] Right-wing, anti-immigrant rhetoric attempted to co-opt this language, such as during Trump's first State of the Union Address in January 2018, when he said "Americans are Dreamers too."

The Trump administration officially canceled DACA on September 5, 2017. Several court cases ensued, with some rulings in early 2018 requiring USCIS to resume processing DACA renewals and extensions. Other cases arose as well, including the suit Texas and six other states brought against DHS secretary Kirstjen Nielsen to cancel DACA. That case was sent to the federal court at Brownsville, Texas, on the eastern edge of the border with Mexico. There, on August 31, 2018, judge Andrew S. Hansen ruled against the immediate cancellation of DACA. However the legal grounds for his ruling were unstable, and in November 2019 the U.S. Supreme Court began hearing oral testimony on DACA.

The continuation of the DACA program is in the balance. "My anxiety level is rising; I've had difficulty sleeping. I've had difficulty talking with my siblings," said Vivian Acedo, a political science major in her senior year at Northern Illinois University, speaking at a Coming Out of the Shadows event on campus.[16] Organized by DREAM Action every spring, these events are centered on undocumented people sharing their stories. In March 2017, this was the first since Trump took office two months prior. Vivian continued, "I question my own worth and my rights to live in this country. Any rights I had with DACA got pulled from right underneath my feet. I had certain plans for my future but now I am afraid. I don't have the assurance that I'm not being deported. I feel I can't share these worries with faculty and staff on this campus. And it's affecting my classes."

The channels for legal migration are increasingly difficult. It can take twenty-three years to complete, not to mention stiff legal fees. Using our anthropological imagination allows us to see the parallels between this very particular, complex, and increasingly terrifying situation playing out along the U.S.-Mexico border and other crises in other parts of the globe.

From "Illegals" to "Shitholes"

To many within the United States, "illegal" immigration has become synonymous with "Mexicans."[17] Language shapes how we think about the issue of immigration, and indeed all issues. Using the term "illegals" conveys stigma and abjection, limiting people's ability to see the system and the humanity of people caught within it and confronting it.[18] "Illegals" become archetypal outsiders, people who don't deserve sympathy and certainly not common resources. The "I" word also reinforces the link between immigration and criminality in people's minds, normalizing a punitive response. The focus on Mexicans, and the stereotypes surrounding them, also prevents recognition of other immigrant communities and their experiences. Different immigrant groups to the United States are experiencing other crises.

"With TPS [Temporary Protected Status], it's like you live under fear," thirtysomething aspiring nurse Michaëlle shared in an interview held in Brooklyn. "You don't know what's going to happen. I live with stress because of that." Michaëlle's situation worsened on April 20, 2017, when ICE recommended canceling TPS for 59,000 Haitian people living in the United States.[19] TPS was made possible by the Immigration Act of 1990, a law that allowed the attorney general to grant unauthorized residents temporary stays in the United States because they were unable to safely return to their own country following a disaster or armed conflict.

After the 2010 earthquake in Haiti, President Obama granted temporary relief to undocumented residents from Haiti who had arrived in the United States before 2011. Given the slow pace of recovery efforts and subsequent disasters, notably the cholera epidemic that killed almost 9,500 by 2017, and Hurricane Matthew that hit Haiti the previous October, TPS has been extended several times.[20] It was set to expire on July 22, 2017.

In essence, Trump's proposed policy would amount to kicking out of the United States 59,000 people who had, despite their fear, put their faith in the U.S. government and applied for TPS. Wideline, a child care provider in her fifties and mother of three children in New York public schools, is one of those people. She recalled that undocumented Haitian people like her were told, "Tell all fellow Haitians they don't need to fear because [the U.S. government] are going to give Haitians who are illegal in this country papers so they can work." Wideline specifically acknowledged her fear that TPS would become, in effect, a pipeline to deportation: "People spread fear, arguing that the papers were so that the U.S. government can identify Haitians living in the country in order to deport them. And this is why some people didn't do it." Given the switch in presidential administrations, signing up for TPS, like registering for DACA, placed a target on people's heads. TPS, like DACA, rendered people visible to the federal government and thus more "deportable."

Most TPS holders, like Wideline, have been in the United States for decades, according to a Cornell University study.[21] Wideline raised children in Brooklyn and is now a grandmother. Collectively, people like Wideline and Michaëlle send over two billion dollars to Haiti in remittances, which represents one-third of Haiti's economy.[22] Michaëlle, like other TPS holders from Haiti, Honduras, and El Salvador, contribute to the United States through their labor and consumption.[23] Many people like Michaëlle report having worked in the undocumented labor force, but after receiving TPS they are able to apply for better paying jobs, albeit still below minimum wage. But these jobs require that their TPS be current, which costs four hundred dollars every eighteen months.

Ending TPS would cause a deep wound in the Haitian community in the United States, ripping apart families, and punishing people who have endured sub-minimum-wage jobs because they believed the government would let them stay. As meager as it is, TPS has been meaningful and affirming to those, like Michaëlle, who possess it: "I feel grateful because I am in this country. I have the ability to go to school and to work."

When the Trump administration announced that TPS would be ending, the Haitian community in the United States mobilized, holding demonstrations, writing letters, publishing op-eds, and circulating a petition authored by elected officials, including New York City Council member Dr. Mathieu Eugene, calling for then–DHS secretary John F. Kelly to renew TPS.[24]

On May 22, 2017, despite the tough talk and apparently mixed signals coming from within the Trump administration, Kelly extended TPS for undocumented Haitian people in the United States for an additional six months, from July 23, 2017, when the plan would have run out, to January 22, 2018. As a sign of just how important Kelly's work was on implementing the new president's policies around immigration, President Trump named him as chief of staff on July 31, 2017.

As the extended deadline for TPS for Haiti loomed closer and people within the administration started discussing what to do again, highly racially charged statements were allegedly uttered by the commander in chief. On December 23, 2017, the *New York Times* quoted an anonymous source that reported that Trump said, "All Haitians have AIDS."[25] While this was obviously false, in fact Haiti has made great progress in slowing the disease, tarring the whole country of Haiti with AIDS was a familiar swipe.[26] When the epidemic was finally acknowledged in 1982, the Centers for Disease Control and Prevention identified what they considered high-risk populations where one might more easily catch the disease. These groups included men who have sex with men, intravenous drug users, hemophiliacs, and people from Haiti. However, Paul Farmer noted that epidemiological evidence actually showed the reverse, that Haitian men were recipients of the virus from U.S. sex tourists.[27]

Less than two weeks before the TPS deadline, Trump dropped another load. On January 11, 2018, the day before the anniversary of the deadly 2010 earthquake, the *New York Times* reported that in a meeting with Senator Dick Durbin of Illinois, the president had called Haiti, El Salvador, and Africa "shithole countries." Of course, the president's first impulse was to deny the statement, just as he had denied making the statement about AIDS. Durbin confirmed that indeed President Trump had spoken these "hate filled words" many times in a conversation about immigration policy, a fact that was later corroborated by White House aide Omarosa Manigault.[28]

Even though TPS was reauthorized in January 2018, following a public outcry, each six-month extension very well may be the last. And while the world, and particularly Haitian communities in the diaspora as well as on the island, snapped back, the official hate speech from the president of the United States is already having an impact. Now with targets on their heads, people like Michaëlle and Wideline live under constant fear.

While DACA and TPS are structurally different and aimed at different populations, with different migration stories, our anthropological imagination can help us identify common threads. Both laws are presidential attempts to make limited, incremental progress faced with Washington's legislative gridlock. As executive orders, both were temporary and wholly inadequate fixes. And both put people in the crosshairs after the changing of the guard.

The Refugee "Crisis" and Fortress Europe

The singular focus on, disproportionate attention to, and shrill demonization of immigrant communities within the United States by many mainstream media outlets prevents us from being able to see what's going on elsewhere in the world. One particular issue, the Syrian refugee crisis, has managed to rise to the surface of our attention occasionally. The framing of the issue as a "crisis" singles out a population that happens to be Muslim and from the Middle East and foments a very powerful nativist backlash in those countries where the refugees seek shelter.[29]

Establishing a legal framework for refugees was among the first actions that the United Nations took upon its founding. On December 10, 1948, the three-year-old UN passed the Universal Declaration of Human Rights, of which Article 14 guarantees the rights of any person to seek asylum in another country for fear of persecution in their own. On July 25, 1951, before the massive wave of decolonization in Africa and much of Southeast Asia (though after India became independent), the UN adopted the Convention Relating to the Status of Refugees. The convention defines the term "refugee," spells out the rights of people displaced, and lists the obligations of states to people classified as refugees. The central pillar of the convention is that a refugee must not be returned to the country where they face "serious threats to their life or freedom." The convention has been ratified by 145 states. The 1967 Protocol extended this protection beyond the original mandate of the convention, which was initially designed for migration within Europe that occurred before that date. The UN definition of refugee is "someone who has been forced to flee his or her country because of persecution, war, or violence. A refugee has a well-founded fear of persecution for reasons of race, religion, nationality, political opinion, or membership in a particular social group."

In no small part, the UN was motivated by the atrocities of the Second World War. Hitler's Third Reich targeted and oversaw the systematic execution of minority populations in the lands that it controlled. His terrifying state apparatus killed over six million Jewish people and five million others, including Poles, Russians, communists, lesbians and gay men, "Gypsies," and people confronting mental illness, among others. These marginalized people were first sent away, hidden at Auschwitz and Belzec and other concentration camps elsewhere on the periphery of the German-occupied territories, mostly in Poland. These atrocities and the fighting and destruction from the war triggered the migration of twenty to thirty million people who sought asylum.

According to the UN High Commissioner for Refugees (UNHCR), charged by the UN to monitor refugee affairs and member states' responses, there were 68.5 million refugees, internally displaced persons, or asylum seekers by the end of 2017, a record high.[30] This number of "persons of concern" is roughly equivalent to the population of France, according to the website of the UNHCR. It is also twice the number from January 2011, less than seven years prior, when the number was 33.9 million.[31]

The decision of the UNHCR to use France's population as an example in this comparison might have been coincidental, though in France's 2017 presidential election, ultra-right candidate Marine Le Pen was catapulted to a runoff by the votes of people full of racial anger and the fear of foreigners entering the French republic. Le Pen, a former member of the European Parliament, said, "Immigration is an organized replacement of our population. This threatens our very survival. We don't have the means to integrate those who are already here. The result is endless cultural conflict."

Le Pen's rise to the second round of the election was part of a rightward, nationalist, anti-immigrant wave across Europe. On June 23, 2016, a slim majority of U.K. voters, disproportionately elderly and from England, voted to leave the European Union. Anti-EU sentiment, specifically anti-immigrant criticism of the EU's response to the massive influx of refugees, also led to gains by right-wing nationalist parties in Germany, the Netherlands, Austria, Sweden, and Switzerland. In April 2018, ultranationalist Viktor Orbán in Hungary won a landslide victory for a third term in an election dominated by the topic of immigration. And in June 2018, a coalition populist-nationalist government took control of the Italian Parliament.

However, on May 7, 2017, French voters rejected Le Pen's brand of xenophobia by an almost two-to-one margin, electing young, "centrist" businessman Emmanuel Macron. Macron's win marked a small victory, especially for the millions of people seeking refuge in Europe.[32] Macron ran on an immigration platform that commended German chancellor Angela Merkel's "generous" refugee policy and promised to prioritize asylum issues in France during his first six months in office.[33]

But not everyone sighed in relief. Four thousand miles southeast of Paris, in Nairobi, Kenya, Ifrah, a Somali refugee, waits for news on her pending resettlement case. She has been waiting for seven years already and is becoming less and less hopeful that she will ever be resettled. "There is no hope for us anymore," Ifrah explained. "We knew it after Trump got elected, and then we knew surely after he banned Somalis. And in Europe, there are too many Syrians so they are not accepting [refugees] from Kenya. I think maybe Australia is the only place left." Indeed, the situation in Europe is disjointed.[34]

Some particular EU member states, which represent the eastern flank of "fortress Europe," have seen what anthropologist Andria Timmer calls "Trumpism before Trump."[35] On October 16, 2015, Orbán sealed the border to Serbia, erecting barbed wire to block Syrian migrants.[36] Orbán successfully controlled the media narrative in his country, especially through a public billboard campaign, rejecting humanitarian reactions to the Syrian crisis in favor of national security.[37]

Across the border, Croatia, a Catholic-majority country, rose to the challenge of processing refugees passing through their borders, at least from September 2015 to March 2016, a process called the "humanitarian corridor." And then the situation changed. "Humanitarian principles started to erode as the borders within Europe started closing, and in the past few months, there have been reports of asylum seekers forcibly returned to Serbia," Laura Heideman explained in 2017. "It's a lot easier to provide short-term humanitarian aid to people only passing through than integrating people long term."[38]

Heideman takes issue with the dominant discourse of the "refugee crisis," saying, "This is not a crisis of resources. This is a crisis of political will." European countries are far from their capacity to absorb immigrants, unlike Lebanon, for example, where 183 of 1,000 people were refugees in 2017.[39] Anthropologist Linda Rabben also questions the exceptionalism behind labeling the wave of Syrian migrants to Europe a "crisis." She points out that following the Second World War, between twenty and thirty million people were assimilated into Western European nations. While the process took between five and fifteen years depending on the country, political leaders and civil society rose to the challenge.[40] They can do so again.

One key difference between then and now, however, is the "desirability" of the refugees in question. More specifically, racial, ethnic, and religious differences and stereotypes about today's migrants mark Syrians and those fleeing from the Middle East and North Africa (MENA) and Horn of Africa regions as "Other" and potentially "terrorist." Right-wing nationalist governments exploit stereotypes of "dangerous refugees" to justify their restrictive immigration policies.

People seeking to migrate have a different understanding of the word "crisis." Many countries in the Global South have been managing massive and abrupt flows of refugees for far longer and with far fewer resources than Europe. And even with the current wave of people fleeing Syria, more than 90 percent of refugees reside in the Global South. And that percentage has grown. In January 2011, just before the current wave of European migration, three million asylum seekers resided in Europe, just under 9 percent of the total.[41] Five years later, four million refugees resided in Europe, representing just 6 percent, compared to sub-Saharan Africa's 29 percent and MENA's 39 percent.

Our anthropological imagination can help us center Ifrah's experiences, putting Europe's supposed "crisis" into context. Centering another point of view, that of people migrating, we can identify material outcomes from Europe's discourses and policies. For example, European nations' restrictive asylum policies have not gone unnoticed by those who have hosted the bulk of refugees. To many, Europe and the United States are shirking the "burden-sharing" responsibilities outlined in the 1967 Protocol Relating to the Status of Refugees. Because of this double standard, on May 6, 2016, Kenya, the seventh largest refugee hosting country, announced its intent to close its camps and phase out hosting refugees, citing "economic, security, and environmental burdens," and disbanding its Department of Refugee Affairs.[42] Karanja Kibicho, Kenya's principal secretary for the interior, argued, "International obligations in Africa should not be done on the cheap; the world continues to learn the ruinous effect of these persistent double standards."[43] In addition to helping us see the hypocrisy of Europe and the United States, our anthropological imagination demands that we push our analysis further.

Beginning with the lived realities, experiences, and analyses of Vivian, Ifrah, or Michaëlle, we can use our anthropological imagination to explore connections between their very different cases. These women all said how being targeted by anti-immigrant policies has caused them stress and trauma. Having an anthropological imagination encourages a deeper analysis of the structural roots of the migrant "crisis" as well as the material impacts on migrant people's lives.

The Uses of Immigration

Having an anthropological imagination allows us to see connections between specific local issues. As they develop, immigrant communities build social ties around anchoring institutions, such as the Catholic Church, the farmworkers union, a soccer club, and businesses ranging from restaurants to wire transfer services. Many immigrants build active ties within society at large, what Renato Rosaldo and Aihwa Ong each called "cultural citizenship."[44] Given the precarity of economic opportunities for immigrants, especially for undocumented workers, people's social ties from back in their home communities influence their recruitment into the informal labor market, creating local diasporas. Anthropologists have long pointed out these transnational ties, what anthropologist Michel Laguerre called "diasporic citizenship."[45] For example, in addition to the remittances they send home, Haitian people living abroad have created dozens of "hometown associations," supporting development projects in Haiti and maintaining social ties both "here" and "there" through Catholic patron saint festivals, *fèt chanpèt*.[46]

We can use our anthropological imagination to pluralize what a U.S. "culture" means and to celebrate the diversity within it. In addition, to confront the increasingly shrill attacks on immigrant communities, a holistic look is necessary, particularly to see the roots of immigration within the global economy.

Global Capitalism

In addition to these ways that a holistic perspective is useful, using an anthropological imagination sharpens our focus on the global capitalist system. This economic system is based on seeking profit, typically by driving costs of production down. The *global* economy offers corporations incentives to outsource production overseas, allowing them to exploit the inequalities across national borders. A movement in the United States is gaining steam to call for a $15 minimum wage. As of 2020, eleven countries have higher minimum wages than the United States' $7.25 per hour. South of the border, Mexico's minimum wage is $6.36 *per day*. Factory workers in Haiti receive $4.56. This inequality is foundational to the global economy. Borders play an important role in maintaining this difference and keeping workers put.

This system kills. The Sonoran Desert itself does the dirty work for the U.S. government.[47] Crossing that arid stretch of land is dangerous business for migrants, and often results in death. But as Ruth Gomberg-Muñoz argues, the current U.S. immigration system is not "broken."[48] In fact, it works very well for those it was designed for. It helps support capitalist endeavors by suppressing workers' wages and organizing. Private contractors in the United States, for example, who secure contracts to build detention centers for the government to house detainees, make huge profits on the centers they construct and run, particularly with a law guaranteeing 34,000-person-per-night minimum occupancy. In addition to this multibillion-dollar industry, called "crimmigration" or the "border" or "homeland security industrial complex," the current militarization of the immigration system reinforces borders, defines who has entitlement to what wealth, and maintains the global economy while simultaneously reinforcing inequality.[49] Using our anthropological imagination, we can see the connection between these kinds of specific circuits of inequality and the uneven development built into the global capitalist economy that drives migration— legal or undocumented—in the first place.

Migration has been shaped by global capitalism. More than that, capitalism was built on migration and continues to depend on migration. As Eric Williams shows in *Capitalism and Slavery*, British colonial policy toward migration worked in tandem with penal codes to regulate the labor market.[50] In times of labor surplus, stiffer sentencing laws put more people in what were then openly called "debtors' prisons." As an alternative to jail time, poor whites were sent to work as indentured servants in the tropical fields of the Caribbean sugar colonies and later places like Australia.[51] And slavery, which tore over fifteen million people from Africa, was central to the development of capitalism.

Once brought together in this uneven, lopsided, and brutal exchange, economies remained linked in markets for labor, capital, and goods for sale. As Cecil Rhodes, diamond prospector and conqueror of Rhodesia (now Zimbabwe), said, "We must find new lands from which we can easily obtain raw materials and at the same time exploit the cheap slave labor that is available from the natives of the colonies. The colonies would also provide a dumping ground for the surplus goods produced in our factories." This is still true today. For example, despite the much-touted "bailout" of Puerto Rico following its debt, the island still sends fourteen times as much wealth back to the United States as received, by design, starting with the 1900 Foraker Act, when the United States took the island from Spain.

These economic relationships between nations, however exploitative, establish circuits of migration. In the expansion of the U.S. West, for example, premised on the wars of extermination bluntly called "Indian removal," recently arrived Chinese laborers were selected to work in railroad construction, particularly the part crossing the dangerous Rocky Mountains. California agribusiness has employed Mexican workers as farm hands, picking fruit and vegetables or spraying pesticides, for over a century. Colonial relationships linked France to Algeria, and the United Kingdom to the Indian subcontinent, as well as countries all over Africa and the Caribbean. Boasting that "the sun never sets on the British Empire," exploitative political, economic, and human ties were set up around the world to the deliberate benefit of British society.

Predictably, in periods of intense interconnection and increased labor demand, migration tends to increase. For example, according to the USCIS, the United States admitted 14.5 million immigrants in the first two decades of the twentieth century, the number peaking after World War I.

Formal decolonization did not end exploitative international relationships. The North American Free Trade Agreement (NAFTA), signed by lame-duck president George H. W. Bush on December 17, 1992, came into effect on January 1, 1994. The terms of the agreement forced Mexican farmers to compete with heavily subsidized U.S. agribusiness. U.S. agricultural goods flooded the Mexican market, upending 4.9 million Mexican family farmers.[52] While one can debate whether this was intentional, destroying Mexico's family farms increased the number of migratory farm laborers in the United States.[53] And the circuits are not random. For example, DeKalb County, Illinois, is a world leader in pork production. When NAFTA bankrupted the Mexican pork-producing regions of Jalisco, Veracruz, and Michoacán, those laid off workers came to DeKalb. Working in factory farms, concentrated animal feeding operations, is hazardous.[54] Cleaning pens holding thousands of pigs within a single poorly ventilated enclosure, and then slaughtering them, cannot be described as anything other than "dirty work," the kind that U.S. American citizens turn their nose at, or try to.[55]

Without migrant labor to do these kind of unpopular tasks, the wheels of agribusiness get stuck in the mud.[56] Just ask Georgia's peach growers. In 2011 the state passed a racial profiling bill, HB 87, terrorizing Mexican Americans, modeled after Arizona's much more notorious law of the same type. In Georgia, the law triggered a $140 million loss in agricultural production. Migrant labor, and yes *undocumented* migrant labor, is central to the peach industry. The bill aimed at cracking down on undocumented migrants resulted in a 40 percent labor shortage when Georgia's farmers needed it most, during harvest. So peaches rotted on the ground, as even pro-business *Forbes* noted.[57]

Our anthropological imagination allows us to understand the connections between migration patterns, imperialist politics, and economic globalization. For example, people from the Northern Triangle countries of

Central America (Guatemala, El Salvador, and Honduras) were the largest group migrating extralegally to the United States during the first years of the Trump administration. They also made up much of the group of migrants that the media famously labeled the "Caravan."[58] Many in the Caravan were fleeing drug violence, fueled by U.S. demand for the product; land dispossession, driven by gold mining industries owned by Canadians, U.S. Americans, and Europeans annexing their homes; economic instability and currency devaluation, accelerated by CAFTA (the Central American Free Trade Agreement); and various U.S.-backed civil wars and random paramilitary violence.

Two large shocks in crude oil prices in the 1970s triggered temporary cash flow problems for Latin American governments, and U.S. investors sent high-interest loans to help keep those governments afloat. When financial markets changed, these countries that had been told to borrow funds to "catch up" to the so-called developed world suffered a massive default. Seizing this opportunity, international financial institutions like the IMF and the World Bank imposed Structural Adjustment Programs (SAPs) on these countries. SAPs have two essential components: "austerity" measures, forcing governments to reduce social spending, for health care, schools, arts, and infrastructure, and "macroeconomic reforms," forcing countries to reduce barriers to "free trade" such as privatization and lowering tariffs. As a result of these force-fed neoliberal economic policies, capital can go wherever it wants but workers are not free to do the same.[59] This fundamental hypocrisy and injustice triggered a downward spiral, widening the gap between rich and poor nations, and between rich and poor people within nations.

At the end of the day, is immigration policy labor policy? Not quite, say anthropologists Ruth Gomberg-Muñoz and Laura Nussbaum-Barberena, but almost.[60] Neoliberal policies globalized all aspects of production *except* labor. While this may or may not be intentional, these restrictions render the immigrant labor force far more vulnerable to deportation or harassment, making labor organizing more difficult. In the United States, the federal government has extraordinary and unprecedented power to intervene in the lives of immigrant workers; E-Verify is but one example. However, government policy enforcement rests in the hands of employers, like those in Cortland, Illinois, where we opened the chapter. The local community there could only guess who tipped ICE off to the eight undocumented workers. The county sheriff, a Republican who ran unopposed in November 2018, made no secret of his views on undocumented individuals. But how could he have known about who worked at each and every employer in the county? The most common guess for who turned these people in was that it was either the owner or a sacked employee, but so far no one has come forward. As the ICE raid in Cortland highlights, just taking a job, let alone speaking out, can result in deportation. Without the right to organize, worker safety laws, and a guaranteed minimum wage, undocumented workers are forced to tolerate substandard working conditions and wages, and live with constantly heightened stress and fear.[61]

Josiah Heyman, who has studied the U.S. Border Patrol for three decades, argues that while global capitalism—what he calls global apartheid— shapes immigration policy, racism prevents its smooth functioning.[62] Fractures within the global capitalist class are exposed as interests collide with one another. Heyman points out how legal border crossings are chronically underfunded and understaffed, by contrast with the expensive and ineffective border wall and largely idle Border Patrol. The immense traffic jams and delays at the legal crossings render a net loss for Boeing in its role as binational manufacturer, despite its profits made as a contractor for Trump's border wall. Cities along the border between Mexico and the United States have grown as traffic has increased between the two countries following NAFTA. A million Mexican laborers are employed for U.S. companies, and the border cities function as a valve, or "arbitrage of value in the world system."[63] Just south of the border are *maquiladoras*, factories run in Mexico, by foreign companies, whose goods are created for export to those countries, where mostly women work subcontracting for U.S. clothing manufacturers at or very near Mexico's minimum wage, and antiunion violence is palpable.[64]

Similarly, the border dividing Haiti from the Dominican Republic polices inequality, separating vastly different economies. Also, not coincidentally, this border reinforces racial hierarchies.[65] For miles along the Dominican side of the border, sugar plantations, called *batèy* in Haitian Creole, employ tens of thousands of Haitian workers. Before harvest, border security often loosens up to accommodate plantation owners' needs for cane cutters. But after, the border is sealed shut, often before the Haitian farmworkers receive their pay envelopes.

Our anthropological imagination thus helps us see in clear relief the intimate connection between global capitalism and migration. The current system isn't "broken" so much as fragmented, serving particular interests: borders reinforce and augment the class, racial, ethnic, and national inequalities embedded in global capitalism. Any attempt at system reform that fails to acknowledge these inequalities will at best be temporary and partial, and at worst fan the flames of racism.

The State System

Arbitrating—and yes, one can say impeding, sometimes violently— migration while still facilitating the flow of goods and capital falls to the task of states—that is, national governments. Immigration is central to the state system, but our anthropological imagination helps us see other ways of organizing human society.

There are few places on earth off-limits to a Schengen Area (European), U.S., Canadian, or U.K. passport. Cuba is, at the time of this writing, one place that U.S. citizens must jump through hoops to visit, but major U.S. air carriers still have regular flights.[66] And given tensions in the Middle East, U.S. airlines often let local partners in their global network burn the fuel to operate those flights, but people from the U.S. can still travel there.

Once in a while, countries such as Haiti, India, and Brazil put up visa barriers specific to U.S. passport holders, but not often. A visitor to Haiti has to hand over ten dollars for an entry tax, but no one stops them from coming. Long-term *permis de sejour* (Haiti's "green cards") do require people to produce police reports, medical reports, and bank statements.

It's possible that this policy is designed for U.S. government employees to have empathy. More than just producing all these documents, potential Haitian visitors to the United States—for any length of time—have to shell out $160 in a nonrefundable deposit to a local bank. They must wait in line all day in Haiti for their several-second interview with a U.S. consular official, whose judgment on whether they are worthy to come to the United States is final. The vast majority—almost everyone—is denied. I have sent students in Haiti letters of support verifying that a branch of the U.S. government financed the research that they needed to present at a conference in the United States, attendance at which was instrumental to the publication of the research and also financed by said U.S. government agency. These letters were complemented by support letters from the director of the Haitian Studies Association and the ranking Democrat on the Senate Foreign Affairs committee, who happens to be my senator, Dick Durbin. Still nothing. Apparently all four of my master's students—and nine others—were deemed a "flight risk." They were poor and/or couldn't offer a "compelling reason" to return to Haiti and/or had a distant relative somewhere in the United States. The Haitian Studies Association definitely felt their absence. What if there was a U.S. conference on Africa and *no one* from the continent showed because of visa issues? This isn't hyperbole; it *actually happened* in March 2017.[67]

Also seemingly too nightmarish to be true was Trump's so-called Muslim ban. Following Trump's executive order, signed January 27, 2017, only a week after his inauguration, people from seven Muslim-majority countries (Iran, Iraq, Libya, Somalia, Sudan, Syria, and Yemen) were banned from entry to the United States for 90 days. Refugees from these countries were denied entry for 120 days, except for Syrian refugees who were denied indefinitely. Trump cited the 9/11 terrorist attacks as justification, even though the authors of the attacks mostly came from Saudi Arabia, many of whom had long-standing ties with the Bush family and administration. Many travelers were informed of this new policy only when they arrived and were denied entry to the country.

Northern Illinois University alumna Nazanin Zinouri came to the United States in 2010. She received her master's degree from NIU and, following that, a doctorate from Clemson University. She was prohibited from entering the United States following a three-week trip abroad. She said, "I was planning on enjoying time with family and taking care of family business."[68] Zinouri was unable to return to work in the South Carolina start-up technology firm that employed her and was left concerned about her family, her job, her apartment, her car still parked at the airport, and the dog she left behind.[69] NIU administration also identified twenty current students from these seven countries, advising them not to travel outside the United States. Also because of this bigotry, a new faculty hire in a short-staffed STEM discipline had to wait in Canada for clearance for over a year.

Aside from the obvious toll on the people affected, these policies, used against people who are actually following the law and are in the United States legally, not only hurt companies that employ people with non-U.S. passports but also hurt public universities, which depend on international students to pay tuition and make up a diverse student body. Immediately following the executive order, many foreign students became fearful of being targeted by the U.S. government and spent their tuition dollars and $32 billion in living expenses elsewhere.[70]

As horrific as these policies are, it is dangerous to think of Trump and his obviously racist policies as exceptional. They are an extension of the repressive state apparatus built over time. The United States first began regulating immigration in 1790, with the Naturalization Act, limiting citizenship to free whites "of good moral character." The Chinese Exclusion Act of 1882 barred entry to all Chinese workers. Following the influx of migrants after the First World War, the U.S. government enacted laws establishing quotas and restricting immigration from certain countries. This discrimination based on national origin—thinly veiled racism—ended during the civil rights era with the 1965 Immigration and Nationality Act, the same year the Voting Rights Act passed. In 1986, the U.S. government granted amnesty to approximately 2.7 million undocumented immigrants with the Immigration Reform and Control Act.

Since then, a coordinated backlash has led to a rising climate of xenophobia and border enforcement in the United States. Following 9/11, the "Latino Threat narrative" became fused with antiterrorism discourse.[71] Activist writer Tram Nguyen's book *We Are All Suspects Now* argues how this antiterrorism engulfed other immigrants and beyond.[72] The Department of Homeland Security was created to secure the nation from the newly perceived threats. Border enforcement growth slowed during this time, but in 2005 "a vigorous new anti-Mexicanism emerged within the US right wing, likely as a form of distraction from the fiasco of the Iraq War."[73] The Latino Threat narrative helped catapult Donald Trump, a wealthy outsider to politics, ahead of other right-wing candidates in a very crowded pack of Republican contenders in 2016, including Tea Party darling, senator Ted Cruz. Announcing his candidacy, Trump called for a "giant wall" on the U.S.-Mexico border to keep out people he called "thugs" and "criminals."

It is no coincidence that Trump's most visible targets were immigrants. Whether he was talking about the "bad hombres" from Mexico, the Muslims he banned, or the people from "shithole countries," these racist slurs speak to a white working class whose anxieties were embodied by scapegoats. It's important to remember that these stereotypes are fomented by those in the ruling class like Trump himself, who made regular use of undocumented laborers, to whom he paid substandard wages. Immigrants are archetypical outsiders.

This racial profiling and targeting is not at all unique to the United States. Trump's talk about ending "birthright citizenship" takes a cue from the Dominican Republic. A September 2013 Dominican Supreme Court decision stripped the Dominican citizenship of Haitian-descended people born after 1929. Ending birthright citizenship rendered an estimated 250,000 people stateless. In June 2015, the Dominican government followed up this decision with a terrifying purge of people not deemed "Dominican" enough. Faced with what the government called "repatriation" to Haiti, as many as 70,000 people fearful of government or vigilante violence fled across the border.

While Haiti was still rebuilding from the 2010 earthquake, many people being expelled from or fleeing the Dominican Republic swelled makeshift camps in Anse-à-Pitre, just across the Dominican border and all but inaccessible to the rest of Haiti except by a harrowing two-hour boat ride. Amnesty International reported that 27 percent of camp residents there were born in the Dominican Republic, many from parents who were also born in the Dominican Republic. Most of these couldn't speak a word of Haitian Creole. After the 2013 court decision, they became stateless people. In addition to being stateless, they were isolated, traumatized, frightened, and confused.

They had good reason to fear: looming large in collective memory, in 1937, Dominican president Rafael Trujillo ordered the massacre of 35,000 Haitian people.[74] Trujillo expanded his state power in the Dominican Republic through his anti-Haitian violence. Trujillo's racism went so far that he banned "African drumming" from the radio airwaves. By scapegoating the racialized Other, Trujillo played on nationalism to minimize opposition to his rule. Trujillo enjoyed twenty-three years in power after the 1937 massacre, whereas his murder of three Dominican human rights activists crossed the line.[75] The Mirabal sisters' death on November 25, 1960, is now designated by the UN as International Day for the Elimination of Violence against Women. Trujillo was assassinated six months later.

While Trump and Trujillo are admittedly extreme examples, national elites and political leaders often gain legitimacy by recourse to nationalism, using immigrants as foils. Archaeological evidence suggests that nationalism is a central tool within the state system itself: disrupting solidarity between like communities, members of oppressed groups are encouraged to identify instead with the ruling classes. This is true today. The dying breed of the family farmer in the Midwest has more in common with peasant farmers in Haiti than it does with the multinational corporations taking over the land. More to the point, farmers who often find themselves leasing their land to seed companies have more in common with Mexican (or Jamaican, Haitian, or Salvadoran) agricultural workers than the companies that put others out of business or the government that made that possible. Having an anthropological imagination helps us pierce the fog, to identify these commonalities, these human connections, which help us forge shared interests and build bonds of solidarity. Rather than seeing migration as the problem, an anthropological imagination helps us refocus the discussion on nationalism, on the state system itself.

Humanity

Migration has been a core part of our human heritage, a key to our survival. An anthropological imagination helps us to bring humanity back to the fore of this issue. First, by helping us see how humanity has been on the move, we can disrupt the "good" and "bad" dichotomy within the migration discussion. By tacking back and forth between the local and global scales, we can use our anthropological imagination to better explain large-scale migration patterns rather than accepting reductionist ideas about "illegal" immigrants. And by putting a human face on the complex issue, we can use our anthropological imagination to bring the issue "out of the shadows" of dehumanizing, legalistic, and reactionary rhetoric.

On the Move

The modern system of borders is out of step with humanity's propensity to move. Seen in an anthropological timeline, the modern state system was created very late, in 1648, with the Peace of Westphalia, the last day in humanity's thirty-year life so far. This form of state—and the formal sovereignty that it implies—did not become universal until after decolonization following the Second World War. As late as 1947, most of the world's population was still colonized.

By contrast, humanity's oldest survival and adaptation strategy was and is still mobility. Humanity has been, and continues to be, on the move. Archaeologist Michael Frachetti said that migration has become ubiquitous, "at the heart of archaeological discourse."[76] Throughout history, people's complex motivations to move, and their specific modes of doing so, may not be fully visible in what people left behind, and so perhaps not accessible for archaeological study.[77] However, humans clearly responded to large-scale events such as a massive drought, volcanoes, or earthquakes by moving. The most dramatic, that is to say, bloody, instances of contact between different sets of people, like the repopulation of Europe following the Ice Age, often dominate our understanding of "human nature," supposedly universal. However, the archaeological record is also full of examples of solidarity between groups. In Papua New Guinea, long-term reciprocal relations between groups facilitated the welcoming of communities fleeing a volcano.[78] In the shadow of the Inca Empire, trade relationships between groups facilitated ties that proved essential following periods of intense drought in the Andes.[79] Migration might well be humanity's single best adaptive response to disasters.[80] Discussing a megadrought that began 4,200 years ago, Harvey Weiss calls this survival strategy "habitat tracking."[81]

Using an archaeological imagination, we see that putting up barriers to mobility cuts off our best chance for survival. Anti-immigrant xenophobia may make for short-term political gains for some, capitalizing on people's worst fears and fanning their racism, but in the long run sealing off borders can only hasten our species' demise. The fact that all habitable land is already occupied by humans is a testament to migration: human beings originated in the Horn of Africa.

However, even the most cursory glance at humanity's earlier migration patterns would reveal that much of this migration was not by choice at all, as the horrors of the transatlantic slave trade dramatize. This raises the question, how much "choice" does one have fleeing acts of genocide, or crimes against humanity?[82] Fleeing a dictator? Fleeing a multiyear drought? Fleeing endemic joblessness caused by multinational policies and treaties such as NAFTA?

In other words, using our anthropological imagination we can disrupt the "good" and "bad" migrant characterization, as "good" migrants are often portrayed as mere victims who take pains to do things "the right way." As soon as one makes the choice to migrate with or without papers, then one is vilified. In reality, human beings are complex, and our decisions are multifaceted and shaped by local and global contexts. This good/bad distinction falls apart because of the systematic ways in which global neoliberal capitalism, heir to colonialism, creates not only "push" factors like NAFTA but also "pull" factors: the global capitalist economy concentrates wealth in "global cities" that pull people to them in search of jobs.[83]

Further, to migrate is to be human, and thus migration should be a human right. We have been on the move for millions of years. This simple fact is deliberately ignored by those whose vision of society excludes those who are different from themselves, and those whose hyphenated identities diversify our communities. To directly confront the prejudice that clouds the judgment of those in power and those who support them, we must also humanize the individuals who are caught in the system.

The Humanity of People

ICE agents teargassed asylum seekers—without warning—at the U.S.-Mexico border the Sunday after Thanksgiving 2018, less than three weeks after the so-called blue wave of the midterm elections. People who want to be in solidarity with migrants need to begin by valuing the specificity of human lives, of real, living, human beings, by helping to identify and reclaim their humanity.

Faced with a rising tide of nationalist xenophobia worldwide, what is to be done? One strategy is clear: anyone in opposition to this racism should have an inspiring vision that brings people out to vote. Such a vision cannot be only an assortment of what we are fighting against but must articulate what we are fighting *for*. "Humanity" not only has emerged as a specific rallying cry within various seemingly unconnected social movements, but has become a strategy. Reclaiming our humanity can turn the tide of what pundits call "public opinion."

For example, the act of "coming out" helps shift the public conversation, and eventually impacts policies. "Coming out of the closet" was a tactic in the 1990s for LGBTQ+ people to gain visibility. Nineteen years after the Defense of Marriage Act passed with 84 percent of congressional votes, the U.S. Supreme Court upheld the legality of same-sex marriage. The NCAA's 2017 boycott of North Carolina over the state's so-called bathroom bill targeting transgender people helped force the state legislature to scuttle the legislation.[84]

Undocumented activists are taking a cue from this success and Coming Out of the Shadows. Leo Chavez notes that there may be signs of similar shifts in public opinion regarding migrant communities. In 1994, California governor Pete Wilson championed Proposition 187, aimed at cutting off services to undocumented families such as access to education, health care, and workers' rights protection. The one-term Republican governor in a difficult reelection contest both rode the wave of and fomented anti-immigrant rhetoric. The measure easily passed with a two-thirds margin of votes before being thrown out in court.[85] Now, California is 180 degrees from Prop 187. Chavez points to demographic shifts, but also the dedication and organizing of Chicano-Latino groups within the country's most populous state. While xenophobia and nativism gave Trump the electoral edge overall, Californians, who amount to one in eight U.S. Americans, resoundingly rejected this anti-immigrant panic, giving Democrat Hillary Clinton a margin of victory of over four million votes, almost twice Trump's (61.73 versus 31.62 percent).

Students in my Anthropology and Contemporary World Problems class had an assignment on empathy, first tried out in 2018. They were to either interview an immigrant they personally knew or to transcribe a Coming Out of the Shadows testimony. They were asked to reflect on the person's migration stories, trying to put themselves in the other's place. A white man from the class shared that he empathized with family separation because of his own family's divorce and move across state lines. A white woman, a mother, from a small town felt the melancholy of an undocumented mother forced to choose between being physically there for her children or being able to provide material support. Some Coming Out of the Shadows narratives particularly struck a nerve in the class. Larissa Martinez was the valedictorian at McKinney Boyd High School in Texas. She came out as undocumented during her speech at graduation, in June 2016, a month before Trump officially became the Republican nominee.[86] Mayte Lara Ibarra was another valedictorian from Texas whose testimony wasn't posted on YouTube, but whose story parallels Martinez's. Both Martinez and Ibarra were targets of hate by social media trolls, forcing Ibarra to cancel her Twitter account. Esther Lee's story shatters stereotypes as an Asian American migrant, supposedly the "model minority." Lee's family fled Taiwan to escape domestic violence. As she shared, "Had we returned to Taiwan we would have returned to certain death." Mohammed, a gay undocumented man from Iran whose family settled in Detroit, detailed the pain at having his dream to go to college come true, only to be smashed five minutes later when the admissions counselor discovered their mistake.[87] Mohammed and others created the website dreamactivist.org, a community of over 300,000 activists from around the United States. In their reflection papers, many of my students reported that they would likely have been too afraid to come out. But many also described their anger and frustration at the injustice of the system for not letting people have a chance to succeed in the United States. They were able to identify things they had in common with the individuals whose stories they heard: concerns about their future, their family status, finding a good job, supporting their families.

One of the most powerful faces and voices inspiring a radical empathy was only five years old. Sofi Cruz wound her way through the crowd and hand delivered a note and T-shirt to Pope Francis when he spoke in Los Angeles in September 2015. The note called upon the pope, in his first visit to the United States, to speak with President Obama and Congress to legalize undocumented immigrants. Speaking to the press, Cruz said, "All immigrants, just like my dad, need this country. They deserve to live with dignity. They deserve to live with respect. They deserve an immigration reform because it benefits my country. . . . Don't forget about the children, or anyone that suffers because they don't have their parents." Sixteen months later, Cruz was the youngest speaker at the overcapacity crowd at the Women's March on Washington, the day after Trump's inauguration.

Putting a human face to the statistics, a radical empathy can underscore the human costs of dehumanizing policies. My own experience with this issue began with an ordinarily straight-A student I'll call Celina missing an assignment. Celina also sat in the back row that day, unengaged and on her cell phone despite the clear policy against that. When I asked her about her behavior after class, after everyone else had filed out, tears welled up in her eyes. She said that her *abuela*, her grandmother, had just passed away. I expressed my condolences. Celina wasn't finished with her story. She was angry that she couldn't attend the funeral. She paused, looked me in the eye, and asked, "Can I trust you?" I'm sure my response was awkward and unconvincing, but she apparently did. Celina came out to me as undocumented. She couldn't go to the funeral because she couldn't risk crossing the border a second time. Celina first came to the United States when she was too young to remember. Her story is a reminder that well before Trump's zero-tolerance policy, undocumented people still faced a form of family separation. Like Vivian, Celina graduated and is now a graduate student at a top-tier public university.

As amazing as the courage of Martinez, Lee, Vivian, and Celina is, some undocumented people bristle at discourse of "DREAMers" being model minorities used by politicians for their own ends. Obviously not everyone can be a valedictorian. The steep fees to apply for DACA, not to mention that it is mostly relevant for people who have made it to college, sets up a two-tiered system within the undocumented community. Many Coming Out of the Shadows testimonies specifically take issue with this, arguing that they need to be allowed to be fully human, flaws and all, like #ProtectionForAll organizer Maria Torres: "Who do you see when you say 'DREAMer'? And I want you to think even harder. Who are you leaving out? And do those people deserve to be left out? It continues to perpetuate this idea that there's people who just magically are super achievers and who deserve more than other people who are not. There's many other stories. I'm one of 11 million; I don't think I'm that special."[88]

Just like some within the LGBTQ+ community or the civil rights movement thought that by presenting themselves as paragons of society, mainstream society would be more accepting, some undocumented activists espouse a "respectability" framework.[89] Other activists like Maria Torres, also an NIU alum, deny outright the notion of illegality, of abjection or stigma, rejecting the label of "good" versus "bad" immigrant.[90] Deliberately challenging the discourse of blame, many activists and artists have been spreading the slogan "undocumented and unafraid." Some specifically add "unashamed" or "unapologetic" to reject story lines that blame their parents or criminalize their communities.[91] Some activists take a cue from queer politics by explicitly challenging the politics of abjection, of stigma.[92] And "undocuqueers" demand that their full humanity, including their multiple identities, be respected. For example, Luis Nolasco says, "I've had to come out of the shadows twice; telling people that I identify as queer was hard at first, but I've grown to fully accept it and love my two identities. I pride myself on them. I'm 'Undocuqueer.'"[93]

Coming out of the shadows does pose significant risk to undocumented individuals, especially their parents, who don't have DACA's same legal protections. The risks were different for coming out as queer in the 1990s. Also, while both types of coming out are about affirming one's identity and humanity, one takes as the starting point one's inner self, and the other focuses on the legal system and an external status. However, both can be effective as a collective political tool. DREAM Action NIU leaders like Vivian and Celina made significant inroads in people's understanding of issues around migration, humanizing not only themselves but the issue itself. Republican state representative Bob Pritchard, now a trustee at NIU, ran unopposed in his last four elections. When DREAM Action first met with Pritchard, he vehemently opposed undocumented rights. As he put it, he didn't know any undocumented people. But once students like Maria Torres, Vivian, and Celina put human faces on the issue, Pritchard could see how precarious their situations were, how courageous they were to face hostility and systematic exclusion, and how they deserved a chance at success. Pritchard signed on as the sole Republican cosponsor of the ACCESS Bill, which would allow DACA-eligible students to pay in-state tuition and qualify for limited sources of funding.

Putting a human face on complex social issues is the very core of having and using an anthropological imagination. This kind of radical empathy is a powerful tool to change the conversation around larger issues. While focusing on the humanity of an issue is absolutely essential, it is only one aspect of changing people's actions. As Vivian notes, "If you consider yourself an ally to the undocumented community, act as an ally. Do not self-declare yourself an ally without doing the work."

Solidarity

A principled politics is based on humanization and empathy. Using our anthropological imagination offers us conceptual support so we can build bridges across our differences. It helps us articulate our solidarity with others. While specific local struggles for justice each have their particularities, our anthropological imagination can help us identify commonalities and explore connections among them.

In Illinois, even with some Republican support, and even with a near-veto-proof majority of Democrats, the ACCESS Bill stalled. The two-year, six-day budget impasse certainly didn't help, but the momentum was lost within the Democratic Party. While there are always personal histories and politics behind the scenes in legislative bodies, in this case there was a coalition breakdown between core constituencies within the Democratic Party. Because the party has a more conservative element and there was the threat of veto, "centrist" Democrats wanted to keep the ACCESS Bill limited to valedictorians, the poster children of DACA. Some members of the Democratic Black Caucus saw parallels between undocumented status and the disenfranchisement of Black males in their communities. Some members asked that the bill include provisions for former offenders of a nonviolent crime. However, organizers like Sandy Lopez had difficulty finding enrolled college students willing to testify as former offenders. And given the ways in which "undocumented" equates to "Mexican" in the minds of many U.S. Americans, undocumented Black people, including Haitian Americans, were rendered invisible. Given the zero-sum nature of formal political processes (where if one wins, another has to lose), competition between different communities of color rather than cooperation started, and ACCESS became framed at least in part as a "black versus brown" issue, implicitly leaving white lawmakers off the hook.

One response to the urgent threat of deportation is sanctuary, setting up spaces where individuals can seek refuge.[94] Citing their moral duty and the separation between church and state, many churches began offering sanctuary to individuals in fear of deportation, like Jeanette Vizguerra, who sought sanctuary in a Denver church in February 2017. Cities, counties, and even states have since passed sanctuary resolutions, preventing local law enforcement from getting involved in deportations and requiring ICE agents to obtain arrest warrants. Preempting this, Trump signed an executive order his first week in office withholding federal funds to "sanctuary cities." Some local jurisdictions have objected, suing the administration. On November 30, 2018, a federal court ruled that the administration could not withhold public safety funding from sanctuary cities. Many of the country's largest cities became sanctuary cities, including three in Texas: Dallas, Houston, and Austin.[95] Some resolutions are stronger than others. Among the strongest, drawing the most ire from President Trump, was California's SB54. The bill declared the entire state, the world's sixth largest economy, a sanctuary, and it passed the Senate with a vote of 27–12 on April 4, 2017, along party lines.[96]

Sanctuaries are an important emergency measure for contemporary injustices, but true justice obviously demands more. The current moment's urgent threats to humanity require people to be not only allies but *accomplices*. An ally is someone who uses their privilege, their status as member of a majority group, to support people being targeted or discriminated against. "Allyship" does not directly challenge the structural inequalities that marginalize or target certain communities, and as such allies maintain privilege. An accomplice is someone willing to put their own body on the line and take risks, in effect ditching their majority privilege, challenging and dismantling it. Alliances can shift, but an accomplice is there till the bitter end. As Indigenous Action defined it, "When we fight back or forward, together, becoming complicit in a struggle towards liberation, we are accomplices."[97] Rather than speaking on behalf of a group, an accomplice works alongside targeted communities as a specific form of solidarity.

Solidarity means identifying the shared humanity in particular communities in struggle and acknowledging that advancing human liberation requires supporting them and the particulars of that struggle, while identifying common roots and multiple connections between "us" and "them." Solidarity is about recognizing ourselves in the other, understanding that we too struggle against the transactional bodily relations capitalism imposes. Those of us located within imperial powers have a responsibility to dismantle the system from within, disrupting processes of violence and accumulation. Solidarity is practicing love, building connections that do not depend on capitalist accumulation, corporate media, militaristic and imperial states, or the system of nations set up to justify and endorse these processes of dehumanization.

Moving well beyond mobilizing compassion and empathy, solidarity is acknowledging that specific forms of oppression intersect with others, and that moreover, at the heart of these systems is dehumanization. It means truly believing, like Lilla Watson, who began chapter 1, that your liberation is tied to the liberation of others. The inverse of being a "citizen of the world," giving "voice to the voiceless" or what Teju Cole called the "white savior industrial complex," solidarity is believing in and understanding the indivisibility of justice.[98]

One example of this happening is that younger, intersectional, queer-inclusive social movement organizations have been building multiracial Black and Latinx coalitions in Chicago. Mayor Rahm Emanuel, who left his post as Obama's White House chief of staff to inherit the infamous "Daley Machine" as mayor of Chicago, outbid Latinx challenger Jesús "Chuy" Garcia for his 2015 reelection in part by suppressing reports of police killings of young African American men, including seventeen-year-old Laquan McDonald, killed on October 20, 2014. Four years later, following a determined effort by community activists demanding that video evidence be released, a jury found Jason Van Dyke, McDonald's killer, guilty of second-degree murder and sixteen accounts of aggravated assault. This was on October 5, 2018.[99] Emanuel announced that summer he would not seek a third term.

Some other ways that these community groups are showing solidarity for one another include the work that activists with Organized Communities Against Deportation are doing with Black Youth Project-100 on a campaign to "erase the database," seeing common cause in police overreach and the ways in which the so-called gang database was legal cover for police brutality and profiling in both Black and Latinx communities.[100] In cities across the country, the gang database is a multiagency designation of suspected affiliation with gangs. In a classic case of administrative overreach, people with the same name as one person arrested, almost all Black and Latinx, are swept into the database; not even proof of innocence can get someone removed.[101] Activists have also been identifying parallels between deportation actions, drug laws, and the capitalist private prison system, called the prison-industrial complex.[102] For example, as drug sentencing laws are changing, new quotas for minimum numbers of deportees in private prisons have begun.[103] Using our anthropological imaginations, we see that all of these phenomena are connected.

Pulling It Together

This chapter has offered a distinctly anthropological look at immigration because for all but the very last bit of human history, we have been on the move. National borders are a recent phenomenon. If we use our anthropological imagination to see the connections between issues, we can at once value the particularities of a specific local campaign and defend the rights of people caught in the system, at risk of deportation, or at the mercy of mercenaries and violence, while also identifying common patterns, exploring connections, and confronting the system that keeps people on the margins. The current international migration system and the racist, xenophobic reaction it engenders serves many interests. This system reinforces national borders, defines who has entitlement to what wealth, and maintains a global economy while simultaneously buttressing inequality. Capitalism is built on upholding private property. At the same time, we must also firmly root our anthropological imagination in the real experiences of people who are just trying to get by, to humanize those who have been used as scapegoats, and to inspire empathy. Specifically, using our anthropological imagination we can

- Identify commonalities among particular targets of current immigration policy.
- Expand our understanding of the issues beyond the focus on the legal system. Immigration policy is also intimately connected to labor policy, housing, and education.
- Render visible people's motivations to migrate, particularly the vast inequalities within global capitalism.

- Sharpen our focus on the state apparatus itself. The modern state system is centered on the ideology of sovereignty, expressed most vividly in the maintaining and patrolling of borders.
- Remember not to exceptionalize the Trump administration. Those reactionary policies were a long time in the making.
- Remind people (such as policy makers) that humanity has always been on the move. It was one of our earliest adaptations.
- Disrupt the distinction between "good" and "bad" immigrant.
- Refocus the discussion about migration on people's humanity, inspiring empathy—radical empathy. This moment calls for more than being an ally, it calls for being an accomplice.
- Outline the contours of a coalitional politics.

We have a shared interest in defending immigration: for our species to survive, humans need to keep being human, allowed to move. In this way we can make humanity's last stand, moving beyond constant defensive reactions and short-term fixes to a lasting, sustainable future. We must first, as Vivian implores, do the work. The next chapter discusses why these battles are being waged on universities, and what those of us who find ourselves there can do.

5

Dismantling the
Ivory Tower

> I insist that the object of all true
> education is not to make men carpen-
> ters, it is to make carpenters men.

As we've seen throughout the book, when we use our anthropological imagination, we can highlight commonalities and points of connections between what often seem like disparate, particular local issues. Spaces, both physical and virtual, that encourage the deliberate coming together of different groups to forge coalitions like the ones discussed in the previous chapter are becoming rarer. Therefore, education is emerging as one of the most important topics within a range of contemporary social movements.

Public education in the United States owes a debt to the African American community, as schools were first widely made public during Reconstruction following the Civil War. Then, as now, community leaders debated the role and function of education, including higher education. Booker T. Washington, who founded the Tuskegee Institute in Alabama, argued for a vocational role for universities, training people who had been enslaved or their children skills deemed useful in getting a job. W. E. B. Du Bois, one of the founders of the NAACP, argued the reverse. The passage beginning this chapter was first published in 1903, in his essay "The Talented Tenth."[1] The language is gendered, and several scholars have pushed back on this elitist vision of focusing on the top "tenth." However, public universities can be, and since at least Du Bois's time have been articulated as, spaces for human liberation and inclusion. They give people the freedom to imagine solutions to tomorrow's problems because left to itself "the market" will not investigate potential solutions to the problems it causes, systematically studying them and weighing options.

The privatization of space and resources has been growing, as spaces for the public, the commons, are under assault. We need to defend the commons against further encroachment. One important site of the struggle is public education.

Universities, particularly public universities that depend on public funds to operate, are under siege. Funding is drying up, and academic freedom is eroding, particularly for those whose identity and/or research finds itself in the crosshairs of current U.S. administration policies. To counter this, we should be reviving Du Bois's vision: universities *can* be sites for encounter, for coming together, for debating and identifying coalitional solutions, and then for educating and mobilizing the public.

However, in its current neoliberal, imperial form, higher education is far from ideal. Universities, and particularly underfunded public universities, reinforce the inequalities and injustices within society at large. In order to fulfill universities' promise and potential, we need to dismantle the ivory tower, reimagining and rearticulating an alternative university in defense of the public, in the service of humanity. Anthropology in particular needs to continue "cleaning house from within."[2] As Faye Harrison implored twenty-five years before Trump's election, anthropology needs to be decolonized and continue its self-critique.[3] Anthropologists who believe in liberation need to change the rules of the game and support engagement with the public. They need to build synergies with organizers and get involved. In addition to actually practicing reciprocity, anthropologists need to build collaborative relationships and structures of accountability.

Decline of the Public

Who is "the public"? As feminist scholars point out, the term implies exclusion of the "domestic" or "private" sphere.[4] The U.S. Constitution literally excluded everyone who wasn't white, male, and owned property from the public. This exclusion was part of the design of "democracy"—a Greek term, based on the city-states of old. Like that created by the original U.S. Constitution, the democracy of ancient Greece was based on the exclusion of the vast majority of the population: not only were women formally excluded from politics, many subject to Greek city-states were enslaved. Social movements have long engaged in the struggle to crack open these old forms for spaces of inclusion.

The long civil rights movement—the generations-long struggle against formal racial segregation that followed informal policing of spaces through acts of terror such as lynching—has made significant inroads into equality under the law. So, rather than just accept a multiracial future, white elites are eroding the public altogether. Neoliberalism, the belief in the free market to solve everything, was their tool, followed by media outlets, think tanks, policy makers, and international institutions as fervently as evangelical Christians follow the Bible. Their actions resulted in a retrenchment of inequalities as public spaces and goods became privatized. When the federal government forcibly desegregated public schools in the landmark 1954 *Brown v. Board of Education* decision, some districts, like Prince Edward County in Virginia, sacrificed educating their white children by instead shutting the whole school system down for five *years*, from 1959 to 1964, rather than desegregate.

In northern centers of power 1968 was a momentous year. For some, 1968 symbolizes revolution, with the protests at the Democratic National Convention in Chicago and the student revolts in Paris. This was also the year that Martin Luther King Jr. was assassinated, along with the leading Democratic presidential candidate and attorney general Bobby Kennedy, while openly white nationalist governor George Wallace of Alabama went on to split the Democratic vote and handed the close election to Richard Nixon. During his first presidential term, Nixon called for a return to "normalcy," declaring a War on Drugs in 1971. This war, which has so far cost a trillion dollars, was at the very best a stalemate, as drug use rates have remained steady over its four decades.[5] In addition to supporting right-wing military dictatorships in drug-producing countries, the real war was against the societal gains of urban Black and Latinx communities, particularly the civil rights they'd recently won. Tellingly the funds for the War on Drugs also heralded the stagnation and decline of support for public education.

Education and the Public

The decline in the support for U.S. education is linked to intentional priorities of the people in power. For example, funding for education has been drying up since the War on Drugs started in 1971, while funding for prisons has skyrocketed. Public funding for higher education has diminished, leaving universities to fend for themselves. State government funding has decreased by over a third, from 14.6 percent of general tax levy budgets in 1990 to 9.4 percent in 2014.[6] This reflects a changing set of priorities for those in power: when adjusting for inflation, funding for corrections went up 141 percent between 1986 and 2013, while funding for public universities increased by only 5.6 percent.[7] In eleven states, funding for the prison system has surpassed that for public universities.[8] This downward spiral accelerated following the Great Recession of 2008: state support for public universities had decreased by 20 percent five years later. Cuts to research universities were even greater, 26 percent.[9]

Inequalities in the education system are part of its original design: Based around the family model of a white, middle-class, patriarchal household with a stay-at-home mom, the burden of "child care" was placed on families, particularly mothers. The state took over "education" at first grade—at least until around 3 P.M. For the majority of families this economic arrangement is very challenging. It forces families to leave kids at home alone while their parents finish the work day, or it means a parent (likely the mother) must take time off of paid work or pay for child care.

Public education also reproduces inequalities in wealth accumulation over generations, as funding mechanisms are based on local property taxes.[10] Since rich neighborhoods have a stronger property tax base than poor ones, this means that per pupil funding for public schools is wildly disparate.[11] For example, the Chicago Ridge School District spent $9,794 per pupil in 2013, whereas an hour's drive north, the Rondout School District spent almost three times as much, $28,639.[12] And this inequality is growing. In 2017, Rondout spent almost four times per pupil more than another district even in the same suburban county.[13] Until this fundamental inequality is addressed, no pre-K catch-up plan or privately funded after-school clubs or mentoring program can equalize children's chances. At best, individuals who are mentored might leap past their classmates, but that's change on a very small scale, one person at a time, when by equalizing the funding in schools, far fewer children would be "left behind." Seeing the deck stacked against them, Black parents who also wanted their children to go to college created historically Black colleges and universities (HBCUs) when they weren't accepted to already established schools. But society's general expectation of Black, Latinx, or Indigenous children is that they will probably not make it to college; that they will, if lucky, hold a steady working-class job; and if not, the private prison system will coerce their labor.[14]

The inequalities found in the K–12 education system are reinforced in college. Well-to-do parents expect their children to go to "good" schools. It is no surprise that the most exclusive and expensive colleges are also typically considered "the best" schools, particularly the private universities in the Ivy League. Study after study has confirmed parents' suspicions: connections people make in college, "social capital," are foundations of their career success.[15] The majority of U.S. ambassadors, for example, are Ivy League school alums, and almost a third of U.S. presidents went to these eight schools. While someone like Mark Zuckerberg can drop out of college and still become one of the world's eight wealthiest individuals, the fact that he started with an enormous amount of privilege and social capital during his Harvard years is critical to his—and Facebook's—success. President George W. Bush was able to succeed in life despite his dismal GPA at Yale in no small part because of his privilege and the social network gained from his very exclusive, all-white, and all-male social club. His father's connections certainly helped. And it is no coincidence that the first nonwhite president of the United States was educated at Harvard Law School, chosen by his overachiever peers to be editor of the *Harvard Law Review*, one of very few service opportunities there where women don't predominate.[16]

As private institutions, Ivy League schools rely on three main sources of income: tuition, philanthropy, and endowments. Since 2014, the annual cost to attend over fifty private colleges has surpassed $60,000, more than the salary of over half of U.S. households. Wealthy individuals, feeling a connection to where they met their future business and life partners, disproportionately donate to their alma maters. This wealth inequality is even further magnified across the generations through endowments: donations from previous years collect interest as investments, including in the stock market. According to the *U.S. News & World Report*, which ranks what it considers to be the best universities, the ten largest endowments are at what they call "national universities" that have PhD programs and focus on research.[17] Not surprisingly, their ranking of "good" schools tends to correspond with the overall endowments at those schools. In addition, only two of the top ten endowments are public, Texas A&M University and the University of Michigan. Harvard University tops the list with an endowment of over $40 billion, an amount greater than the economy of Paraguay and 101 other countries. By contrast, many public universities were originally founded to educate future teachers, whose pay is often barely or not enough to make ends meet, to say the least about their ability to give back to their alma mater. Public colleges rely as much on state and federal funds for higher education as they do on tuition, and are therefore also more vulnerable to funding cuts.

Taking a look at education, then, is also taking a look at the public, and vice versa. Inequalities are structured into the system.

Universities as Sites for Struggle

Following the end of World War II, the public university played a central role in crafting what Tom Brokaw named the "Greatest Generation," creating the middle class and solidifying U.S. dominance in the world (the word used was, and still is, "leadership"). This was also when the GI Bill, which included tuition support for veterans, was instituted. In the decade after World War II, two million vets went to college. A college degree, which was now attainable and financially reasonable, was the surest ticket to upward class mobility.

During the Cold War, universities saw an increase in public investment, particularly among the hard sciences, as what U.S. president Dwight Eisenhower termed the military-industrial complex needed researchers to staff its many new initiatives. Federal investment in education during the Cold War directly supported war technologies, like nuclear physics and petrochemicals like Agent Orange.[18] Such research made universities responsible for the war machine, with direct financial interests in maintaining and increasing it. In addition to the natural sciences, the humanities and social sciences also received a boost with the creation of "area studies" in order to amass knowledge about foreign enemies, or potential enemies. The Department of Defense offered Foreign Language and Area Studies (FLAS) grants to universities, and the Department of State offered Fulbright awards to individuals to conduct research abroad. Today, accounts of the "decline" in anthropology's relevance peg this Cold War period as the discipline's hey-day.[19] Anthropologists like Margaret Mead and Ruth Benedict were general household names, consulting for high-level members of the federal government.[20]

The rising tide lifted the university from local educational centers to the status of national institution, with great public support, including not only financial backing from the government but also great political capital and moral authority.[21] In some accounts, certainly from those who pine for a return to anthropological "relevance," special interests and identity politics destroyed the institution, costing it public support.[22] The reality is quite different.

Exclusions within the Cold War University

The "Cold War University" was a central actor within the military-industrial complex.[23] In a reflection of the turbulent times, students were attacked and even killed on campus for protesting: in February 1968, three students were killed at South Carolina State University, and in May 1970, four were killed at Kent State and two at Jackson State.

Students weren't the only targets of the Cold War top-down, authoritarian militarism. Many professors were also caught in the crosshairs. U.S. senator Joseph McCarthy of Wisconsin led witch hunts around the country from 1950 until 1954, destroying careers of those he accused of being communist.[24] In addition to individuals, whole groups of people became targets.[25] Area studies, so vital to the growth of anthropology and other humanities and social sciences after World War II, tended to "fix" societies and cultures into types, often reproducing and perpetuating stereotypes.[26] Columbia University professor Edward Said denounced these processes as "Orientalism."[27] Knowledge production is used to control the Other—the creation of the "West" depends on a vilified "East." Far more than being merely academic concerns, these stereotypes were often called up and used by the military at a moment's notice, especially during a lead-up to a U.S. invasion or other military intervention. For example, the Taliban's oppression of women suddenly became important, with images of the *burqa* (the full-body covering worn by Muslim women) plastered all over U.S. media in 2002, conveniently just as the United States geared up for the invasion of Afghanistan.[28]

During the 1960s social upheaval, activists who risked their lives on the streets joined with university students. This exchange fueled an energetic surge in antiwar protests, as many college students, disproportionately people of color, were drafted to serve in Vietnam. This connection also fueled students to call for knowledge about and institutional support for oppressed peoples. Women's (now often women's, gender, and sexuality) studies and ethnic studies programs were created by student and community demands that their universities create spaces for inclusion. San Francisco State University hosted the first Black studies program in 1968, as part of the School (now College) of Ethnic Studies founded the following year. The school also included Asian American studies, American Indian studies, and Latina/o studies. That same year at California State College (now University) at Los Angeles, the first Mexican American studies (later Chicano studies) program was founded. In 1969, faced with a student strike that called for free tuition and open enrollment for New York City high school graduates, the City University of New York (CUNY) responded with the establishment of a Department of Urban and Ethnic Studies, and in 1971, Puerto Rican studies. The first official women's studies course was in 1969 at Cornell University, and in 1970, the first women's studies program was established at San Diego State College (now University).[29] Begun as concessions by reluctant administrations, gender and ethnic studies are almost never embraced by the university and are usually given fewer resources than more established core departments. And certainly universities still remain attached to Enlightenment ideals of personhood, supposedly universal, but actually white, European, male, heterosexual, capitalist, and colonizer ("Western" is the polite term).[30] This association is so powerful that women of color faculty are often "presumed incompetent."[31]

Support for public universities began to erode at the same time that women and people of color began entering the university in larger numbers, as students, as professors, and into the curriculum as the subject of courses. The institution itself was transformed into what many call the "neoliberal university."[32]

The "Neoliberal University"

Universities are far from immune to capitalist values. The three pillars of public universities—research, teaching, and public service—have all seen a dramatic turn toward private capitalist interests in recent years, having been left with limited public resources while at the same time the structure of the university itself has become "like a business."[33] Like all institutions, the "neoliberal university" is a product of society, reflecting changes within it.[34] But it has also been attacked further, a result of a deliberate, targeted, coordinated, and well-funded effort from conservative elements in the United States. These changes have eroded full-time tenure-track positions while swelling administrative positions and passing the cost on to students, who already carry an unsustainably heavy debt burden.

Noted above, state legislatures have steadily rolled back support for public universities. This stresses the system, reinforcing existing inequalities and exclusions, notably patriarchy and white supremacy.[35] When public universities cannot depend on public funds to operate, administrators refashion them to start acting like a business. Businesses constantly seek to lower costs, and one of the biggest costs in the university is that for instruction. Tenured and tenure-track faculty are steadily being replaced by contingent labor, whose salaries are much lower, often without benefits. This erosion of tenured faculty diminishes the mission of universities to advance knowledge. Tenure-track and tenured faculty, whose jobs include contributing to new knowledge through research, making decisions about departmental curriculum, and participating in the "shared governance" of the overall university, have been significantly reduced. The percentage of instructional faculty employed full-time has decreased sharply, from almost 80 percent in 1971 to 50 percent in 2011.[36] In 2015, part-time lecturers accounted for 40 percent of the teaching staff, with an additional 30 percent of classes taught by instructors who weren't on the tenure track.[37] By 2016, almost three-fourths (73 percent) of faculty positions were off the tenure track.[38] The American Association of University Professionals reported that "over the past four decades, the proportion of full-time tenured positions has declined by 26 percent and full-time tenure-track positions has dropped by 50 percent."[39]

Under neoliberal capitalism, universities are set against one another to compete for limited resources. This competition is deliberately fostered, and reward structures are put in place to encourage and reproduce capitalist values such as competition, individual achievement, entrepreneurship, specialization, and, especially, bringing in money.[40] Not surprisingly, colleges of business and engineering tend to be prioritized by universities, which can clearly be seen in the salaries of incoming faculty in those departments. Science, technology, engineering, and math (STEM) departments have received particular attention. With our tech economy, there are more and larger funding opportunities for STEM. At my institution, within the college of liberal arts and sciences, junior faculty in the anthropology department are paid $12,000 per year less than those in natural sciences departments.[41] Starting assistant professors in the college of business have a mean salary of $13,767 per month—though the lowest paid professors in the college earn less than half of the highest paid. This average amount is over twice that of an assistant professor in the college of education ($6,815 per month) or the college of visual and performing arts ($5,335 per month). Given the bean-counting nature of employment, this capitalist logic of production encourages quick research methods, and professors are under pressure to "publish or perish."

However, not all changes to the university kept costs low. Administrative positions swelled by 60 percent between 1993 and 2009.[42] The largest university in the United States, California State University (CSU), is a good example. From 1975 to 2008, CSU added 405 full-time faculty members, an increase of 3.5 percent, and an additional 8,383 administrators, a 220 percent increase. Administrators now outnumber full-time faculty at CSU. As of 2012, the published salaries for university presidents or chancellors, which conveniently doesn't include a range of nontaxable benefits like housing, was $370,470, almost five times (4.7) the average salary for tenured professors.[43] For PhD-granting university systems, the average presidential salary was $431,575. Tellingly, the highest paid university position is often the football coach.

When cutting state budgets for university support, state legislators calculated that universities could and should generate their own income. So university presidents became fundraisers, turning universities into quasi-businesses. One source of revenue is, of course, student tuition. In response to cuts in public funding, many universities simply pass students the bill by raising tuition costs. On average, in-state tuition has more than tripled over the past thirty years, from $3,190 in 1987 (adjusted for inflation, using 2017 dollars) to just under $10,000 ($9,970) in 2017.[44] While some may say that this is just the cost of higher education today, scholars have argued that it is a result of deliberate public policy over a long period of time.[45] The United

States is out of step with its peers, or "competitors" in capitalist language. Students in Montréal, Québec, Canada, held a mass general strike for almost seven months in 2012, stopping planned tuition increases. An organized student movement in Chile that included general strikes forced the government to concede free tuition in 2016.[46] A college education has been free in Germany, the Czech Republic, Sweden, Denmark, Norway, Finland, Iceland, and Estonia, some with incentives to keep students on track. In France, tuition is less than two hundred euros a year. In Cuba, education is free through the doctorate level.

With lenders preying on parents' and young people's fears and hopes, student debt has skyrocketed, disproportionately benefiting for-profit online universities like Phoenix. And unlike other forms of debt, student loans are almost impossible to default on since the Bankruptcy Abuse Prevention and Consumer Protection Act of 2005 was passed, signed by President Bush.[47] As of 2017, 44.2 million people in the United States owed $1.31 trillion in student loan debt, up to $1.5 trillion in 2019. The average debt carried by the class of 2016 is $37,172. This debt is also being felt more within communities of color. According to a Demos Foundation report, 54 percent of young Black families have student loan debt, compared to 39 percent of white families.[48] Borrowers sued Secretary of Education Betsy DeVos to implement legal protections so that predatory lenders wouldn't scam them. However, instead DeVos opened the door for private lenders to cash in on even more of this lucrative "market."

Meanwhile, neoliberal global capitalism has pulled the rug out from under U.S. workers. A college education no longer guarantees a stable, professional, middle-class career as it once might have, but it often guarantees debt for a long time, particularly for communities of color.

In addition to debt, high tuition triggers other negative consequences: USA Today reported on a series of websites for older men who prey on cash-poor female college students, offering them money for sex.[49] Large amounts of debt pressure individuals and limit their choices. Collectively debt also keeps a large segment of the population in a quasi-permanent status of being "liminal"—on the margins, outside. Therefore, given the poverty and forced obedience to the system that student loan debt triggers, struggles within the university are directly linked with those "outside," and vice versa. Like town-gown activist coalitions of marginalized groups in the turbulent 1960s, today's activism needs to be both "in" and "of" the university, as Charlene Carruthers, activist and cofounder of Black Youth Project 100, argued.[50]

Specific Targets in the "Imperial" University

As argued in the second chapter, and by many, many other people, capitalism is founded on, and continues to foment, racial inequality, xenophobia, and patriarchy. These capitalist values have deliberately and increasingly been sown into public universities. With fewer resources flowing into the university overall, the modest gains of traditionally underrepresented groups within it have come under siege. Muslim students are facing increasing surveillance. Undocumented students struggle with the financial aid system and increasingly the terror of deportation looms. Transgender students face threats to their safety in bathrooms and other campus spaces. Women students face pervasive sexual harassment, and one in five is sexually assaulted. Black students are racially profiled on and off campus. They risk becoming another statistic, like NIU student Quintonio LeGrier, shot and killed by Chicago police officer Robert Rialmo on Christmas Day, 2015, while unarmed.

Along with other right-wing individuals, Lynne Cheney, wife of Dick Cheney, vice president to George W. Bush, and Joe Lieberman, a conservative Democrat who now supports Donald Trump, cofounded an organization called the American Council of Trustees and Alumni (ACTA) to take the neoliberal agenda and the culture wars to the university. This right-wing neoconservative think tank took aim at what it saw as the most "dangerous" professors (those with the most "radical" views), "political correctness," and challenges to Zionism, among other things. ACTA is just one right-wing group coordinating systematic, well-funded attacks on the university's independence.

In addition to these attacks, many faculty members have additional burdens.[51] Women's and gender studies (WGS) scholars are often pressured to provide additional service to the university on top of their teaching duties.[52] They have also borne the brunt of therapeutic activities for students who have experienced assault. Before women's centers on campus existed, these professors provided frontline services, and still do.[53] Many have double service expectations as "joint hires," serving two academic units, since many university administrations devalue this interdisciplinary program with an activist history. In addition, they mentor junior colleagues, graduate students, and undergraduates while often being expected to run "extracurricular" service programs. A grad school colleague of mine, one of only a few full-time WGS faculty at a teaching-heavy public university, always fell seriously ill at the end of March, Women's History Month.

Ethnic studies scholars face the same burden, especially if they are one of only a few POC faculty members for others to turn to. At NIU, Black History Month had over twenty events each year. The director was not even a full-time faculty member in Black studies and for years taught an overload to ensure there were enough classes to keep the program alive. Another trap for these scholars is official university-wide committees that they often get tapped to participate on, particularly those addressing diversity.[54]

As feminists of color since Ann DuCille, Dána-Ain Davis, Chandra Mohanty, Cherrié Moraga, Gloria Anzaldua, and others have demonstrated, women of color are especially taxed.[55] Reflecting on systemic exclusions, Patricia Hill Collins detailed the pains of being an "outsider within."[56] It seems too obvious to mention, but alas, it isn't within the scope of a corporatized bean-counting university: an intersectional analysis of one's job value is necessary, as queer people, people of color, immigrants, those who are differently abled, and/or women face multiple pressures. Carole Boyce Davies called universities the most colonized spaces.[57] This colonization structures systemic racism within the academy.[58] Gina Athena Ulysse demonstrated the ways in which not-so-subtle racism surrounded her early career.[59]

As pre-tenure faculty, Tami Navarro, Bianca C. Williams, and Attiya Ahmad were supposed to keep quiet and not participate in the official conversation so as to not endanger their tenure bids.[60] But they spoke out about the subtle and sometimes not-so-subtle racist comments they faced from other faculty members, the need they felt to dress up when older white men in their departments got to wear whatever they wanted, and the feeling of having white students actively challenge their knowledge and authority— being "presumed incompetent."[61] Williams professed to still be "in love with anthropology," but wondered whether a "long-distance" relationship might be more sustainable, working within departments of radical ethnic studies with other faculty of color. This is the same point Robert Alvarez made over twenty-five years ago.[62] Jafari Sinclaire Allen and Ryan Cecil Jobson warn that people *move* from places they are not welcome: "Many of us will continue to occupy anthropology as forgotten or unwanted mortgagors, even as we build new places of residence."[63]

While administrators and some senior colleagues might be tempted to dismiss these concerns as strictly anecdotal evidence, these inequalities are structured within the academy, as products of the society that produces it.[64] In a *Boston Review* forum "Black Study, Black Struggle," leading Black studies scholar Robin D. G. Kelley made this same point. Kelley and several respondents detailed multiple ways that universities are hostile environments for students of color as well as staff and faculty. Kelley warned people—particularly people of color—against overidentification with the institution, "incapable of loving them—of loving anyone," and he argued for a revival of Fred Moten and Stefano Harney's concept of the "undercommons," where radical activist students are *in* the university, not *of* it, that it is a site of temporary refuge, and not "home."[65] The full debate (http://bostonreview.net/forum/robin-d-g-kelley-black-study-black-struggle) is well worth the time to read—multiple times—and contributor Derecka Purnell offers a reading list (http://bostonreview.net/reading-radicalism) to start one's self-education in the style of the civil rights era Freedom Schools. Contributors to the debate hone in on the multiple legacies of systematic exclusion in the academy, hammering home the idea that universities, especially public universities, are part of the society that produces that racist legacy, a point made by many others as well.[66] Discussing two universities in St. Louis in the wake of the 2014 Ferguson Uprising, Sarah Lacy and Ashton Rome detailed how universities profited directly off of racism, which Zoe Todd demonstrated regarding Indigenous peoples.[67] As an integral part of society, universities reflect society's inequalities and injustices, but can also be sites of struggle against them.

In their roles as fundraisers, university presidents often pitch conservative, in an effort to attract what they perceive to be "mainstream" donors. They become susceptible to manipulation and pressure, agents of rolling back academic freedom, for example like University of Illinois chancellor Phyllis Wise, who canceled new—tenured—faculty member Steven Salaita's job offer when he tweeted about the Israeli military's 2014 shelling of Gaza. Piya Chatterjee and Sunaina Maira have assembled firsthand accounts of racial profiling and other forms of targeting of radical voices within what they call the "imperial university."[68] Ironically, Salaita's chapter in that volume, also published in 2014, critiques the use of universities to increase state power, enforcing anti-Arab and particularly anti-Palestinian policies.[69] Salaita's case, chilling as it is, particularly given the asphyxiation of higher education in Illinois, is far from unique: Lara Deeb and Jessica Winegar interviewed over 120 anthropologists who work in the region, many of whom report a consistent pattern of marginalization and even bullying.[70]

As this discussion hammers home, contemporary universities are far from safe spaces for many. And they are not just a deliberate battleground in the "culture wars" in the country but also sites for struggle over the definition and elaboration of policy. Anthropology emerged within this contradictory and fraught context as a clear example of the historical tensions discussed above.

Anthro-apologies

Anthropology is and always has been complex and contradictory, rendering any simplistic, all-or-nothing defense or rejection difficult. For example, anthropology has played a special role providing support for U.S. empire, and yet many anthropologists actively opposed militarism, in the United States as well as Israel, some at great risk to their careers.[71] This will be only the briefest of introductions to the debate within the field of anthropology, as people outside universities don't necessarily need to be steeped in the details of much of these issues. However, many millennial activist groups of color already know that anthropology does indeed have a colonial history.[72] In addition to the ways in which U.S. anthropology as a whole benefited from the Cold War University and specifically area studies programs, British anthropologists have also been collaborators within colonial administrations and U.S. anthropologists with the government's Bureau of Indian Affairs.[73] Witting or not, anthropological knowledge has served militaristic ends. Within the Cold War, anthropologists were engaged in counterinsurgency efforts in Vietnam and Latin America, a role reprised during the Global War on Terror, particularly in Afghanistan and Iraq within the Human Terrain System, which sent social scientists alongside combat units to conduct research identifying potential insurgency threats.[74]

This colonialism is unfortunately not only in the past either. Mwenda Ntarangwi, a graduate student from Kenya at a U.S. university, detailed the ways in which race and racism shape the discipline, reproducing hierarchies.[75] As Gilberto Rosas said, "The haunting expropriations of land, labor, and loved ones are still the backbone of the discipline, along with the pilfering of ideas."[76] In the summer of 2018, as the United States was pulling out of the Paris Agreement and Trump was escalating his war on immigrant families, including instituting his family separation policy, several anthropologists were mired in a scandal, only one of many #MeToo, triggering a flurry of critique and analysis from within the discipline. David Graeber, who attracted a large following among activists and anarchists because of his role in #Occupy, issued a public apology for the journal he helped create. The journal's editor was accused of abusing a female assistant. Responses—particularly by anthropologists of color, many untenured—moved well beyond the initial trigger. The journal was named *HAU*, based on a concept in the foundational text in economic anthropology translated from Maori as "reciprocity." As a group of Maori scholars pointed out, Marcel Mauss—whose career took off by his use of this concept—did not practice reciprocity when he popularized that term, and the Indigenous group did not reap the rewards of Mauss's extraction and dispossession (and incomplete translation) of the concept.[77] Neither, as it turned out, did the team behind *HAU*.

E-Racing Black Anthropology

Anthropology has also colonized "internalized" others, who Black feminist sociologist Patricia Hill Collins calls "outsiders within."[78] The very term "anthropology" signifies racism in some quarters.[79] The term itself was first used by those who ranked various peoples along a single evolutionary line. As a discipline, anthropology has done more to elevate "folk" theories of race into science than any other.[80] A French aristocrat who called himself an anthropologist, Arthur de Gobineau, used craniometry (the measurement of skulls) to "prove" innate differences in intelligence among people he categorized as belonging to distinct "races." His 1853 book on the subject justified the European colonization of Africa and Asia. Slaveholders in the U.S. South like Leonardo DiCaprio's character in the movie *Django Unchained* used craniometry and de Gobineau's book to vindicate what they euphemized as the "peculiar institution" of slavery.

A generation later, a man also educated in France used what he called "positivist anthropology" to directly refute de Gobineau's claim. Anténor Firmin was born and raised in the only country in the world to have arisen from a slave revolt. After his 1885 book, he returned to his native Haiti to launch a political career. Firmin's *The Equality of the Human Races* did not go viral like the book it critiqued did. The message of racial equality, or perhaps just the messenger—an educated Black man from not just a Black-majority nation, but also the world's first—was hard to swallow for members of "polite society" who wished to pretend that racism was a thing of the past since the end of plantation slavery.

Only after Franz Boas, a German-born Jewish immigrant to the United States, came on the scene could the idea be widely received that "races" were not inherently unequal. Boas, trained as a physicist, assembled the "four fields" of anthropology (physical or biological, sociocultural, and linguistic anthropology and archaeology) in the service of his vision of refuting racism, xenophobia, and anti-Semitism. The conclusion of Boas's life's work, that race is not biological but a social construct, directly challenged prevailing racialism, or the "naturalness" of race and racial inequalities. However, this did not prevent the rise of "Aryan" superiority later or the horrors of the Holocaust. And however important his contribution to the field, Carolyn Fluehr-Lobban has called "Papa Franz" to task for pilfering the ideas of his Haitian predecessor without proper acknowledgment.[81] Fast-forward to the present—saying that race does not exist biologically has since become a conservative, even at times reactionary argument. Racism most definitely exists within society, whether or not "race" exists biologically. As Junaid Rana argues, this trivialization of white supremacy continues within anthropology, even though it has clear material consequences.[82]

As former president of the American Anthropological Association Leith Mullings argues, Boas's "color blind" vision limits anthropology's contributions to the study of racism.[83] Generations of anthropologists were trained to not "see" race. Within anthropology, the subfields most dedicated to the scientific study of race—biological anthropology and archaeology—are the least diverse. They are nearly all white.[84]

The marginalization of African Americans and other people of color within anthropology began at least as early as the period when Boas was working. Boas built his career and a legacy of anthropology in the United States as a critique of what he called "armchair" anthropology—research conducted in the library, cobbling together sources written by others, usually missionaries, colonial administrators, or wealthy adventure seekers. The way his work is typically taught to anthropology students today, Boas conducted his famous research among the Kwakiutl people in British Columbia himself. However, Ella DeLoria, a Yankton Dakota scholar, conducted most of this research. Boas chose her as his assistant because of her Indigeneity. Sadly, this story resurfaced only among several specifically feminist, activist, revisionist histories of the discipline.[85]

Zora Neale Hurston herself was an innovator in ethnographic research and writing, penning studies of the folklore and community history of Eatonville, Florida, Jamaica, and Haiti. Hurston studied anthropology under Boas, who saw an opportunity to expand his research into African American communities, particularly with research that was considered sensitive and even racist like craniometry.[86] However, Hurston's unique approach to her research and writing, which blended in her own story and used fictionalizing accounts and literary flourish, was too forward-thinking for anthropology. As Gwendolyn Mikell analyzed, "If anthropology as a discipline would not accept the lifestyle and research approaches necessary to produce the texts of black culture, she would abandon it."[87] And she did, in 1936. Two years later, she published her ethnography of Jamaican and Haitian folklore, *Tell My Horse*.[88] The irony is that since the 1980s, anthropology has been engaged in a self-critique that has created spaces for methodological and textual innovation, which Lynn Bolles says "are not particularly new from a Black feminist anthropological perspective."[89] Fortunately for Hurston, she went on to have a significant career in American literature.

Continuing Boas's legacy, and his habit of silencing Black women, his student Melville Herskovits became the power broker in African studies within anthropology.[90] While not himself Haitian or Black, Herskovits had the final say on who would receive fellowships to study in Haiti. In addition to Hurston, Herskovits worked with another Black woman anthropology student who was also an artist, who also abandoned her PhD. Fortunately for Katherine Dunham, she had a successful career outside anthropology as a successful dancer/choreographer and human rights activist.[91] Herskovits also wielded this power over other Black women anthropologists, such as Johnnetta Cole, who eventually became president of Spelman College, an HBCU.[92]

This marginalization of people of color continued within anthropology. For example, the textbook in my 1995 undergraduate theory class included works from twenty-three anthropologists. All but one (Ruth Benedict) were male and *all* were white. Fast-forward to 2018, and graduate students still cite this book. Ira E. Harrison and Faye V. Harrison sought to correct this erasure in their 1999 collection, *African American Pioneers in Anthropology*.[93] This erasure started in the beginning; while Boas himself didn't receive his degree in anthropology, his status in the field remains unchallenged. However, W. E. B. Du Bois is rarely claimed as an anthropologist despite his contributions to our understanding, including the concept of empirical study and an understanding of worldview and the perception of self and other within society—what he termed "double consciousness."[94]

Anthropologists of color were relegated to studying their own culture and were often marginalized for doing so. St. Clair Drake's *Black Metropolis* and Allison Davis's *Deep South*, both early systematic studies of racism within the United States, were seen as not being "anthropology" (read: exotic) enough.[95] Even though the full title of *Black Metropolis* includes "anthropology," the publisher lists it in their sociology section. An exception to this rule of what Brackette Williams called "homework" was Delmos Jones, who worked in Vietnam during the U.S. war, and whose ethical decision to protect the community by not publishing his research cost his career dearly.[96]

Anthropologists like Jonathan Rosa and Yarimar Bonilla, Jafari Sinclaire Allen and Ryan Cecil Jobson, Bianca Williams, and Orisanmi Burton are reimagining and rearticulating what anthropology in the service of human liberation would look like, what we would do, and how we can change our praxis.[97] Acknowledging that activists are now writing in their own name, Burton writes, "They are reflecting back on the strengths and limitations of their actions and as they speak for themselves, the anthropologist's ethnographic authority is called into question."[98] Finding new roles for anthropologists alongside or behind activists requires humility and reflection. And it does require sincere long-term commitment. Before this is possible, anthropologists must decolonize the discipline.

Decolonizing Anthropology

Anthropologists—led particularly by women, queer people, and/or people of color—have been engaging in a self-critique for over a generation. Interested readers can follow this discussion in the many thoughtful, insightful, necessary critiques that have already been written, some of which are cited below. But briefly, feminist anthropologists challenged the ways that androcentric (male-centered) biases creep into the field's methods and theories as part of the assumptions scholars make when they do their research *and* about whose lives are worth studying.[99] Anthropologists of color have waged a long struggle to decolonize anthropology.

Eve Tuck and K. Wayne Wang insist that decolonization is not just a metaphor, that anyone attempting to "decolonize" must support Indigenous communities' reclaiming sovereignty and land rights.[100] Faye Harrison argues that decolonizing anthropology requires working to end the inequalities between First World and Third World anthropologies. Harrison argued that we must "empower those most alienated from and dispossessed of their rights to democratized power and the material benefits of economic justice."[101] Decolonizing anthropology challenges the false distinction between "pure" and "applied" anthropology, as well as the supposedly "neutral" and "detached" production of knowledge. The goal is to "free the study of humankind from the prevailing forces of global inequality and dehumanization and to locate it firmly in the complex struggle for genuine transformation."[102] More recent radical feminist, queer, and/or people of color anthropologists have pushed the boundaries, bridging scholarship with activism from outside the academy, such as Gina Athena Ulysse, Bianca Williams, Zoe Todd, Orisanmi Burton, Yarimar Bonilla, and many others. Dána-Ain Davis and Christa Craven published a couple of books together advancing feminist activist anthropology.[103] Aisha Beliso-De Jesús and Jemima Pierre offer specific examples of the ways that anthropology reproduces white supremacy.[104] However, because of the evisceration of universities just discussed more than a fifth (21 percent) of PhDs in anthropology are working as tenure-track professors.[105] Given this, it is clear that an approach to scholarship that attempts to separate the university from the community is no longer even possible.

Self-Interrogation

So where do we go from here?

The first step in dismantling the ivory tower and unleashing a liberatory anthropological imagination involves anthropologists turning our ethnographic gaze on ourselves. Much good recent work written discusses this. As Jaskiran Dhillon says, "Those of us who occupy [academic] spaces ought to be deliberating long and hard about what we are doing with/in them."[106] Navarro, Williams, and Ahmad agree: "Anthropology possesses tools—such as a willingness to look inward—that may prove invaluable in dismantling oppressive environments. The work that remains to be done is applying these tools to the discipline itself, looking starkly at its embedded assumptions and hierarchies."[107] The *HAU* scandal offered an opportunity for such self-reflection. And what was reflected back wasn't pretty: "Many of [anthropology's] current practices have worked to constitute the conditions of possibility for colonialism, settler colonialism, conquest, and both past and present dispossessions."[108] The discipline is going to need more than simple reflection in order to "clean house from within."[109]

Where does this house cleaning start?

Rewarding Hierarchy

Cleaning house requires changing the rules of the game and the reward structures that prop up the status quo. As trained social scientists, we should be able to analyze these reward structures just as we analyze systems of bride-wealth, rites of passage, or informal exchange. At a star-studded "presidential" panel at one of the first American Anthropological Association (AAA) meetings I attended, a prominent anthropologist put out a call especially to the grad students in the audience, many of whom were there to get a glimpse of our academic heroes in person, to conduct an ethnography of the AAA itself. I volunteered. I should not have been surprised that my email was never returned. In retrospect, his speech was a performance of self-critique by a senior white man who gained status through the system as it already existed. His vision for change involved more of the same.

Like all professional associations, the status economy in the AAA is often tied to the real economy. Thousands of us descend on a particular city, eating out and staying in hotels, which makes hosting a meeting an attractive option for cities that maintain convention centers. But it can be hard to justify for anthropologists who are not well funded at their institutions. For example, with required annual membership dues and conference registration, it costs a midcareer professor over $600 just to attend the conference. The AAA secures blocks of rooms for its members in large corporate hotel chains, with "discounted" rates of $179 and up per room per night (plus taxes). Those whose universities can afford to foot the bill get to have informal meetings in the hotels, where "elevator pitches" are often at least as important as formal meetings to secure a job or book deal.[110] Tenure-track professors at less well-funded universities, who usually have to individually fork over at least some of the total cost of attending the conference, can afford to stay at a "budget" hotel close by. Contingent faculty, folks who teach at community colleges, and/or graduate students, are often forced to stay in other neighborhoods farther away from the convention center and main conference hotels, or might take the risk and book an apartment share where they pay in advance before knowing the final conference schedule.

My current annual cost to attend the AAA ($1,800 per year on average) is between two-thirds and three-fourths of what my salary was for the entire semester teaching a course as an adjunct at my partner's public university.

With graduate students and even some full professors unable to attend the annual meetings of the AAA, the biggest networking event for all anthropologists, is it any wonder that activists are excluded from this corporate cloister? Every time I have attempted to break down the conference walls and bring in local activists, the registration fee, upward of $500 each for nonmembers, presented significant barriers. Many scholars coming from outside the United States aren't even allowed in the country to attend the meeting either. Some professional associations have addressed this by passing resolutions against holding future meetings in the United States until these restrictive travel policies are lifted.

At some point in transition from exploited graduate student to liminal postdoc to hushed-up untenured assistant professor to tenured faculty, many people learn to internalize the current reward structure of tenure and promotion and start believing it has some inherent value, that it is a meritocracy. Departments, university presses, peer-reviewed journals, fellowships and grants, and even field sites are ranked, sometimes only implicitly, on a prestige scale. And how successful you are on this prestige scale often translates into opportunities for better employment, publishing possibilities, or grants. Graduates from the top fifteen PhD programs in the United States compose a majority of tenure-track professors.[111] While women PhDs in anthropology now outnumber men two to one, men are disproportionately hired in tenure-track jobs, a statistic that has increased since 2009.[112] This gap is also more pronounced for PhD-granting institutions, yet to hear some older white men tell it, women of color are taking over the discipline.

Changing the Reward Structures

While individuals can and must be accountable for their actions, collectively we have a shared responsibility to change the rewards for maintaining the status quo inherent in the academy. I would be honestly surprised if most students—to say the least about activists in the community—are aware of these reward structures, so the following discussion might feel like "inside baseball." But these collective sets of decisions *do* influence what gets approved to be taught—how, by whom, and to whom. How can we support tomorrow's activists addressing humanity's urgent crises head-on if we can't sustain this activism within the university, support it, and diversify our ranks?

Those of us who get tenure, especially we white men, need to do our part to make structural changes. Academic promotion, including what gives someone tenure, varies quite widely by discipline. Anthropologists can rewrite the rules about what counts as acceptable for promotion within our department. For example, since faculty of color tend to be overburdened by service, departments should not expect everyone to be "super minorities" with sympathetic white colleagues advising them to "just say no," some actually meaning it. Typically, service counts the least in personnel decisions; we should change this, stepping up so that more faculty share the service burden. Given the need to support diverse student bodies, we should also prioritize hiring more faculty of color, which will also benefit departments by increasing the diversity of viewpoints. Strength in numbers also helps actually shift the running of departments. Karen Brodkin, Sandra Morgen, and Janis Hutchinson have outlined specific ways to challenge the "white public sphere" in anthropology, beginning at the department level: white faculty need to be proactive in addressing issues of race and racism, making it an explicit priority.[113]

Anthropologists should also have something to say about what counts as "good research." We can at the very least value other activities in addition to receiving large external grants, which university administrations love because universities can take upward of an additional 60 percent in "indirect costs"—basically a tax to run the management of grant activities. The achievement most highly weighted in many a scholar's quest for tenure is still the peer-reviewed article, but only if it appears in one of a very few highly ranked journals. Peer-reviewed articles written in languages other than English, published in journals from the countries where anthropologists work, are often considered inferior. The very least those of us who work abroad owe communities whose time, analyses, and personal stories make our careers is to share our findings with them, yet many departments don't reward this, let alone require it. And access to these high-prestige articles is often locked behind a paywall, despite the fact that researchers happily give the companies the text to publish for free and also give our free labor to them as peer reviewers. One way to get around this restriction is to give articles that are open access to anyone the same respect that we give those published in corporately funded journals. Anthropology faculty should also devise some formula for increasing the value given to other scholarly productions, like videos, blogs, testimonies to governmental bodies or expert witness accounts in court, interactive websites used by activists, or museum exhibits, and not just "count"—that is to say, dismiss—them as service. Departments could give faculty members incentives to work collaboratively, to publish with their interlocutors, both abroad or in the United States. Research arising from community-identified needs could be given extra weight, particularly that which challenges the bias of colonial priorities.[114]

Scholars should be specifically encouraged to cite local experts, women, and/or scholars of color.[115] That would ensure people actually read their works in the first place, allowing some to join what Louise Lamphere called "the discipline's patriarchs" on required reading lists.[116] Some anthropologists have already been pushing for this. Ira Harrison and Faye Harrison, Lee Baker, and others have attempted to bring attention to the contributions of "African American pioneers" by writing them back into the history of anthropology.[117] In Aoteoroa (the Indigenous Maori name for New Zealand), a multiethnic coalition of scholars has come together to support Indigenous anthropologists, self-consciously bringing Maori works as well as their epistemologies (ways of knowing) to the fore. And in addition to Jaskiran Dhillon, Indigenous anthropologists like Zoe Todd, Kim Tallbear, and Vanessa Watts have similarly chipped away at the hegemony of so-called Western epistemologies.[118]

These are just a few ways scholars can change the rules of the game. If we acknowledge that the status economy is real and has material consequences, we can actively disrupt it. In addition to talking about the importance of "public" anthropology, we can identify and remove barriers to engagement with the public. Actually defending the issues bridging town and gown requires more than just engaging with the public. It requires *organizing*.

Organizing

The university system is part of society, its fate intertwined with that of the public. Global capitalism, particularly in its current neoconservative, imperialist variant, has made systematic assaults on public institutions and "the commons," resources like water, air, land, and their symbiotic relationship (collectively "the environment") that belong to us all. Activists and scholars alike are grappling for bigger solutions: rather than a constant game of whack-a-mole with specific issues, where can we dig in our heels and turn the tide against these forces now fully out in the open?

One potential vehicle for solidarity is the faculty union, requiring professors to ditch our false consciousness and identify ourselves as workers. Faculty working conditions are student learning conditions. Being part of a union also puts us in the same room as other teachers, public employees, and other workers, full stop. As the victories won in 2019 by Chicago Teachers Union and Kentucky Education Association members highlight, unions can be vehicles for solidarity and transformative social justice.[119] Engaging our full selves and helping craft a collective self-interest, unions can move the needle, helping professors move from "allies" to "accomplices." Well-funded conservative commentators on talk radio constantly attack public universities since they are battlegrounds for a range of issues. It is high time a town-gown coalition mobilizes not just for activism but for *organizing*, helping particular groups and communities to transform their relations of power. Our anthropological imaginations might have something to offer.

Praxis

There are several strands of organizing praxis, each with distinct approaches to issues, and the relationship among the group, the "constituency." But all activist organizing has at its core the goal to identify then transform structures of power.[120] All groups to varying degrees involve establishing and tending to relationships. In its best moments, anthropology has affinity with organizing. For example, key methods in sociocultural anthropology identify structures of power, offer tools for mobilization, frame issues and identify connections between them, and build connections between various communities.

As Harrison implored us almost thirty years ago, anthropology's praxis can and should embrace the most marginalized among us, to center the perspectives of and humanize those under siege.[121] An embodiment of Black feminist praxis, Gina Athena Ulysse pushes through boundaries of art, activism, and scholarship, simultaneously publishing in three languages.[122] Aimee Cox, an anthropologist at Yale University, draws inspiration from Black feminism and particularly Hurston and Dunham noted above: "The centering of narrative, learning in and from community, and the practice of theorizing through experience are aligned as methodologies in Black feminism as I have studied and lived it as praxis."[123] Women activist scholars of color Maya Berry, Claudia Chávez Argüelles, Shanya Cordis, Sarah Ihmoud, and Elizabeth Velásquez Estrada argue, "Our colleagues, both women and men, must share the responsibility of centering queer, trans, and feminist epistemologies in their teaching and advising practices."[124] However, aligning anthropology and organizing requires actually doing the work of social change. Dhillon, quoting political scientist and scholar of color Malinda Smith, argued that "we actually do something (not just think progressive thoughts) to make it happen . . . we need to ask ourselves *where our political commitments lie.*"[125]

Like many others, such as Karen Brodkin, Dána-Ain Davis, Hillary Haldane, Susan Hyatt, Vincent Lyon-Callo, Jeff Maskovsky, Leith Mullings, Ida Susser, and Jennifer Wies, I came to anthropology via community organizing. When I was an organizer, I saw synergies between anthropology and long-term social justice organizing. Anthropologists talk with and listen to the world's most marginalized people, whom other disciplines tend to ignore, silence, or translate into statistics. Sociocultural anthropology's core methodologies most resemble those of grassroots activism: participation, patience, holistic listening, and a humanistic approach to caring, understanding, and working with real people. Organizing inspires critical transformations in people, and marginalized, formally uneducated people, when included in the planning and executing of activism, often have sharper analyses than professionals.

Anthropology also seemed then, as it still does now, an ideal space to support long-lasting, grassroots social change—an antidote to not only the constant barrage of corporate fear mongering on the right but also self-righteous, top-down, single-issue Marxist theorizing. Anthropologists have a global reach, enabling anthropology to explore how global phenomena, such as the contemporary global economic crisis, are impacting people everywhere—how these phenomena are understood, how they intersect with local realities, and how humanity is confronting them. Like it or not, the global capitalist system has already turned the world into a single market, with a few complicated exceptions and asterisks like Cuba. Like it or not, one of capitalism's outputs—climate change—is impacting our entire species, though some people definitely have a few extra generations before directly, individually, paying the consequences.

In other words, our trained anthropological imagination is ideally positioned to do away with the entire logic of the "least common denominator" and instead articulate a vision of the "greatest common good."

Collaboration

Long-term organizing for justice is not easy work, and it's always collaborative. This absolutely requires attention to reciprocity, and those of us within the academy not only need to work against the tendency toward accumulation of achievements and status but should actively disrupt institutional power dynamics and hierarchies. We need to examine the inherently unequal power contexts in our work and move beyond a goal of simple reciprocity.[126]

Collaborations by their nature tend to be fragile, requiring shared commitment and upkeep between all the parties involved. And collaborators must always check their privilege and "saviorism" at the door. This is often hard for scholars, particularly white male scholars, whose privilege is often an unexamined part of our background and opportunities, lining up along several different types of inequality. To face the extreme challenges of this moment in history, people need to move beyond being *allies*, where privilege remains intact, to becoming *accomplices*, putting one's own body on the line, disrupting and dismantling privilege.

The systematic undoing of public higher education may have the unintended consequence of shoving more people with an anthropological imagination into the world well beyond the ivory tower. However, for that to work we need to heed the advice of radical Puerto Rican scholar/activist/educator Jessie Fuentes. She said at an organizing training for NIU students that one should always enter spaces as a learner. For long-term organizing work to succeed, those trained as scholars indeed have much to learn. Organizers should share their toolkit as part of the required preparation of anthropologists. Especially since almost four-fifths of anthropology PhDs are going to do something else other than work as a professor, skills such as writing grants and understanding and navigating multiple bureaucracies would be valuable for the grads themselves as well as their communities, organizations, and employers. Writing for different audiences, through blogs, letters to the editor or to policy makers, and even through tweets, might prove essential to social change work. Experience and preparation for "public engagement" like facilitating meetings, conducting needs assessments, understanding how power works, identifying strategies and issues, organizing constituent groups, practicing antiracism, uncovering and dismantling privilege, working across unequal identity groups, building coalitions—in short, organizing—offer potential to address the very inequalities that have been systematically undermining both the "public" and education.

University professors should not only strengthen our own ties to "organic intellectuals," Antonio Gramsci's term for people who come to knowledge about their own social group through experience and reflection, not official credentialing, but also change our value systems to respect their contributions to the world of knowledge.[127] While liberal arts still exist in what remains of the public university, organic intellectuals can provide insights, experiences, and training to complement those of professional anthropologists. Top-down buzzwords like "engagement" and "service learning" are often not fully thought through when it comes to the work needing to be done in the community. As part of capitalist "bean-counting" metrics of the university, priorities are expressed through the *number* of hours that students volunteer, not the *impact*. U.K. universities have the Research Excellence Framework, inspiration for the "audit culture," so professors there too are under pressure to document their achievements in a numerical calculus, rather than through the impact of their work.[128] Requiring so many hours of student "engagement" risks tapping out local agencies' abilities to manage student volunteers. The concern on campuses across the United States is not the tangible outcome and results but students' engagement and experience—what activists critique as a "laying on hands" approach, voyeurism, poverty pimping, or white saviorism.

The antidote to this mismatch is an organic relationship between universities and community organizations, with professors being active members of the collectives and movements in the first place.[129] Bringing activists in as paid instructors, as equally valued as the professor, makes a powerful statement about what gets counted as knowledge.[130] It would first make sure that activists are paid, literally valued. And that they do more than "babysitting" students. Another powerful statement for scholars like anthropologists to make would be to work with organic intellectual colleagues on shaping the research agenda in the first place, an approach long promoted in participatory action research (PAR).[131]

However, the women scholars of color trained in "activist anthropology" cited above encourage us to move beyond PAR. They argue that "our training must entail grounded discussions of the particular challenges non-male, non-white, non-hetero, and non-cisgender bodies face in order to be better prepared as researchers."[132]

Completing the research-teaching-service trifecta requires copublishing as equal coauthors. Like anything, this requires careful tending to relationships, in no small part through active participation, putting the time in.

Accountability

Dismantling the ivory tower to unleash the liberatory potential of public universities requires actually doing the work to make change. Scholars need to be in the room where it happens: going to community meetings and engaging our neighbors, discussing what is to be done, establishing relationships, and building trust. As anthropologists, we should be open to learning, challenging our own assumptions and worldview, and not always act as "experts." It is not enough to change the rules within the academy to reward "activism." We must make sure that those of us who attempt it have to check in with those most affected, who should be leading the charge. As Dhillon asks, "To whom are we accountable, as individual scholars, as departments, and as a discipline?"[133]

Barbara Ransby argues for a "radical recalibration of what universities owe—and not only to students and faculty, but also to campus workers and to communities beyond the campus."[134] Maya Berry and colleagues "envision a critical feminist activist anthropology that holds us politically accountable to our interlocutors as well as to our own embodied reality, as part of the same liberatory struggle, albeit differentially located along the continuum of black and Indigenous liberation."[135] Charlene Carruthers says, "Activists must be both in this world and of it if we want to transform it." Those of us seeking temporary refuge within universities need to address the structural inequalities within them and at the same time try to dismantle the ivory tower. Working with communities on today's pressing issues requires both/and, not either/or, action.

Accountability to marginalized individuals and communities is key to dismantling the ivory tower. It requires changes to professorial reward structures, and having a transformative, radical reciprocity behind a true spirit of community collaboration. To reiterate,

- Today's urgent world problems require intentional collaborations between scholar/activists in the university and those in the community.

- Resources of the university need to be defended as public goods, and shared equitably among students and communities, particularly marginalized groups.
- Public universities should fulfill their role as spaces of encounter and discussion, so people can deliberate there on the urgent issues facing communities, identify solutions, and then train and mobilize the community.
- Organizing offers potential synergy with an anthropology dedicated to human liberation and developing our anthropological imaginations.
- Before any of this is possible, individuals within the university need to divest from internalized capitalist, colonialist, racist logics of inequality. Particularly those most privileged within the system need to do the necessary work to acknowledge—and then dismantle—our privilege.
- Decolonization must always be accompanied by action, to change the institutional structures and rules of the game. It should be accompanied by real, concrete action to redress dispossession.
- Activist and community partners need to be coproducers of knowledge, having a say in crafting the research agenda, empowered to call professors out, keeping us accountable.

Activist/scholars from Du Bois onward have urged universities to join humanity's struggle for liberation. Sadly, until now, universities in general and anthropology in particular have failed to answer the call.

People within the academy can—and must—transform scholarly institutions, changing the reward structures and lowering financial barriers like entry fees, to encourage community participation in scholarly endeavors. At the same time, by learning lessons from activists confronting ever complex and intersectional crises, together we can create new, deliberately inclusive spaces for town-gown organizing. These collaborative spaces can connect activists and movements across the globe or across the tracks, engaged in local, national, and international struggles for justice, to explore the ways in which these concerns are interwoven and learning from one another about the specifics of local issues, and about possible parallels, challenges, strategies, to identify connections.

Let's get to it.

Conclusion

Anthropolitics

> Everything that has a beginning
> has an end.

Are we headed for extinction?

Human beings evolved from being prey to predator, from living in the forest to the savannah to ever growing concrete jungles. We are now our own primary threat. As Agent Smith mused while interrogating Morpheus in the movie *The Matrix*, "Every mammal on this planet instinctually develops a natural equilibrium with the surrounding environment, but you humans do not. You move to an area and multiply and multiply until every natural resource is consumed, and the only way you can survive is to spread into another area."

We're out of space, running out of time.

It's high time we develop a new platform, one centering on our species, on defending humanity: *anthropolitics.*

Humanity is on the losing end of so many struggles that it often feels impossible to stay engaged. The forces of capital, deploying the best resourced and deadliest military apparatus ever created, white supremacy, the seductive power of consumption, the distractive power of for-profit media, and a rising tide of populist nationalism that is enveloping the most powerful countries, are winning, overwhelming principled movements defending humanity—at least for now. How indeed do we turn the tide in this struggle for the future of our species, our planet? For a more just and equitable distribution of resources?

So, more than just blithely asserting that "we are all connected" and affirming people's humanity, that human lives matter, especially those most marginalized by the capitalist system, we need to use our anthropological imagination to help us think through messy and complicated issues if it's to be useful.

Stunningly, *The Matrix* came out at the end of the last millennium, when, at least in the United States, there were seemingly limitless opportunities in technology to solve apparently everything: economic growth, world hunger, disease, and many others. Instead, the tech economy left many workers obsolete as traditional engines of industry rusted out. Some still hold hope that technology will somehow magically by itself fix the world's problems. We can't expect to buy our way into solutions. That has to come through struggle.

Naomi Klein's *This Changes Everything: Capitalism vs. the Climate* begins with an otherworldly gathering of scientists trying to identify technological solutions to global warming at a conference funded by deep pockets. Some geoengineering ideas included impractical and alarming solutions such as spraying chemicals like sulfur to cool the rays of the sun. What Klein calls "magical thinking" can also be seen in a spate of films that have come out in the last decade, like *Interstellar* and *Lost in Space*, depicting another potential solution—sending people into space, essentially giving up hope for Planet Earth. At least in the film *Elysium* there is some acknowledgment that only a few rich folks will get to escape. As for the rest of us....

Dystopian visions of the future are far more commonplace these days, after a seemingly endless Global War on Terror and a long recession. No figure captures this fear of the apocalypse greater than the revival of a piece of Haitian folklore. The *zonbi* or zombie, was initially an enslaved person's escape from the plantation and slavery. In Hollywood's hands, it became our primary metaphor for encroaching doom. Our neighbors, our family, or ourselves could be turned next, becoming the very evil that is surrounding us. Zombies stand in for globalization, dehumanization, the postindustrial economy, urbanization, anomie, atomization, alienation, secularism, and so on.

Some of these plunges into depths of human despair include a hero designed to prevail, like Katniss Everdeen, the heroine of *The Hunger Games*. The opulence of the capital in that alternate United States echoed prerevolutionary France, with the royal court famously disconnected from the reality of everyone else, contrasted directly with the muted, emaciated workers in the districts. Unfortunately, in reality, faced with rising nationalism, violence, white supremacy, pervasive gender violence, and a decidedly anti-intellectual, anti-science, knee-jerk climate denialism amounting to a mass cover-up of humanity's destruction by fossil fuels, the odds are *not* ever in our favor.

Apocalypse Now

Unfortunately, Hollywood's obsession with humanity's pending demise is pallid next to the real horrors facing specific people and communities. Right now, not in some ill-defined future. It's ironic that Agent Smith concluded his monologue by likening our species to a virus—as the book is going to press in mid-March 2020, COVID-19 has just been declared a pandemic. Thousands of people across every inhabited continent are affected. Whole cities like New York are moving toward a lockdown, following whole countries like Italy. Airports, subway systems, universities, public schools, public gatherings of *any* kind are being suspended as panicked consumers ravage stores for anything they have left. The word *apocalypse* has become everyday talk—at least from people in the United States who are unaccustomed to scarcity, precarity, and large-scale catastrophe. *Is* our way of life going to be around when the virus finishes its rapid spread across human societies?

It's too soon to tell, of course. But hopefully it's not too *late* to finally recognize that phenomena like the coronavirus bring home the point: we truly are one human race, our fates intertwined. We ignore the fate of the "other" at our own peril. That we have something desperately to learn from one another.

Experiencing these all at once, without a break, it may well be overwhelming; seeing them as connected, as different battlegrounds within humanity's last stand helps inspire solidarity. We are not alone. We are never alone.

And our struggles mean something for others, the stakes always local and global at once.

For example, because of the U.S. government's family separation policy, children are forced to defecate in front of one another, separated from their parents, for no reason other than the fact that they were brought by their parents fleeing to the United States. Halfway across the world, the right-wing Hindu nationalist government of India has denied Muslim people citizenship, all refugees from Bangladesh, Pakistan, or Afghanistan. Muslims make up 15 percent of the population of India and have vigorously rejected the law that discriminates against them, but allows Hindus, Jains, Christians, Sikhs, and Buddhists a path forward to citizenship. The head of the party in power threatened to throw them in the Bay of Bengal.

It's fitting that I wrote this conclusion in the summer of 2019 in Haiti, which was facing a protracted political and economic crisis that ground the country to a halt. Beginning in September, for nine weeks people stayed at home, schools and clinics shuttered, gas stations out of fuel, power outages for days on end—for several months the government didn't turn on the water taps, and trash kept piling up because the municipal government ran out of funds to haul it away. I can't even count anymore the number of my colleagues, friends, neighbors, comrades, and students who declared that "Haiti is finished" or "the capitalist system has reached its end."

Haiti appears in foreign for-profit media only when calamity occurs, when there's death, destruction, and carnage. In fact, there seems to be no other possible fate for the country that rose up against slavery and pushed out its colonizers. The revolution here was in 1804 and made Haiti the second independent nation-state in the Americas. The Haitian Revolution was literally "unthinkable," so powerful were the prevailing ideologies of white supremacy, so effective the reduction of human beings to "tools with a soul" that the French planter elites were caught off guard.[1] As human beings, were the rebellious enslaved workers subject to France's laws not entitled to the fruits of the French Revolution, of liberty, equality, and fraternity?

In Haiti, it's easier to see with greater clarity the global connections to and roots of the current "crisis." Literally thousands of families are on the brink of starvation.

Haitian people fought back against an IMF-sponsored increase in gas prices in July 2018, gaining steam as they demanded accountability from the government, which had received billions in aid. The mobilization brought together people of different class backgrounds, united behind the question,

#KòtKòbPetwoKaribeA? Where did the funds from PetroCaribe go? Street protests and social media solidarity forced the hand of the government and led to the high court's publication of a report detailing corruption. The social movement ignited because PetroCaribe is an example of South-South solidarity, and movement actors refused to accept the oversimplification of the cause as "corruption." Haiti's president publicly declared his allegiance to the United States and neoliberalism while asserting that he was staying put in the National Palace, destroyed ten years ago in the earthquake, still rubble.

Haiti is not an exception, an outlier. Our anthropological imagination can help us see how Haiti's case is an early warning system, a real, human, consequence of the current system of global capitalism and the horrors of slavery that it was built upon, and the continued injustices of colonialism and white supremacy. This is where the global capitalist economy is heading—those in power holding all the cards and refusing to help those in need without huge payoffs just because they can. Haitian activists/scholars have also organized solidarity actions with the people of Puerto Rico, Venezuela, Palestine, Charleston, and El Paso, among others.

Also in August 2019, another white supremacist in the United States opened fire on a group of mostly people of color in a Walmart in the border town of El Paso, Texas. The suspect had posted an anti-immigrant manifesto twenty minutes before the first 911 calls in which he denounced the "Mexican invasion of Texas." He killed at least twenty people. And within thirteen hours of that, there was another mass shooting in Dayton, Ohio, killing at least nine people.

Several media portrayals characterized the killings as "senseless" or "unthinkable." They are not senseless . . . they are targeted. They are racist. They are reflections of the failed promises of whiteness and masculinity, allowed to fester in a society built on these inequalities and celebration of individualism. Of the erosion of the social fabric and contract that held that hard work and perseverance leads to individual achievement. Lots of white men fear their future will not be as bright as the past. Trump fueled this rage to bully his way to the top of the list of a crowded field of Republican contenders and win the presidency. With no experience in government, his simple "Make America Great Again" slogan struck a raw nerve, pushing him over the edge in the important Rust Belt states that the capitalist system, and the Democratic Party's pandering to it, failed.

Indeed, one might well ask, why can't the United States join the rest of the industrialized or postindustrialized world to regulate deadly weapons, or at least check in on who has access to them? The multimillion-dollar lobby of the National Rifle Association (NRA) absolutely plays a central role, but so does the collective memory of the nation's founding by a rebellious group of white slave owners and capitalists who bristled at state control getting in the way of their individual accumulation of wealth—which included maintaining slavery. The founding mythos of John Locke's phrase "life, liberty, and property," which Thomas Jefferson translated as the "pursuit of happiness," weaves an unbridled individualism into the "culture." Individualism at once erases any analysis of social structure, including inequalities like white supremacy and patriarchy, and it glorifies the wealthy as global capitalism consolidates wealth and power at an alarming rate.

Feminist millennials brought the phrase "toxic masculinity" to our language, spiking the punch of "patriarchy." As feminists point out, when men are raised to view themselves as providers and protectors and see that ability wither away as the capitalist system renders their labor obsolete, they tend to strike out. #BlackLivesMatter brought similar analyses about toxic whiteness and white fragility to our attention.[2] Combine the NRA-encouraged, puffed-up Second Amendment hands-off approach to gun control with the systematic underfunding of education and health care, particularly mental health services, and El Pasos and Daytons are going to keep happening, like the shootings in Las Vegas, Parkland Springs, Sandy Hook, and Columbine before. With what happened in El Paso we also need to see how these acts of violence serve particular interests, maintaining capitalism's racial order, like the violence in Charleston, Pittsburgh, and Christchurch. And we must act in principled solidarity, not as distant observers because this global economic system—not to mention our climate—is rotting before our very eyes.

Solidarity

Seeing the violence as unthinkable, exceptional, or tragic and "sending our thoughts and prayers" frankly don't cut it. We need to move beyond being allies, to becoming accomplices. We need to put our full selves into the effort of changing society, seeing how our own self-interest is connected.

For example, in addition to marching against gun violence, like an impromptu group of moms who held a midnight vigil at the White House did minutes before the shooting in Dayton, we need to put together the pieces of what is happening all over: these are specific outcroppings of an empire in decline, of the global capitalist order reaching its limit, of the ways that gender and race trick those of us endowed with specific privilege into identifying with not just the "1 percent" but the world's 0.0000001 percent. Trump tapped into, validated, and whipped up fears of an emasculated white working class, including the "birthers" who simply couldn't believe that a Black man could be president, the Minutemen lashing out against undocumented migrants who brave death to cross the Sonoran Desert, and the white nationalists like Dylann Roof, opening fire in a crowded Black church.[3] Trump's tweets point the finger at Black, Latinx, and Muslim others, just as Hitler whipped up German working poor men's anger against specific "others" like the Jews.

Martin Niemöller, a Lutheran pastor and initial supporter of the Nazi regime, famously named these others: "First they came for the Communists, and I did not speak up because I was not a Communist." Several versions of his warning about the necessity of defending the oppressed and targeted, a "bystanders' manifesto," name different people: Jews, trade unionists, the mentally ill, Catholics, Jehovah's Witnesses, social democrats, and socialists.[4] All end with the warning: "And then they came for me . . . and by that time there was no one left to speak up."

Niemöller's poem—in its many iterations—became a touchstone as Trump issued his "Muslim ban" within a week of taking office. The sentiments behind the speech are rooted in empathy, but they stop short of what humanity needs. Bystanders like Niemöller can choose when—and whether or not—to engage, because they see themselves as separate from the people being targeted. Now more than ever we need to push past a distanced bystander stance if we as a species are to survive.

By using our anthropological imagination, we can see the ties that already bind us together in solidarity. The water I drink, the food I eat, the clothes I wear, the carbon I burn for my electricity and transportation, the specific consumer choices I make as to where to live and what other things I buy that are not necessities, not only affect an abstract "Earth" or "environment" or "climate" but also connect me with specific others: human beings who pick the fruit, human beings who sew my clothes, human beings displaced for me to live where I do and the overseas investments my mortgage facilitates (if I indeed have one), human beings who mine the coal or live by the power plant burning fossil fuels for my electricity or by the landfill that accepts my trash, the community displaced or flooded to give me access to water—we are all connected, our lives already entwined. I can't claim innocence or separation like Niemöller. To support justice for people in Palestine or Haiti or Myanmar, a solidarity response, guided by our anthropological imagination, requires that we first see the connections already intertwined, and that we disrupt the circuits of domination, inequity, oppression, dispossession, repression, and exploitation that already connect my body and my consumer choices to the global capitalist system. In addition to "the carbon footprint" we need to be able to see the slavery quotient or oppression index of our consumer choices.

Solidarity is not "speaking up" on behalf of someone else; it is working to identify the ways that we are already connected. It is learning the specific contours of a community, an identity, an issue, or a struggle for ourselves, and not demanding that others teach us. It is working to join forces from a collective self-interest, acknowledging and working through differences. It is following the lead of local groups and communities, being present and adding your body and resources in the struggle because you understand that you are also impacted, your own liberation is at stake. It is taking this knowledge and experience from collective action and engaging in your own community, and through that local activism helping identify more connections. Solidarity supports specific people's struggles, demanding constant self-evaluation and critique. Through our actions and commitments, we establish relationships of trust, and break down engrained barriers, helping construct this ephemeral "humanity."

There Are Alternatives

The wealthy, privileged few within our current global economy own the media, and they use it to bombard us with constant messages urging us to buy our way into happiness. They literally bank on their ability to limit our imagination by constantly reinforcing the message that global neoliberal capitalism is the only game in town. However, by using our anthropological imagination, we can identify *other* ways of being connected to one another. Building solidarity ties should include a solidarity economy, disrupting what Marx called "alienated labor."

Middle-class consumers pay top dollar for the experience of visiting a coffee estate or eating "farm to table." The experiences of seeing firsthand the connections to the humans behind our consumption have become a multimillion-dollar tourist industry.[5] In the United States, people spent

$1 billion at farmer's markets in 2013.[6] The fact that these experiences are profitable is testament to human beings' desire to uncover and reactivate our ties with one another. Yes, we can (and should) join (or start) cooperatives, or support community-supported agriculture, but we should also think about whom this excludes, and how this can be rectified—what specific policies, processes, and aggregate of consumer choices feed the global capitalist growth machine, and push family farms out of business in the first place and limit access to low income communities of color, for example?

At its most basic, by using our anthropological imagination we can see that there are other alternatives. Humanity's 99 percent of existence before global capitalism shows us many ways we might exist, imperfect as the models may be. Truly, we need to look outside of capitalist society for options of how to scale down our consumption and survive. Many human societies have powerful cultural mechanisms to prevent individuals from getting ahead at the expense of their neighbors. A famous example is that of people in the Kalahari (!Kung San or Dobe Ju'Hoasi) insulting the meat brought by hunters, to keep their egos in check. Fears of witchcraft being used against them also motivate people to be generous when needed, and not seek individual gain at the expense of others. In her work, Margaret Mead discussed cultural sanctions being invoked against someone being "precocious" in Samoa.[7] In Haiti and all over the post-plantation Caribbean similar belief systems came together to keep inequalities within rural, peasant communities in check.[8] Looked at in an unkind light, some scholars have likened peasants to crabs in a bucket, pulling others down if they get too far up.[9]

Particularly since we *need* to go on a low-carbon diet, it behooves us to learn from societies that have been forced to live with less or chose to like the Kayapo in Brazil or the people of Bhutan. By using our anthropological imagination we can see past the romanticism of the "noble savage" to deal with the messy details as well. Embodying and practicing a radical empathy requires us to have an ability to know, envision, and create different ways of being.

Changing the Rules of the Game

It doesn't take long to find the concept of "human nature" lurking behind any justification of war, violence, rape, or transphobia.[10] If there's one thing anthropology has contributed to our understanding of "human nature," it is the idea that human beings are diverse and flexible. We respond to the reward structures put in front of us. The task for us going forward therefore is to ask who wrote the rules and how (and why) they're enforced.

Human beings are neither inherently selfish nor collective minded, neither peaceful nor violent. Poverty should not be romanticized, and people should not read resistance into everyday survival. Other commentators see a "psychic unity" of humankind by pointing out the ways that so-called primitives behave just like people in advanced capitalist societies, which is not only backward but misses the point.

Human beings *are* capable of violence and aggression on a truly horrifying scale, as our current time period all too clearly shows. But we are also capable of resistance to war and tyranny, as well as modeling solidarity, community, and support. While we clearly have the capacity for murder and genocide, human beings have also in key moments offered shelter to enslaved people escaping to freedom or to Jews being sent to concentration camps or to undocumented immigrants seeking protection from deportation.

And we have demonstrated the capacity to resist exploitation by others and to imagine (and create) other societies. The first generation of enslaved African peoples resisted their enslavement. In Panama, the first mention of a slave revolt was in 1525. Those who escaped created a maroon community, from the Spanish *cimarrón*, led by a man named Bayano. The maroons cultivated their own land and negotiated treaties with the Spanish colonial government, surviving as an independent, recognized community for decades.

This spirit of self-help, autonomy, and communal ownership of the means of production as part of a social justice project inspired several successful community transformations, at once resistance against and alternatives to neoliberal capitalism. In Brazil, over two million landless peasants occupied unused land claimed by large landowners or corporations. The Landless Peoples' Movement, MST in the original Portuguese, offered support to peasant social movement organizations across the region, including in Haiti. The beginning of the end of the single-party rule of the PRI (the Institutional Revolutionary Party, nominally communist) in Mexico was an Indigenous revolt in Chiapas that began in 1994, the day NAFTA took effect; the Zapatistas there fought for community control and Indigenous liberation, resisting global capitalism, building a network of schools, clinics, and other social services for their own communities while also seizing control of the land. Soul Fire Farm in Upstate New York and Plant Chicago on the South Side of Chicago are examples of community developments in food justice, facilitated by Black, Indigenous, and people of color activists and organizations. Detroit has a network of community gardens reclaiming lots abandoned by the failure of racial capitalism and particularly the 2008 subprime mortgage collapse. Jackson, Mississippi, has a bottom-up network of cooperatives supported by the city government. Indigenous activists have built on ideas from Alexandria Ocasio-Cortez's "Green New Deal" to promote a "Red Deal," which centers on ending the occupation of their lands, reclaiming Indigenous sovereignty, and gaining or keeping access to natural resources like land and water.[11] Common threads in these contemporary models for justice are leadership by marginalized groups, self-determination, community control, and linking social movement activism with collective production.

With all these examples, using our anthropological imagination can help us highlight alternative models for organizing our planet-wide human society that specific sets of oppressed peoples have already created in their own liberation.

Organizing

Drawing on lessons from organizing, our anthropological imagination should begin where people are: How do people live? What moves us as individuals? What excites us? What prevents our full humanity from being recognized and prevents us from realizing our full human potential? What limitations do we have in common? Who or what binds our eyes, our feet, our voices?

Tracking back and forth from the lived experience—our own individual bodies—to the species level, it is absolutely important to be conscious on both levels of how we feed, clothe, and shelter ourselves, and how we manage limited resources like fresh water and clean air. Each and every dollar spent now is a vote for the kind of world we live in, the kind of human we aspire to be. That dollar spent, our economy, is also at its fundamental level an exchange, a relationship. Do we want to support a faceless global conglomerate, belching pollutants into our common resources of clean air and water? Or should we take the time to look for worker-owned collectives or farmers' cooperatives? Sure, it takes a little more time and effort to read the label. But if a future in which we don't kill everyone off or choke the planet is worth creating, we should share in the collective labor. We could reappropriate technology and crowd-source solutions across the globe. But we also need to keep in mind that not everyone has access to technology, and so some of us actually need to seek people out and have real-time dialogues, even if it means learning another language.

We must also think about how our individual bodies reproduce or challenge privilege: Do I get stopped by police or followed by store security? Do I feel safe walking on campus or in my neighborhood at night? Can I safely go to the bathroom without having to expose myself or having to choose a gender identity? Can I physically enter a building without a ramp? Am I breathing or drinking toxins because the only home that I can afford is by the site of a dump? Should I get sick or injured, can I access and afford appropriate treatment? Dismantling privilege begins with people who have been granted it being willing to transgress that boundary and add our bodies to the struggle.

COVID-19, belatedly for some, taught the importance of self-care. While taking care of our bodies we need to not get into the trap of capitalist consumerism. Melissa Harris Perry encouraged us to go further, "squad care."[12] We are not isolated individuals. We share space with other humans. We can choose to ignore those around us while focusing on our screens, or we can be more conscious of this human connection and actually build communities. "Community" has long since become a buzzword, drained of its meaning. Being part of a community doesn't mean that we all have to be like one another—to look alike, dress the same, eat similar food, speak the same language, or even think the same—and it doesn't even mean that we have to like one another. But it means that we agree to be respectful and conscious about sharing space, and agree to disagree, or more accurately, agree to engage one another in conversation about our differences. One of the best, most empowering aspects of community organizing is the sense of collective power created when people get to know each other, to meet folks with whom we share common interests. Being part of a vibrant community is one of the best antidotes to the isolation and powerlessness stoked by our current economic system. This isolation renders us susceptible to division and fear mongering. Actually knowing and sharing with people who are Muslim, queer, trans, or undocumented helps break down stereotypes.

For some people, having vibrant communities is the end goal to their organizing or analysis. However transformative communities can be, though, it is important to keep going beyond "building community" and also engage power structures. School boards make important decisions about what textbooks to buy for their students, which online resources will be offered, how diversity will be addressed, how they will respond to claims of bullying, sexual harassment, or safety for trans people, and whether they will be welcoming and provide services to undocumented students. City councils can rein in local police, demanding oversight, accountability and transparency of them, and require not just that they demonstrate cultural competency but have implicit bias training as well. They can also work to diversify the police force or declare their cities sanctuaries. Or cut the funding. Local planning commissions decide whether to offer incentives to megacorporations to build big-box stores or small, locally owned businesses who can make decisions about what's on the shelves. Whether one is concerned about organic food, worker rights, or minority-owned businesses, filling out an anonymous online comment to a corporate office thousands of miles away, where it may or may not even be read, is far less effective than talking to the owner herself. Local businesses can also support local production, supporting jobs and reducing the carbon footprint of transport.

Some platforms, including anthropology texts, stop here. It does feel good to go local. It also is something that we can grasp. But we need to stretch our (anthropological) imaginations. Going local as the only solution privileges those who profit on land stolen from Indigenous peoples and those to whom resources flowed, like those in imperialist core countries. The United States also has a lot of arable land for agriculture, and if people adopted a vegan diet, the United States could feed the entire planet. But this solution also forgets that some tracts of land were ruined by slavery, by toxic chemicals, or by warfare.[13]

Far from retreating into local isolationism, having an anthropological imagination inspires us to reach out, to reappropriate the tools capitalism built to facilitate transfer of wealth in the service of humanity, offering not just transactions but exchange of ideas, experiences, worldviews, and analyses. Using our anthropological imagination reminds us of our already-existing global connections and a shared humanity. Fighting for justice for workers in places like Mexico, the Philippines, and Haiti helps workers in Cleveland and Detroit. Protecting environments in the Amazon and Shanghai cleans the air we all breathe, including keeping more trees around to inhale the carbon dioxide. Working on complex issues like conservation is also always at once a struggle for human rights, livelihood security, equity, and social justice.

We need to focus on the specific circuits of capital already connecting us. Engaging in solidarity also means that we all need to confront the same seed company, the same global food conglomerate, the same investment firm, the same manufacturer who is driving down wages; polluting Black, Latinx, and Indigenous communities; swallowing up land farmed by generations of families; and shackling millions of students with trillions of dollars in debt—oppression *here* (wherever that is) is also oppressing people *there*. Pulling at this local thread will help unravel the global system of oppression ensnaring communities in Bangladesh, Somalia, and Guatemala. Using our anthropological imagination helps us illuminate these connections—it's up to us to also tend to these relationships, actually communicating, sharing strategies, and focusing our energies when pressure is needed. Inhumanity and injustice are always advanced in local spaces, where and when we can't always predict: Auschwitz, Selma, Standing Rock, McAllen, Texas, Krome Detention Center, Gaza. . . .

Our anthropological imagination—like organizing—helps us focus on being effective: Where exactly should we apply our pressure? What are our connections? Where is the dehumanization machine attempting to advance? Where is the weak link? Where are people fighting back?

We also need the courage and insight to be able to directly confront the source: the global capitalist economy, built on Indigenous genocide and African slavery, expanded through colonialism, maintained by xenophobia and patriarchy, turning everything into private property, reducing commons like the air we breathe to "externalities" that can be polluted because it increases profits.

Once in a while we need to actually put our bodies on the line when humanity is at stake. In addition to protesting in a courtroom or city hall, or filling the streets of the capital or the steps of the capitol, sometimes that means chaining yourself to a bus on its way to deport migrants or blocking a shipment of dirty fuel, shutting the port down. We need to calibrate our actions according to what our bodies and embodied privilege protects us from . . . or not. We can also use our humanity to protect and care for those on the front lines, like providing food and medical or legal assistance. As South African revolutionary Nelson Mandela reminds us, "[People] who take great risks often suffer great consequences."[14] Sadly, the consequences of our failure to act are even greater. We have no time to lose.

If we develop our anthropological imagination, we can see that there are, in fact, alternatives. Urgent local issues are part of the same global struggle to defend humanity. An anthropolitics, collectively forged to defend our species and shared humanity, requires that we change the rules of the game, rekindling our human connections across groups and organizations, and put our bodies on the line for one another. True, we need to get actively involved in the systems of power that currently exist, including not only registering people to vote but actually running for office, telling our own stories in the established media. We must also create. A solidarity-based anthropolitics connecting local struggles lays the groundwork for building new systems.

While dismantling the old order we must simultaneously lay the groundwork for the world we want to live in, through our conscious, embodied choices as well as the principled solidarity relationships we build through our anthropolitics. Rebellions are indeed built on hope. Truly, another world is possible and ready to be created. We are limited only by our imagination. Hopefully this book has in some small way helped expand yours.

Now, while we still can, let's change the world.

Notes

Foreword

1 Please see NASA 2003a; MacDonald 2016; "Earth's Magnetic North Pole" 2019; Kaplan 2019. The U.S. government magnetic model update is located at www .ngdc.noaa.gov/geomag/WMM/DoDWMM.shtml. See also NASA 2011; "Anthropologist Contributes to Major Study" 2019; Conniff 2010.
2 NASA 2003b. See also Choi 2013; American Institute of Physics 2019; de Wit et al. 2018.
3 European Climate Declaration 2019.
4 "Open Letter to UN Secretary-General" 2012.
5 Kennedy 2018.
6 There were many operations within COINTELPRO whose official declassified documents are located online at https://vault.fbi.gov/cointel-pro. COINTELPRO was a Department of Justice counterintelligence program that targeted political dissenters for dirty tricks, harassment, and even assassination. The definitive book examining the official government documents was written by Churchill and Vander Wall ([1990] 2002).
7 Please see McKinney 2013.
8 Schambach 2019.
9 Hornsby 1986.
10 Quijano 2000.
11 Dr. Jeffrey Perry's work is located at www.jeffreybperry.net.
12 Allen 2012.

Preface

1 Bauer 2020.
2 Vélez and Villarrubia 2018.
3 Abebe 2020.

4 Benjamin 2020; Chotiner and Hammonds 2020; Crenshaw 2020.
5 Taylor 2020.

Introduction

1 Sixteen, actually, but that number was quickly revised.
2 But *not* his racial profiling of people who "looked" like they could be Mexican.
3 Nike's virtue signaling is not entirely on the up and up, as they very publicly engaged prison labor to make its products. A 1995 article cites Oregon state representative Kevin Mannix openly courting Nike to work in prisons: http://people.umass.edu/~kastor/private/prison-labor.html. This 2017 report—https://glitch.news/2017-03-01-left-leaning-microsoft-and-nike-both-rely-on-prison-labor-camps-to-produce-high-profit-products.html—and a flurry of articles making this particular connection appeared in October 2018.
4 See, for example, Harrison 2012a; Kuklick 2006; Magloire and Yelvington 2005; Maurer 2003; Orent 1970.
5 Gershon 2011.
6 BCE means before the common era, replacing BC, "before Christ."
7 Lamphere 2018.
8 Sanday 1998; Willis 1982.
9 This concept was actually voiced by sociologist Herbert Spencer.
10 Publishing at least as early as 2005, Dyson called it what it "sounds like when it speaks in public" (Dyson 2005, 203).
11 Sandoval 2000.
12 Abrams 2010; Chaudry 2009.
13 Davis 2014.
14 Cole 2012.
15 Mills 1959.
16 Gramsci 1971.
17 Hurricane Cleo in 1964 swiped Haiti, doing less damage.
18 See Trouillot 1997 for critical discussion.
19 Ulysse 2008, 122.

Chapter 1   Structuring Solidarity

1 King 1968.
2 Williams 1944.
3 Mintz 1977, 1984.
4 Patterson 1982.
5 Polanyi [1944] 2001.
6 And while there have been same-sex relationships throughout history, John D'Emilio (1983) argued that in similar ways capitalism produced the conditions in which a gay *identity* was possible.
7 Engels [1884] 1986.
8 Sacks 1975.
9 Slocum 1975.
10 See Desai 2002.
11 Zinn 1995.

12 See di Leonardo 1999; Moyneur 2013; Traube 1993; Weedman 2006
13 Rosie is also—perhaps only coincidentally—the name of the Jetson's robot, subhuman servant doing household chores.
14 National Partnership for Women & Families 2020.
15 National Partnership for Women & Families 2019.
16 Sacks 1975; Slocum 1975.
17 Von Rueden et al. 2019; Wrangham 2019; Boehm 1997.
18 Scott 2009, 2014.
19 Gamble 1988.
20 Gibbons 2009; White, Suwa, and Asfaw 1994.
21 Gibbons 2017.
22 The most cited—and translated—was his first book, published in 1520 (Casas 2004).
23 Equiano 2009; Haley 1976; Rediker 2007.
24 Beckles 1989.
25 Williams 1944.
26 Stolberg 2019.
27 They also sourced cotton from India, after successfully destroying the country's textile production and reducing it to a producer of raw materials.
28 Rodney 1972.
29 The phrase was co-opted, originally Mexican activist Gustavo Esteva's critique of the mainstream development paradigm.
30 According to a *Business Week* executive pay survey.
31 AFL-CIO 2015.
32 Hardoon 2017.

Chapter 2   Dismantling White Supremacy

1 See, for example, Remnick 2017.
2 Wynter 2003.
3 Wilderson 2016. Afro-pessimists argue that "humanity is made legible through the irreconcilable distinction between humans and blackness ... [and] the black is positioned *a priori* a slave" (Douglass, Terrefe, and Wilderson 2018).
4 Rosa and Díaz 2020.
5 O'Neal 2016. Some cite 52 percent (CNN 2016).
6 Pew Research Center 2018a.
7 See, for example, "Russian Hacking and Influence."
8 Savransky 2016.
9 Coates 2017, 347.
10 Education level was most significant, with Clinton pulling 55 percent of white voters who had a four-year degree or greater, compared to 38 percent for Trump (Pew Research Center 2018a).
11 Coates 2017, 344.
12 Rosentiel 2008; Craighill and Sullivan 2013.
13 Taylor 2017, 61.
14 Taylor 2017, 63, 62.
15 Carruthers 2018, 3.
16 Carruthers 2018, 4.
17 Coates 2017, 359.

18 Taylor 2017, 1.
19 Macdonald and Doucet 2011; Hsu and Aristil 2014; Sontag 2012; Sullivan and Helderman 2015.
20 At the 1996 Republican Convention, Bob Dole specifically dismissed the idea. Many others have followed suit. See Marcotte 2015.
21 See Equal Justice Initiative 2014.
22 Pew Research Center 2018b.
23 Gambino 2018.
24 Rosa and Bonilla 2017, 202.
25 Kranish and O'Harrow 2016. Trump so relied on the dethroned powerbroker, asking "Where's my Roy Cohn?" when in legal trouble. Mangan 2019.
26 Coded political messages that don't sound like race baiting to the mainstream but send signals to a particular base are like a dog whistle, which is inaudible to humans.
27 See Perlstein 2012 for the full interview.
28 Taylor 2016, 55.
29 Davis 2017.
30 Lord 2018.
31 Gray 2017.
32 Alt-right is a more recent term that veers toward more explicit racism (Beauchamp 2019).
33 Anti-Defamation League 2019.
34 "New Zealand Mosque Attacks Suspect" 2019.
35 Collinson 2019.
36 Several Indigenous Maori leaders pointed out the hypocrisy: as a settler colonial state, New Zealand was founded on white supremacy.
37 Khan-Cullors and Bandele 2017, 168.
38 "Deaths during the L.A. Riots" 2012.
39 Operation Ghetto Storm 2014—the title riffs on Operation Desert Storm, the code name for the 1991 war in Iraq.
40 Pearl 2018.
41 Wagner and Walsh 2016.
42 Prison Policy Initiative 2012.
43 ACLU 2020.
44 Alexander 2012.
45 Schlosser 1998; Flateau 1996; Davis 2000.
46 Khan-Cullors and Bandele 2017, 213.
47 Ransby 2018, 49.
48 Quoted in Taylor 2016, 161.
49 Van Gelder 2015.
50 Ransby 2018, 1.
51 Taylor 2016, 15.
52 Building on insights first articulated in the Combahee River Collective Statement, intersectionality was formalized by Columbia University law professor Kimberlé Williams Crenshaw (2001; Garza 2014).
53 Garza 2014.
54 Davis 1983; Sharpe 2010; Spillers 1987.
55 Crenshaw and Ritchie 2015.

56 Ritchie 2017, 43.
57 Ritchie 2017, 29–30.
58 National Black Justice Coalition 2011.
59 Richardson 2015.
60 Crenshaw and Ritchie 2015, 24.
61 Garza 2014.
62 Köhler 1978; Harrison 1997.
63 Galtung 1980; Farmer 2004.
64 Carmichael and Hamilton 1967. Keeanga-Yamahtta Taylor (2016, 8) defines it as "the policies, programs, and practices of public and private institutions that result in greater rates of poverty, dispossession, criminalization, illness, and ultimately mortality of African Americans."
65 Burton 2015.
66 Sohn 2017. And Hispanics are more than two and a half times less likely to have health care (Castañeda 2017).
67 Centers for Disease Control and Prevention 2017, cited in Hetey and Eberhardt 2018, 183.
68 This is a point W. E. B. DuBois argued in 1899.
69 Bonilla-Silva 2003.
70 Cox 2015.
71 In *18th Brumaire*, Marx said, "Men make their own history, but they do not make it as they please; they do not make it under self-selected circumstances, but under circumstances existing already, given and transmitted from the past."
72 Mamdani 2005; Rana 2020.
73 Ransby 2018, 13.
74 Crawford 2018.
75 Brunkard, Namulanda, and Ratard 2008.
76 Purvis 2015.
77 Khan-Cullors and Bandele 2017, 248.
78 Marable [1983] 2000.
79 Saul Alinsky was a radical labor organizer during the 1930s who later founded a community organizing institution and wrote a book distilling "best practices," his 1971 *Rules for Radicals.* The Midwest Academy was founded in 1973 to train labor, community, and civil rights organizers.
80 Carruthers 2018, 111.
81 Hansberry 1959.
82 Mitchell and Franco 2018.
83 Terkel 1967, 1986; Kotlowitz 1991.
84 Taylor 2016, 103.
85 Carruthers 2018; Ransby 2018; Stovall 2016. A 2016 *Chicago Reporter* article notes that most of the schools that remain vacant, blighting neighborhoods, are in the Black-majority South Side (Belsha and Kiefer 2016).
86 Taylor 2016, 104.
87 Harvey 2014; Smith 1984, 1996.
88 Wilson 1987.
89 Reed 2008, 151.
90 Betancur 2002; Cahill 2007; Mumm 2008; Petterson et al. 2006; Wyly and Hammel 2001.

91 Taylor 2016, 11.
92 Ransby 2018, 159.
93 Gilmore and Gilmore 2016.
94 Hutchinson 2005.
95 Hutchinson 2005; Cox 1948; Robinson [1983] 2000.
96 Robinson [1983] 2000, 2.
97 Inikori 1976; Inikori and Engerman 1992.
98 Hutchinson 2005, 153.
99 Cockacoeske was Powhatan's niece. Powhatan confederated many nations on the then-western border of the "thirteen colonies."
100 Alexander 2012, 24.
101 Ahmed 2006.
102 Coates 2017, 86.
103 Kelley 2002; Robinson [1983] 2000.
104 Brodkin 2000.
105 Harrison 2012b, 241–42.
106 Malcolm X 1992.
107 Carruthers 2018, 29.
108 Malcolm X's political thought is often frozen in time before his 1964 haj to Mecca and visit in Africa. Ideas of the "later Malcolm" move away from theorizing the nation-state (Marable 2011).
109 Du Bois [1903] 1995.
110 Rahier 2003; Whitten 2007.
111 Perry 2020.
112 Thomas and Clarke 2013, 306.
113 Willoughby-Herard 2015.
114 Pierre 2013.
115 Pierre 2020; Wilderson 2016.
116 Beliso-De Jesús and Pierre 2020.
117 Hilker 2012.
118 Beliso-De Jesús 2020.
119 Fanon 1967. Martinique is now a "department," similar to a U.S. state.
120 *A Girl Like Me* is available at www.youtube.com/watch?v=17fEyoq6yqc.
121 Harrison 2002, 55.
122 Clarke and Thomas 2006.
123 Prashad 2007.
124 Harrison 2002, 54.
125 The G8 plus the world's two most populous nations.
126 "Projected GDP Ranking" 2020.
127 Harrison 2002.
128 Rodney 1972.
129 Some of these arguments are made by *RACE: Are We So Different?* (Goodman and Moses 2012), a project of the American Anthropological Association, including a book, video, and museum exhibit.
130 See Maseko 1998 and Sharpley-Whiting 1999.
131 Kelley 2002; Robinson [1983] 2000.
132 Rosa and Bonilla 2017, 204.
133 Kelley 2002.

134 Carruthers 2018, 139.
135 Taylor 2017.
136 Carruthers 2018, 67.

Chapter 3   Climate Justice versus the Anthropocene

1 Moran 2006; Carvalho et al. 2019; Broughton and Weitzel 2018.
2 Alinsky 1971, 10.
3 Bobo, Kendall, and Max 2010.
4 Sen 2003.
5 Klein 2014.
6 Nixon 2011.
7 Crutzen and Stoermer 2000.
8 Haraway 2015; Whitington 2016.
9 Moore 2016. Moore's term has been critiqued as being "Marxish," missing the key element of class struggle: Angus 2016; McKittrick 2013, 2. See also Moore et al. 2019.
10 Davis et al. 2019, 10.
11 Whyte 2018b. See also Whyte 2018c; Davis and Todd 2017.
12 Whyte 2017.
13 Trouillot 2003.
14 Whyte 2018b.
15 See, for example, Fiske et al. 2014; Roscoe 2014; Crate and Nuttall 2009; Howe 2015; Sayre 2012; Hardesty 2007; Maldonado et al. 2013; Marino and Lazrus 2016.
16 Westerling et al. 2006; Running 2006.
17 Logan 2018.
18 Bennardo 2019.
19 Jacques, Dunlap, and Freeman 2008; Powell 2011.
20 Marino 2015; Shearer 2011.
21 Button 2002.
22 Button 2010; Schuller and Maldonado 2016.
23 They were never federally recognized, which some consider a deliberate oversight (Maldonado 2018).
24 Brown 2015.
25 Maldonado 2018.
26 Kelley et al. 2015.
27 Taub 2017.
28 Said 1979.
29 Chakrabarty 2009.
30 United Nations University 2015.
31 See International Organization for Migration 2020 and Randall n.d.
32 Norwegian Refugee Council n.d.
33 Maldonado 2018, 8.
34 Hurricane Cleo, also a category 4, swiped southern Haiti in 1964.
35 Peck 2013; Schuller 2016.
36 United Nations Office for the Coordination of Humanitarian Affairs 2016.
37 United Nations Office for the Coordination of Humanitarian Affairs 2017b.
38 Danticat 2015; Jean-Baptiste 2012; Renda 2001; Schmidt 1971.
39 Nixon 2011; Farmer 2004; Harrison 1997.

40 United Nations Office for the Coordination of Humanitarian Affairs 2017a.
41 Emanuel 2005.
42 Hansen 2009.
43 Galarneau, Davis, and Shapiro 2013; Holland and Bruyère 2014; Webster et al. 2005; López-Marrero and Wisner 2012; Taylor et al. 2012; López-Marrero and Scalley 2012.
44 Checker 2008b.
45 Sheller 2018.
46 Kishore et al. 2018.
47 Bonilla and Lebrón 2019.
48 Puig González, Benacourt Lavastida, and Álvarez Cedeño 2010.
49 Ramos Guadalupe 2005.
50 Thompson and Gaviria 2004.
51 Scott 1985.
52 See Checker 2009 and Checker 2008a; Middleton Manning 2011, 2018.
53 United Nations n.d.
54 Roscoe 2014, 544; Aronoff 2017. Candidate for the U.S. House of Representatives Alexandria Ocasio-Cortez also called for a "Marshall Plan" for renewable energy in the United States, which she later termed the "Green New Deal," also drawing from U.S. history.
55 Sadowski 2018.
56 Fossil Free n.d.
57 United Nations Development Programme 2012.
58 See Wong and McCormick 2016 and Rapoza 2016.
59 Abu-Lughod 2002; Hirschkind and Mahmod 2002.
60 Estes 2019.
61 See, for example, Dhillon and Estes 2016 and Estes 2016.
62 Estes 2016.
63 Estes 2016.
64 Estes 2016.
65 See, for example, https://mazaskatalks.org/#theboycott and https://lastreal indians.com/guide-to-divestment-by-rachel-heaton.
66 Tobias 2017.
67 Dhillon and Estes 2016.
68 LaDuke 2017; Whyte 2019; Estes 2019; Dhillon and Estes 2019; López 2018; Chrisler, Dhillon, and Simpson 2016.
69 Checker 2005.
70 Perkins 2006.
71 Whyte 2017.
72 LaDuke 1999; Wildcat 2009.
73 Johnston 2011; Vélez-Vélez 2010.
74 Brook 1998.
75 Waziyatawin and Yellow Bird 2012.
76 Verma 2017.
77 Shostak and Nisa [1981] 2000.
78 Slocum 1975.
79 Roscoe 2014; Whyte 2018a.
80 Ford and Nigh 2016; McAnany and Yoffee 2009.

81 See also Whyte 2018b.

82 Wildcat 2009.

83 Jailed Italian Marxist Antonio Gramsci (1971) called this process hegemony.

Chapter 4 Humanity on the Move

1 United Nations Secretary-General 2013.

2 De León 2015, 3.

3 Fassin 2011.

4 Inda 2006; Foxen 2007.

5 Chavez 1998; Heyman 1998.

6 Rosas 2018b. Whether administration officials actually believe this, it plays well to their base.

7 "Stop Breaking Up Families" 2018.

8 Jordan 2018.

9 Dickerson 2018.

10 Thompson 2018.

11 Duncan, Heidbrink, and Yarris 2018. The issue offers links to resources by the Anthropologist Action Network for Immigrants and Refugees: www.anthropologist actionnetwork.org.

12 Pew Research Center 2019.

13 Pew Research Center 2011; Pew Research Center 2012.

14 See Gonzáles and Chavez 2012.

15 Hing 2013.

16 This is a pseudonym to protect her.

17 Rosa 2012; Dávila et al. 2016.

18 Rosa 2012, 2013.

19 Gomez 2017.

20 Gladstone 2017.

21 Dubuisson and Schuller 2017.

22 "Haiti—Economy" 2017.

23 Immigrant Legal Resource Center 2017.

24 Ullian 2020.

25 Shear and Hirschfeld Davis 2017.

26 UNAIDS 2020.

27 Farmer 1992.

28 Johnson 2018; "Omarosa Confirms" 2018.

29 De Genova 2017.

30 United Nations Refugee Agency 2020.

31 United Nations Refugee Agency 2012.

32 Murphy 2017.

33 Calamur 2016; Masters and McCurdy 2017.

34 De Genova 2017.

35 Timmer et al. 2018.

36 Lyman 2015.

37 Timmer 2017.

38 Human Rights Watch 2017.

39 United Nations Refugee Agency 2015.

40 Rabben 2016.
41 Wirtz and Schuller 2017.
42 United Nations Refugee Agency 2015; United Nations Refugee Agency 2016.
43 Kibicho 2016.
44 Chavez 1998; Gonzáles 2016; Ong 1996; Rosaldo 1994.
45 Clarke 2010; Gowricharn 2006; Robotham 1998; Slotta 2014; Williams 2018; Blanc, Basch, and Schiller 1995; Stephen 2007; Laguerre 1998.
46 Glick Schiller and Fouron 2001; Pierre-Louis 2006.
47 De Leon 2015.
48 Gomberg-Muñoz 2017, 144.
49 Stumpf 2006; McElrath, Mahadeo, and Suh 2014; Fernandes 2007; Zavella 2011.
50 Williams 1944.
51 Beckles 2013.
52 Weisbrot, Lefebvre, and Sammut. 2014.
53 Gálvez 2018.
54 Thu and Durrenberger 1998.
55 Millard and Chapa 2004.
56 Holmes 2013; Horton 2016; Stuesse, Staats, and Grant-Thomas 2017.
57 Powell 2012.
58 See also AANIR 2018.
59 These "free-market" policies designed by University of Chicago economist Milton Friedman were usually ushered in by SAPs, on the belief that free enterprise was not only the best engine for growth but also the fairest distribution of wealth.
60 Gomberg-Muñoz and Nussbaum-Barberena 2011.
61 Stuesse 2016; Zlolniski 2006.
62 Heyman 2012.
63 Heyman 2012.
64 Churchill 2004; Collins 2003; Mendez 2002; Navarro 2002; Tiano 1992.
65 Simmons 2010; Simmons 2009.
66 This policy changed again in 2020 (Pentón 2020).
67 Levin 2017.
68 Zinouri 2017.
69 ibid. She was eventually let in the following week.
70 "Trump's Travel Ban" 2017.
71 Chavez [2008] 2013.
72 Nguyen 2005.
73 Heyman 2012, 271.
74 Danticat 1998.
75 The sisters—known as the *mariposas* (butterflies)—were involved in the resistance against Trujillo's rule. One of them, Minerva, said, "If [Trujillo] kills me I will reach my hand from the grave and become stronger!" Dominican novelist Julia Alvarez memorialized their story in *In the Time of Butterflies*.
76 Frachetti 2011, 196.
77 Frachetti 2011, 206.
78 Torrence 2016, 2018.
79 Sharratt 2016.
80 Taylor 2015.
81 Weiss 2017.

82 De Genova 2017.
83 Sassen 2001.
84 Boren 2017. Quietly, another similar bill was proposed and passed, slightly modified.
85 ACLU 1999.
86 www.youtube.com/watch?v=PUobmpH74Bk. For the full text, visit https://speakola.com/grad/larissa-martinez-mckinney-boyd-high-2016.
87 www.youtube.com/watch?v=uFdTQWBkiwM.
88 Schamisso 2017.
89 Nicholls 2013 calls these thinkers "bounded" DREAMers.
90 Dávila et al. 2016; De Genova 2010; Heyman 1998; Rosa 2012; Stuesse, Staats, and Grant-Thomas 2017.
91 Villarrubia-Mendoza and Vélez-Vélez 2017.
92 De Genova 2005, 2010; Gonzáles and Chavez 2012.
93 www.youtube.com/watch?v=vGZnXZuhIqM.
94 Yuval-Davis, Anthias, and Kofman 2005.
95 Apsan Law Offices n.d.
96 Park 2017.
97 Indigenous Action 2014.
98 Cole 2012.
99 Incidentally the same day that Senator Flake requested a week for the FBI to complete their investigation of allegations against Supreme Court nominee Brett Kavanaugh.
100 Wences and Gomberg-Muñoz 2018.
101 Bedi and del Valle 2018.
102 Alexander 2012; Davis 2000; Schlosser 1998; Sudbury 2008.
103 Stumpf 2006.

Chapter 5   Dismantling the Ivory Tower

1 Du Bois [1903] 2013.
2 Dhillon 2018.
3 Harrison 1991.
4 E.g., Fraser 1992 and Lamphere 1993, among many others.
5 Pearl 2018.
6 American Academy of Arts & Sciences 2015, 8.
7 American Academy of Arts & Sciences 2015, 10.
8 The eleven states include Michigan, Oregon, Arizona, Vermont, Colorado, Pennsylvania, New Hampshire, Delaware, Rhode Island, Massachusetts, and Connecticut (American Academy of Arts & Sciences 2015, 11).
9 American Academy of Arts & Sciences 2015, 2.
10 Semuels 2016.
11 California's Proposition 13, passed in 1978, capped property taxes, widening racial disparities. A measure to address this is on the 2020 ballot (Toppin 2019).
12 National Public Radio 2016.
13 Griffin 2017.
14 DiMaggio 1982; Bourdieu and Passeron 1990; Willis 1981.
15 Bourdieu 1998; Ruth 2018.
16 A hearty thank you to Jennifer Wies for this analysis.

17 Kerr 2019.
18 Gusterson 2017.
19 Sahlins 1999.
20 González 2004; Low and Merry 2010.
21 This also reflects the university's origins within the church.
22 Gitlin 1995.
23 Lowen 1997. A draft of Eisenhower's famous farewell address included "academic" in this title, ditched that day (Giroux 2007).
24 Gusterson 2017; Schrecker 1986; Newfield 2008; Wax 2008.
25 Price 2004; Nader 2002.
26 Kehoe and Doughty 2012.
27 Said 1979.
28 Abu-Lughod 2002; Hirschkind and Mahmod 2002.
29 Most of these programs were funded by the Ford Foundation (National Public Radio 2006).
30 Wynter 2003.
31 Gutiérrez y Muhs et al. 2012.
32 Ball 2012; Thornton 2015; Greyser and Weiss 2012; Petersen and Davies 2010; Posecznik 2014; LeCompte 2014.
33 Maskovsky 2012.
34 Hyatt, Shear, and Wright 2015.
35 Davis 2015; Byrd 2017; Smedley and Hutchinson 2012.
36 Landy 2013.
37 Flaherty 2017.
38 American Association of University Professors 2018.
39 American Association of University Professors n.d.
40 Lyon-Callo 2015; Shear and Hyatt 2015.
41 Northern Illinois University, University Council 2018.
42 Campos 2015. It is important to note that some of this administrative burden is a legalistic response to reporting requirements by Title IX and others.
43 Higher Ed Jobs 2020.
44 College Board 2019, 2020.
45 Giroux 2013; Gusterson 2017; Lyon-Callo 2015; Maskovsky 2012; Shear and Hyatt 2015. In all, 58 percent of senators in 2015 attended private college: Blake 2015.
46 Given the inequalities of opportunity within Chile, university students were disproportionately children of the elite. Soon after being elected in December 2017, Chile's right-wing government moved to reverse this.
47 The first change was made in 1976, then again in 1984. And fewer than 5 percent of additional students were covered as of 2018.
48 Huelsman et al. 2015.
49 Gusterson 2017, 443, citing Goldrick-Rab and Broton 2015; Hervey 2016.
50 Carruthers 2016.
51 Craven and Davis 2013.
52 DuCille 1994.
53 Wies and Haldane 2011.
54 Ahmed 2006; Davis 2015; DuCille 1994.
55 Davis 2015; DuCille 1994; Mohanty 1988; Moraga and Anzaldua 1983.

56 Collins 1990. Faye Harrison's 2008 collection builds upon this concept, also the title.
57 Davies 2003.
58 Smedley and Hutchinson 2012.
59 Ulysse 2003.
60 Berry et al. 2017.
61 Quoting Edwidge Danticat, Gina Athena Ulysse (2008) called whiteness itself a "three-piece suit" (Gutiérrez y Muhs et al. 2012).
62 Alvarez 1994.
63 Allen and Jobson 2016.
64 Byrd 2017.
65 Harney and Moten 2013.
66 See, for example, Allen and Jobson 2016; Yelvington et al. 2015; Harrison [1991] 2010; Kelley 2002; Brodkin, Morgen, and Hutchinson 2011; Schrecker 1986; Chatterjee and Maira 2014; Smedley and Hutchinson 2012; Ahmed 2006; Greyser and Weiss 2012; LeCompte 2014.
67 Lacy and Rome 2017; Todd 2015.
68 Chatterjee and Maira 2014.
69 Salaita 2014. See also his book (Salaita 2006).
70 Deeb and Winegar 2015.
71 See, for example, Gonzáles 2009; Lucas 2009; Price 2008, 2011.
72 Asad 1979.
73 Deloria 1988.
74 Jaschik 2015.
75 Ntarangwi 2010.
76 Rosas 2018a.
77 Tahi 2018.
78 Collins 1986; Harrison 2008.
79 King 2019; Stocking 1971.
80 Burton 2015; Hutchinson 2005; Baker 1998.
81 Fluehr-Lobban 2000, 2005.
82 Rana 2020.
83 Mullings 2005, 669.
84 Harrison and Harrison 1999.
85 Harrison and Harrison 1999; Lamphere 2018.
86 Stocking 1971.
87 Mikell 1999.
88 Hurston [1938] 1990.
89 Bolles 2013, 64.
90 Baker 2005.
91 Aschenbrenner 1999; Glover 2016.
92 Barnes 2018, 87.
93 Harrison and Harrison 1999.
94 Harrison and Harrison 1999, 13.
95 Drake and Cayton 1945; Davis, Gardner, and Gardner [1941] 2009; Baber 1999; Harrison and Harrison 1999.
96 Williams 1995; Klugh 2018.
97 Rosa and Bonilla 2017; Allen and Jobson 2016; Burton 2015.
98 Burton 2015.

99 Behar and Gordon 1995; Reiter 1975; Rosaldo, Bamberger, and Lamphere 1974.
100 Tuck and Wang 2012.
101 Harrison [1991] 2010, 10.
102 Harrison [1991] 2010, 10.
103 Craven and Davis 2013; Davis and Craven 2016.
104 Beliso-De Jesús and Pierre 2020.
105 Speakman et al. 2018, 3.
106 Dhillon 2018.
107 Navarro, Williams, and Ahmad 2013, 459.
108 West 2018.
109 Dhillon 2018.
110 These are also unfortunately potential sites for sexual harassment, as is recently coming to light.
111 Kawa et al. 2018.
112 Speakman et al. 2018.
113 Brodkin, Morgen, and Hutchinson 2011.
114 Alonso Bejarano et al. 2019; Smith 2013; Archibald Q'um Q'um Xiiem, Lee-Morgan, and De Santolo 2019.
115 In her 2018 Margaret Mead Award acceptance speech, Sameena Mulla asked audience members to #CiteBlackWomen, following Christen Smith's hashtag.
116 Lamphere 2018.
117 Baker 2005; Harrison and Harrison 1999; Harrison, Johnson-Simon, and Williams 2018.
118 Tallbear 2015; Todd 2015; Watts 2013.
119 Balingit 2019.
120 Alinsky 1971; Bobo, Kendall, and Max 2010; Sen 2003.
121 Rosas 2018a.
122 Ulysse 2015.
123 Cox 2018.
124 Berry et al. 2017, 558.
125 Dhillon 2018.
126 Cox 2018; Dhillon 2018.
127 Gramsci 1971.
128 See, for example, Shore and Wright 2000; Strathern 2000.
129 Hale 2016.
130 Heyman, Morales, and Núñez 2009; Todd 2015; Rosas 2018a; Cox 2018.
131 See, for example, Stringer 1996; Whyte 1991.
132 Berry et al. 2017, 559.
133 Dhillon 2018.
134 Ransby 2016.
135 Berry et al. 2017, 558.

Conclusion

1 Trouillot 1995. Aristotle defined slaves in *Politics* as "living tools" (Robinson [1983] 2000, 97).
2 Robin Diangelo (2011, 2018) is often credited with this concept. Scholars of color, including Joseph Flynn (2018), has also written on the topic.

3 De Leon 2015.

4 Marcuse 2016.

5 While this is an older study, before farm to table took off, this article offers statistics estimating its huge market: Schoenfeld 2011.

6 Agricultural Marketing Resource Center 2019.

7 Mead [1928] 2001.

8 Anglade 1974; Barthélémy 1990.

9 Wilson 1973.

10 In addition to books like William Golding's *Lord of the Flies* and Joseph Conrad's *Apocalyse Now* and the attitudes of sentencing judges of the rare rape cases that get tried, the firestorm of protest following the Gillette ad critiquing rape culture that aired during the 2019 Super Bowl unleashed a torrent of "boys will be boys" justification. Even Democrats like Hillary Clinton and Michael Bloomberg resort to divisive stereotypes about trans people. See Diavolo 2019, 2020.

11 Yazzie 2019.

12 Harris-Perry 2017.

13 Under the banner of localism many advances in equality were actively resisted; in addition to NIMBYism pushing pollution to the poor (and/or communities of color), ending Reconstruction following the U.S. Civil War heralded the return to open hostility toward formerly enslaved people and terror mobs.

14 Mandela 1994—with a heartfelt acknowledgment to my dear colleague and comrade, the late Mychel Namphy, for this insight.

References

Abebe, Zemdena. 2020. "The Lesser of Two Evils." *Africa Is a Country: COVID-19 dispatches*, May 26. https://africasacountry.com/2020/05/the-lesser-of-two-evils.

Abrams, Kathryn. 2010. "Empathy and Experience in the Sotomayor Hearings." *Ohio Northern University Law Review* 36:263–286.

Abu-Lughod, Lila. 2002. "Do Muslim Women Need Saving?" *American Anthropologist* 104(3):783–790.

ACLU. 1999. "CA's Anti-immigrant Proposition 187 Is Voided, Ending State's Five-Year Battle with ACLU, Rights Groups." www.aclu.org/news/cas-anti-immigrant-proposition-187-voided-ending-states-five-year-battle-aclu-rights-groups.

———. 2020. "Fair Sentencing Act." www.aclu.org/issues/criminal-law-reform/drug-law-reform/fair-sentencing-act.

AFL-CIO. 2015. "CEOs Paid 373 Times Average Worker, CEO Pay Increased 16 Percent in 2014." May 13. https://aflcio.org/press/releases/ceos-paid-373-times-average-worker-ceo-pay-increased-16-percent-2014.

Agricultural Marketing Resource Center. 2019. "Farmers' Markets." www.agmrc.org/markets-industries/food/farmers-markets.

Ahmed, Sara. 2006. "The Nonperformativity of Antiracism." *Meridians: Feminism, Race, Transnationalism* 7(1):104–126.

Alexander, Michelle. 2012. *The New Jim Crow: Mass Incarceration in the Age of Colorblindness*. Rev. ed. New York: New Press.

Alinsky, Saul David. 1971. *Rules for Radicals: A Practical Primer for Realistic Radicals*. New York: Random House.

Allen, Jafari Sinclaire, and Ryan Cecil Jobson. 2016. "The Decolonizing Generation: (Race and) Theory in Anthropology since the Eighties." *Current Anthropology* 57(2):129–148.

Allen, Theodore. 2012. *The Invention of the White Race*. Expanded ed. New York: Verso Books.

Alonso Bejarano, Carolina, Lucia López Juárez, Mirian A. Mijangos García, and Daniel M Goldstein. 2019. *Decolonizing Ethnography: Undocumented Immigrants and New Directions in Social Science*. Durham, NC: Duke University Press.

Alvarez, Robert R. 1994. "Un Chilero en la Academia: Sifting, Shifting and the Hiring of Minorities in Anthropology." In *Race*, edited by Steven Gregory and Roger Sanjek, 257–269. New Brunswick, NJ: Rutgers University Press.

American Academy of Arts & Sciences. 2015. "Public Research Universities: Changes in State Funding." www.amacad.org/multimedia/pdfs/publications /researchpapersmonographs/PublicResearchUniv_ChangesInStateFunding.pdf.

American Association of University Professors. 2018. "Data Snapshot: Contingent Faculty in US Higher Ed." October 11. www.aaup.org/news/data-snapshot -contingent-faculty-us-higher-ed#.XEfmG81MHIU.

———. n.d. "Higher Education at a Crossroads: The Annual Report on the Economic Status of the Profession, 2015–16." www.aaup.org/report/higher-education -crossroads-annual-report-economic-status-profession-2015-16.

American Institute of Physics. 2019. "The Discovery of Global Warming: Changing Sun, Changing Climate." February. https://history.aip.org/climate/solar.htm.

Anglade, Georges. 1974. *l'Espace Haïtien*. Montréal: Presses de l'Université de Québec.

Angus, Ian. 2016. "Book Review." *Climate and Capitalism*, September 26. https:// climateandcapitalism.com/2016/09/26/anthropocene-or-capitalocene-misses-the -point.

The Anthropologist Action Network for Immigrants and Refugees (AANIR). 2018. Five Things You Should Know About the "Migrant Caravan." American Anthropological Association.

"Anthropologist Contributes to Major Study of Large Animal Extinction." 2019. *Science Daily*, September 20. www.sciencedaily.com/releases/2019/09 /190920124648.htm.

Anti-Defamation League. 2019. "Hardcore White Supremacists Elevate Dylann Roof to Cult Hero Status." February 6. www.adl.org/blog/hardcore-white-supremacists -elevate-dylann-roof-to-cult-hero-status.

Apsan Law Offices. n.d. "Sanctuary Cities." www.apsanlaw.com/law-246.List-of -Sanctuary-cities.html.

Archibald Q'um Q'um Xiiem, Jo-ann, Jenny Bol Jun Lee-Morgan, and Jason De Santolo. 2019. *Decolonizing Research: Indigenous Storywork as Methodology*. New York: Zed Books.

Aronoff, Kate. 2017. "Could a Marshall Plan for the Planet Tackle the Climate Crisis?" *The Nation*, November 16. www.thenation.com/article/could-a-marshall -plan-for-the-planet-tackle-the-climate-crisis.

Asad, Talal. 1979. "Anthropology and the Colonial Encounter." In *Politics of Anthropology: from Colonialism and Sexism toward a View from Below*, edited by Gerrit Huizer and Bruce Mannheim, 85–97. The Hague: Mouton.

Aschenbrenner, Joyce. 1999. "Katherine Dunham: Anthropologist, Artist, Humanist." In *African American Pioneers in Anthropology*, edited by Ira E. Harrison and Faye V. Harrison, 137–153. Champaign: University of Illinois Press.

Baber, Willie L. 1999. "St. Clair Drake: Scholar and Activist." In *African American Pioneers in Anthropology*, edited by Ira E. Harrison and Faye V. Harrison, 191–212. Champaign: University of Illinois Press.

Baker, Lee D. 1998. *From Savage to Negro: Anthropology and the Construction of Race, 1896–1954*. Berkeley: University of California Press.

———. 2005. "Melville J. Herskovits and the Racial Politics of Knowledge." *American Anthropologist* 107(3):524–525.

Balingit, Moriah. 2019. "In a Kentucky Upset, Aggrieved Teachers Flex Their Muscles." *Washington Post*, November 6. https://www.washingtonpost.com/local /education/in-a-kentucky-upset-aggrieved-teachers-made-a-difference/2019/11/06 /35d91e66-00b7-11ea-8bab-0fc209e065a8_story.html.

Ball, Stephen J. 2012. "Performativity, Commodification and Commitment: An I-Spy Guide to the Neoliberal University." *British Journal of Educational Studies* 30(1):17–28.

Barnes, Riché J. Daniel. 2018. "Johnnetta Betsch Cole: Eradicating Multiple Systems of Oppression." In *The Second Generation of African American Pioneers in Anthropology*, edited by Ira E. Harrison, Deborah Johnson-Simon, and Erica Lorraine Williams, 84–98. Champaign: University of Illinois Press.

Barthélémy, Gérard. 1990. *L'Univers Rural Haïtien: Le Pays en Dehors*. Paris: L'Harmattan.

Bauer, George Kibala. 2020. "Beyond the Western Gaze." Africa Is a Country: COVID-19 Dispatches, May 29. https://africasacountry.com/2020/05/beyond-the -western-gaze.

Beauchamp, Zack. 2019. "An Online Subculture Celebrating the Charleston Church Shooter Appears to Be Inspiring Copycat Plots." *Vox*, February 7. www.vox.com /policy-and-politics/2019/2/7/18215634/dylann-roof-charleston-church-shooter -bowl-gang.

Beckles, Hilary McD. 1989. *Natural Rebels: A Social History of Enslaved Black Women in Barbados*. New Brunswick, NJ: Rutgers University Press.

———. 2013. *Britain's Black Debt: Reparations for Caribbean Slavery and Native Genocide*. Kingston, Jamaica: University of the West Indies Press.

Bedi, Sheila, and Vanessa del Valle. 2018. "Chicagoans for an End to the Gang Database v. City of Chicago." MacArthur Justice Center. www.macarthurjustice .org/case/chicagoans-for-an-end-to-the-gang-database.

Behar, Ruth, and Deborah Gordon. 1995. *Women Writing Culture*. Berkeley: University of California Press.

Beliso-De Jesús, Aisha M. 2020. "The Jungle Academy: Molding White Supremacy in American Police Recruits." *American Anthropologist* 122(1):143–156.

Beliso-De Jesús, Aisha M., and Jemima Pierre. 2020. "Special Section: Anthropology of White Supremacy." *Accounting, Organizations and Society* 122(1):67–75.

Belsha, Kalyn, and Matt Kiefer. 2016. "Interactive Map: Closed Schools Still Burden Distressed Chicago Neighborhoods." *Chicago Reporter*, September 14. www .chicagoreporter.com/interactive-map-closed-schools-still-burden-distressed -chicago-neighborhoods.

Benjamin, Ruha. 2020. "Black Skin, White Masks: Racism, Vulnerability & Refuting Black Pathology." Department of African American Studies, Princeton University, https://aas.princeton.edu/news/black-skin-white-masks-racism-vulnerability -refuting-black-pathology.

Bennardo, Giovanni. 2019. *Cultural Models of Nature: Primary Food Producers and Climate Change*. New York: Routledge.

Berry, Maya J., Claudia Chávez Argüelles, Shanya Cordis, Sarah Ihmoud, and Elizabeth Velásquez Estrada. 2017. "Toward a Fugitive Anthropology: Gender, Race, and Violence in the Field." *Cultural Anthropology* 32(4):537–565.

Betancur, John J. 2002. "The Politics of Gentrification: The Case of West Town in Chicago." *Urban Affairs Review* 37(6):780–814.

Blake, Aaron. 2015. "Where the Senate Went to College, in One Map." *Washington Post*, January 30. https://www.washingtonpost.com/news/the-fix/wp/2015/01/30 /where-the-senate-went-to-college-in-one-map/?utm_term=.ad24c4016273.

Blanc, Cristina Szanton, Linda Basch, and Nina Glick Schiller. 1995. "Transnationalism, Nation-States, and Culture." *Current Anthropology* 36(4):683–686.

Bobo, Kimberley A., Jackie Kendall, and Steve Max. 2010. *Organizing for Social Change: Midwest Academy Manual for Activists.* 4th ed. Santa Ana, CA: Forum Press.

Boehm, Christopher. 1997. "Impact of the Human Egalitarian Syndrome on Darwinian Selection Mechanics." *American Naturalist* 150(Suppl.):S100–S121.

Bolles, Augusta Lynn. 2013. "Telling the Story Straight: Black Feminist Intellectual Thought in Anthropology." *Transforming Anthropology* 21(1):57–71.

Bonilla, Yarimar, and Marisol Lebrón. 2019. *Aftershocks of Disaster: Puerto Rico Before and After the Storm.* Chicago: Haymarket Books.

Bonilla-Silva, Eduardo. 2003. *Racism without Racists: Color-Blind Racism and the Persistence of Racial Inequality in America.* Lanham, MD: Rowman & Littlefield.

Boren, Cindy. 2017. "NCAA Ends Boycott of North Carolina after Repeal, Replacement of Bathroom Law." *Washington Post*, April 4. https://www.washingtonpost .com/news/early-lead/wp/2017/04/04/ncaa-ends-boycott-of-north-carolina-after -repeal-replacement-of-bathroom-law.

Bourdieu, Pierre. 1998. *Practical Reason: On the Theory of Action.* Stanford, CA: Stanford University Press.

Bourdieu, Pierre, and Jean-Claude Passeron. 1990. *Reproduction in Education, Society and Culture.* London: Sage.

Brodkin, Karen. 2000. "Global Capitalism: What's Race Got to Do with It?" *American Ethnologist* 27(2):237–256.

Brodkin, Karen, Sandra Morgen, and Janis Hutchinson. 2011. "Anthropology as White Public Space?" *American Anthropologist* 113(4):545–556.

Brook, Daniel. 1998. "Environmental Genocide: Native Americans and Toxic Waste." *American Journal of Economics and Sociology* 57(1):105–113.

Broughton, Jack M., and Elic M. Weitzel. 2018. "Population Reconstructions for Humans and Megafauna Suggest Mixed Causes for North American Pleistocene Extinctions." *Nature Communications* 9(5441):12.

Brown, Dylan. 2015. "Adaptation." *E&E News*, April 21. www.eenews.net/stories /1060017151.

Brunkard, Joan, Gonza Namulanda, and Raoult Ratard. 2008. "Hurricane Katrina Deaths, Louisiana, 2005." http://ldh.la.gov/assets/docs/katrina/deceasedreports /KatrinaDeaths_082008.pdf.

Burton, Orisanmi. 2015. "Black Lives Matter: A Critique of Anthropology." *Hot Spots*, June 29. https://culanth.org/fieldsights/black-lives-matter-a-critique-of -anthropology.

———. 2018. "Organized Disorder: the New York City Jail Rebellion of 1970." *The Black Scholar* 48(4):28–42.

Button, Gregory V. 2002. "Popular Media Reframing of Man-Made Disasters: A Cautionary Tale." In *Catastrophe & Culture: The Anthropology of Disasters*, edited by Susanna M. Hoffman and Anthony Oliver-Smith, 143–158. Santa Fe, NM: School of American Research Press.

———. 2010. *Disaster Culture: Knowledge and Uncertainty in the Wake of Human and Environmental Catastrophe*. Walnut Creek, CA: Left Coast Press.

Byrd, W. Carson. 2017. *Poison in the Ivy: Race Relations in the Reproduction of Inequality on Elite College Campuses*. New Brunswick, NJ: Rutgers University Press.

Cahill, Caitlin. 2007. "Negotiating Grit and Glamour: Young Women of Color and the Gentrification of the Lower East Side." *City and Society* 19(2):202–231.

Calamur, Krishnadev. 2016. "Angela Merkel's Refugee Policy." *The Atlantic*, July 28. www.theatlantic.com/news/archive/2016/07/germany-refugee-terrorism/492011.

Campos, Paul F. 2015. "The Real Reason College Tuition Costs So Much." *New York Times*, April 4. www.nytimes.com/2015/04/05/opinion/sunday/the-real-reason-college-tuition-costs-so-much.html?_r=o.

Carmichael, Stokely, and Charles V. Hamilton. 1967. *Black Power: The Politics of Liberation*. New York: Random House.

Carruthers, Charlene. 2016. "Black Study, Black Struggle." *Boston Review*, March 7. http://bostonreview.net/forum/black-study-black-struggle/charlene-carruthers-charlene-carruthers-response-robin-kelley.

———. 2018. *Unapologetic: A Black, Queer, and Feminist Mandate for Radical Movements*. Boston: Beacon.

Carvalho, Joana S., Bruce Graham, Hugo Rebelo, Gaëlle Bocksberger, Christoph F. J. Meyer, Serge Wich, and Hjalmar S. Kühl. 2019. "A Global Risk Assessment of Primates under Climate and Land Use/Cover Scenarios." *Global Change Biology* 25:3163–3178.

Casas, Bartolomé de las. 2004. *A Short Account of the Destruction of the Indies*. New York: Penguin.

Castañeda, Heide. 2017. "Is Coverage Enough? Persistent Health Disparities in Marginalised Latino Border Communities." *Journal of Ethnic and Migration Studies* 43(12):2003–2019.

Centers for Disease Control and Prevention. 2017. "Sudden Unexpected Infant Death and Sudden Infant Death Syndrome: Data and Statistics." www.cdc.gov/sids/data.htm.

Chakrabarty, Dipesh. 2009. "The Climate of History: Four Theses." *Critical Inquiry* 35(Winter):197–221.

Chatterjee, Piya, and Sunaina Maira. 2014. *The Imperial University: Academic Repression and Scholarly Dissent*. Minneapolis: University of Minnesota Press.

Chaudry, Neena. 2009. "The Sotomayor Hearings: When Did Empathy Become a Dirty Word?" https://nwlc.org/blog/sotomayor-hearings-when-did-empathy-become-dirty-word/.

Chavez, Leo R. 1998. *Shadowed Lives: Undocumented Immigrants in American Society*. Fort Worth, TX: Harcourt, Brace, and Jovanovich.

———. [2008] 2013. *The Latino Threat: Constructing Immigrants, Citizens, and the Nation*. Stanford, CA: Stanford University Press.

Checker, Melissa. 2005. *Polluted Promises: Environmental Racism in a Southern Town*. New York: New York University Press.

————. 2008a. "Carbon Offsets: More Harm Than Good?" *CounterPunch*, August 27. www.counterpunch.org/2008/08/27/carbon-offsets-more-harm-than-good.

————. 2008b. "Eco-Apartheid and Global Greenwaves: African Diasporic Environmental Justice Movements." *Souls* 10:390–408.

————. 2009. "Double Jeopardy: Carbon Offsets and Human Rights Abuses." *CounterPunch*, September 9. www.counterpunch.org/2009/09/09/double-jeopardy-carbon-offsets-and-human-rights-abuses.

Choi, Charles Q. 2013. "Tiny Solar Activity Changes Affect Earth's Climate." *Space.com*, January 16. www.space.com/19280-solar-activity-earth-climate.html.

Chotiner, Isaac, and interview with Evelynn Hammonds. 2020. "How Racism Is Shaping the Coronavirus Pandemic." *The New Yorker*, May 7. https://www.newyorker.com/news/q-and-a/how-racism-is-shaping-the-coronavirus-pandemic.

Chrisler, Matt, Jaskiran Dhillon, and Audra Simpson. 2016. "The Standing Rock Syllabus Project." www.publicseminar.org/2016/10/nodapl-syllabus-project.

Churchill, Nancy. 2004. "Maquiladoras, Migration, and Daily Life." In *Women and Globalization*, edited by Delia D. Aguilar and Anne E. Lascamana, 120–153. Amherst, NY: Humanity Books.

Churchill, Ward, and Jim Vander Wall. [1990] 2002. *The COINTELPRO Papers: Documents from the FBI's Secret Wars Against Dissent in the United States*. Cambridge, MA: South End Press.

Clarke, Kamari Maxime. 2010. "New Spheres of Transnational Formations: Mobilizations of Humanitarian Diasporas." *Transforming Anthropology* 18(1):48–65.

Clarke, Kamari Maxine, and Deborah Thomas. 2006. *Globalization and Race: Transformations in the Cultural Production of Blackness*. Durham, NC: Duke University Press.

CNN. 2016. "Exit Polls." November 23. www.cnn.com/election/2016/results/exit-polls.

Coates, Ta-Nehisi. 2017. *We Were Eight Years in Power: An American Tragedy*. New York: One World.

Cole, Teju. 2012. "The White Savior Industrial Complex." *Atlantic Monthly*, March 21. www.theatlantic.com/international/archive/2012/03/the-white-savior-industrial-complex/254843/.

College Board. 2019. "Trends in College Pricing: Highlights." https://trends.collegeboard.org/college-pricing/figures-tables/tuition-fees-room-and-board-over-time.

————. 2020. "Trends in College Pricing: Resource Library." https://trends.collegeboard.org/college-pricing/figures-tables/2017-18-state-tuition-and-fees-public-four-year-institutions-state-and-five-year-percentage.

Collins, Jane L. 2003. *Threads: Gender, Labor and Power in the Global Apparel Industry*. Chicago: University of Chicago Press.

Collins, Patricia Hill. 1986. "Learning from the Outsider Within: The Sociological Significance of Black Feminist Thought." *Social Problems* 33(6):S14–S32.

————. 1990. *Black Feminist Thought: Knowledge, Consciousness, and the Politics of Empowerment*. New York: Routledge.

Collinson, Stephen. 2019. "Trump Again Punts on White Supremacy after New Zealand Attacks." *CNN*, March 16. https://edition.cnn.com/2019/03/16/politics/donald-trump-new-zealand-white-supremacy-muslims/index.html.

Conniff, Richard. 2010. "Meet the New Species: From Old-World Primates to Patch-Nosed Salamanders, New Creatures Are Being Discovered Every Day."

Smithsonian Magazine, August. www.smithsonianmag.com/science-nature/meet
-the-newspecies-748819.

Cox, Aimee Meredith. 2015. "The Choreography of Survival." *Hot Spots*, June 29.
https://culanth.org/fieldsights/the-choreography-of-survival.

———. 2018. "Afterword: Why Anthropology?" *Hot Spots*, September 26. https://
culanth.org/fieldsights/1539-afterword-why-anthropology.

Cox, Oliver Cromwell. 1948. *Caste, Class and Race: A Study in Social Dynamics*.
New York: Doubleday.

Craighill, Peyton M., and Sean Sullivan. 2013. "The Wide Racial Gap in Obama's
Presidential Elections in 2 Charts." *Washington Post*, August 28. www.washington
post.com/news/the-fix/wp/2013/08/28/the-wide-racial-gap-in-obamas-presidential
-elections-in-2-charts.

Crate, Susan A., and Mark Nuttall. 2009. *Anthropology and Climate Change*. Walnut
Creek, CA: Left Coast Press.

Craven, Christa, and Dána-Ain Davis. 2013. *Feminist Activist Ethnography: Counter-
points to Neoliberalism in North America*. Lanham, MD: Lexington Books.

Crawford, Neta C. 2018. "Human Cost of the Post-9/11 Wars: Lethality and the Need
for Transparency." Watson Institute, Brown University. https://watson.brown.edu
/costsofwar/files/cow/imce/papers/2018/Human%20Costs%2C%20Nov%208%20
2018%20CoW.pdf.

Crenshaw, Kimberlé. 2001. "Mapping the Margins: Intersectionality, Identity Politics
and Violence against Women of Color." Paper presented at the World Conference
Against Racism, Durban, South Africa.

———. 2020. "When Blackness Is a Preexisting Condition." *New Republic*, May 4.
https://newrepublic.com/article/157537/blackness-preexisting-condition
-coronavirus-katrina-disaster-relief.

Crenshaw, Kimberlé Williams, and Andrea J. Ritchie, with Rachel Anspach, Rachel
Gilmer, and Luke Harris. 2015. "Say Her Name: Resisting Police Brutality against
Black Women." New York: Columbia University Law School, African American
Policy Forum and Center for Intersectionality and Social Policy Studies.

Crutzen, Paul J., and Eugene F. Stoermer. 2000. "The 'Anthropocene.'" *IGBP
Newsletter* 41:17–18.

Danticat, Edwidge. 1998. *The Farming of Bones*. New York: Soho Press.

———. 2015. "The Long Legacy of Occupation of Haiti." *New Yorker*, July 28. www
.newyorker.com/news/news-desk/haiti-us-occupation-hundred-year-anniversary.

Davies, Carole Boyce, and Charles Peterson with editorial team: Meredith Gadsby,
and Henrietta Williams. 2003. *Decolonizing the Academy: Diaspora Theory and
African New World Studies*. Trenton, NJ: Africa World Press.

Dávila, Arlene, Leith Mullings, Renato Rosaldo, Luis F. B. Placencia, Leo R. Chavez,
Rocío Magaña, Gilberto Rosas, Ana Aparicio, Lourdes Gutiérrez Nájera, Patricia
Zavella, Alyshia Gálvez, and Jonathan D. Rosa. 2016. "Vital Topics Forum: On
Latin@s and the Immigration Debate." *American Anthropologist* 116(1):146–159.

Davis, Allison, Burleigh B. Gardner, and Mary R. Gardner. [1941] 2009. *Deep South:
A Social Anthropological Study of Caste and Class*. Columbia: University of South
Carolina Press.

Davis, Angela Y. 1983. *Women, Race & Class*. 1st Vintage Books ed. New York:
Vintage Books.

———. 2000. *The Prison Industrial Complex*. Chico, CA: AK Press.

Davis, Dána-Ain. 2014. "What Is a Feminist Activist Ethnographer to Do?" *American Anthropologist* 116(2):413–415.

———. 2015. "Constructing Fear in Academia: Neoliberal Practices at a Public College." In *Learning under Neoliberalism: Ethnographies of Governance in Higher Education*, edited by Susan Brin Hyatt, Boone W. Shear, and Susan Wright, 151–177. New York: Berghahn Books.

Davis, Dána-Ain, and Christa Craven. 2016. *Feminist Ethnography: Thinking through Methodologies, Challenges, and Possibilities*. Lanham, MD: Rowman & Littlefield.

Davis, Heather, and Zoe Todd. 2017. "On the Importance of a Date; or, Decolonizing the Anthropocene." *ACME: An International Journal for Critical Geographies* 16(4):761–780.

Davis, Janae, Alex A. Moulton, Levi Van Sant, and Brian Williams. 2019. "Anthropocene, Capitalocene, . . . Plantationocene? A Manifesto for Ecological Justice in an Age of Global Crises." *Geography Compass* 13(5):e12438.

Davis, Rachaell. 2017. "Dylann Roof: 'I Am Not Sorry, I Have Not Shed a Tear for the Innocent People I Killed.'" *Essence*, January 4. www.essence.com/news/dylann-roof -no-regret-trial-defense.

"Deaths during the L.A. Riots." 2012. *Los Angeles Times*, April 25. https://spreadsheets .latimes.com/la-riots-deaths.

Deeb, Lara, and Jessica Winegar. 2015. *Anthropology's Politics: Disciplining the Middle East*. Stanford, CA: Stanford University Press.

De Genova, Nicholas. 2005. *Working the Boundaries: Race, Space, and "Illegality" in Mexican Chicago*. Durham, NC: Duke University Press.

———. 2010. "The Queer Politics of Migration: Reflections on 'Illegality' and Incorrigibility." *Studies in Social Justice* 4(2):101–126.

———. 2017. *The Borders of "Europe": Autonomy of Migration, Tactics of Bordering*. Durham, NC: Duke University Press.

de León, Jason. 2015. *The Land of Open Graves: Living and Dying on the Migrant Trail*. Berkeley: University of California Press.

Deloria, Vine. 1988 (1969). *Custer Died for Your Sins: an Indian Manifesto*. Norman: University of Oklahoma Press.

D'Emilio, John. 1983. "Capitalism and Gay Identity." In *Powers of Desire: The Politics of Sexuality*, edited by Ann Snitow, Christine Stansell, and Sharan Thompson, 100–113. New York: Monthly Review Press.

Democracy Now! 2005. "Environmental Racism: How Minority Communities Are Exposed to 'Toxic Soup.'" August 30. www.democracynow.org/2005/8/30 /environmental_racism_how_minority_communities_are.

Desai, Meghnad. 2002. *Marx's Revenge: The Resergence of Capitalism and the Death of Statist Socialism*. London: Verso.

de Wit, T. Dudok, B. Funke, M. Haberreiter, and K. Mathes. 2018. "Better Data for Modeling the Sun's Influence on Climate." *EOS: Earth and Space Science News*, September 4. https://eos.org/science-updates/better-data-for-modeling-the-suns -influence-on-climate.

Dhillon, Jaskiran. 2018. "The Future of Anthropology Starts from Within." *Hot Spots*, September 26. https://culanth.org/fieldsights/1532-the-future-of-anthropology -starts-from-within.

Dhillon, Jaskiran, and Nick Estes. 2016. "Introduction: Standing Rock, #NoDAPL, and Mni Wiconi." *Hot Spots*, December 22. https://culanth.org/fieldsights/1007 -introduction-standing-rock-nodapl-and-mni-wiconi.

———. 2019. *#NoDAPL and Mni Wiconi: Reflections on Standing Rock*. Minneapolis: University of Minnesota Press.

Diangelo, Robin. 2011. "White Fragility." *International Journal of Critical Pedagogy* 3(3):54–70.

———. 2018. *White Fragility: Why It's So Hard for White People to Talk about Racism*, with foreword by Michael Eric Dyson. New York: Penguin Random House.

Diavolo, Lucy. 2019. "Hillary Clinton Calling Transgender People New and 'Difficult' Ignores Our History." *Teen Vogue*, October 15. www.teenvogue.com/story/hillary -clinton-calling-transgender-people-new-difficult-ignores-history.

———. 2020. "Michael Bloomberg's Transphobic Remarks Illustrate How Democrats View Trans People as a Political Football." *Teen Vogue*, February 19. www.teenvogue .com/story/michael-bloomberg-transphobic-remarks-trans-people-political-football.

Dickerson, Caitlin. 2018. "Migrant Children Moved Under Cover of Darkness to a Texas Tent City." *New York Times*, September 30. www.nytimes.com/2018/09/30 /us/migrant-children-tent-city-texas.html.

Di Leonardo, Micaela. 1998. *Exotics at Home: Anthropologists, Others, American Modernity*. Chicago: University of Chicago Press.

DiMaggio, Paul. 1982. "Cultural Capital and School Success: The Impact of Status Culture Participation on High School Students." *American Sociological Review* 47:189–201.

Douglass, Patrice, Selamawit D. Terrefe, and Frank B. Wilderson III. 2018. "Afro-Pessimism." *Oxford Bibliographies*. doi:10.1093/obo/9780190280024-0056.

Drake, St. Clair, and Horace R. Cayton. 1945. *Black Metropolis: A Study of Negro Life in a Northern City*. New York: Harcourt, Brace.

Du Bois, William Edward Burghardt. [1899] 2001. *The Philadelphia Negro: A Social Study*. Philadelphia: Chelsea House Publishers.

———[1903] 1995. *The Souls of Black Folk*. New York: Signet.

———. [1903] 2013. *The Talented Tenth*. Scotts Valley, CA: CreateSpace.

Dubuisson, Darlene, and Mark Schuller. 2017. "'You Live Under Fear'—50,000 Haitian People at Risk of Deportation." *Huffington Post*, April 25. www .huffingtonpost.com/entry/you-live-under-fear-50000-haitian-people-at-risk_us _58ff6f7ce4b047ce3ee27c5c.

DuCille, Ann. 1994. "The Occult of True Black Womanhood." *Signs: Journal of Women in Culture and Society* 19:591–629.

Duncan, Whitney, Lauren Heidbrink, and Kristin Yarris. 2018. "Im/migration in the Trump Era." *Hot Spots*, January 31. https://culanth.org/fieldsights/1300-im -migration-in-the-trump-era.

Dyson, Michael Eric. 2005. *Come Hell or High Water: Hurricane Katrina and the Color of Disaster*. New York: Basic Civitas.

"Earth's Magnetic North Pole Has Shifted So Much We've Had to Update GPS." 2019. *Science Alert*, February 6. www.sciencealert.com/navigation-systems-finally -caught-up-with-the-mysteriously-north-pole-shift.

Emanuel, Kerry. 2005. "Increasing Destructiveness of Tropical Cyclones over the Past 30 Years." *Nature* 436:686–688.

Engels, Friedrich. [1884] 1986. *The Origin of the Family, Private Property, and the State*. New York: Penguin.

Equal Justice Initiative. 2014. "The Superpredator Myth, 20 Years Later." April 7. https://eji.org/news/superpredator-myth-20-years-later.

Equiano, Olaudah. 2009. *The Interesting Life of Olaudah Equiano, or Gustavus Vassa, the African, Written by Himself.* S.I.: NuVision.

Estes, Nick. 2016. "Fighting for Our Lives: #NoDAPL in Historical Context." *The Red Nation*, September 18. https://therednation.org/2016/09/18/fighting-for-our-lives -nodapl-in-context.

———. 2019. *Our History Is the Future: Standing Rock versus the Dakota Access Pipeline, and the Long Tradition of Indigenous Resistance.* New York: Verso Books.

European Climate Declaration. 2019. "There Is No Climate Emergency." September 26. https://clintel.nl/wp-content/uploads/2019/09/ED-brochureversieNWA4.pdf.

Fanon, Frantz. 1967. *Black Skin, White Masks.* Translated by Charles Lam Markmann. New York: Grove Press.

Farmer, Paul. 1992. *AIDS and Accusation: Haiti and the Geography of Blame.* Berkeley: University of California Press.

———. 2004. "An Anthropology of Structural Violence." *Current Anthropology* 45(3):305–325.

Fassin, Didier. 2011. "Policing Borders, Producing Boundaries: The Governmentality of Immigration in Dark Times." *Annual Review of Anthropology* 40:213–226.

Fernandes, Deepa. 2007. *Targeted: Homeland Security and the Business of Immigration.* New York: Seven Stories Press.

Firmin, Joseph Anténor, and introduction by Carolyn Fluehr-Lobban. 2002 (1885). *The Equality of the Human Races: Positivist Anthropology.* Champaign: University of Illinois Press.

Fiske, Shirley J., Susan A. Crate, Carole L. Crumley, Kathleen Galvin, Heather Lazrus, George Luber, Lucy Lucero, Anthony Oliver-Smith, Ben Orlove, Sarah Strauss, and Richard Wilk. 2014. "Changing the Atmosphere. Anthropology and Climate Change." Final report of the AAA Global Climate Change Task Force. Arlington, VA: American Anthropological Association.

Flaherty, Colleen. 2017. "The More Things Change." *Inside Higher Ed*, April 11. www .insidehighered.com/news/2017/04/11/aaup-faculty-salaries-slightly-budgets-are -balanced-backs-adjuncts-and-out-state.

Flateau, John. 1996. *The Prison Industrial Complex: Race, Crime, and Justice in New York.* Brooklyn, NY: Medgar Evers College Press.

Fluehr-Lobban, Carolyn. 2000. "Anténor Firmin: Haitian Pioneer of Anthropology." *American Anthropologist* 102(3):449–466.

———. 2005. "Antenor Firmin and Haiti's Contribution to Anthropology." *GRAD-HIVA* 1:95–108.

Flynn, Joseph. 2018. *White Fatigue: Rethinking Resistence for Social Justice.* Edited by sj Miller and Leslie David Burns. New York: Peter Lang.

Ford, Anabel, and Ronald Nigh. 2016. *The Maya Forest Garden: Eight Millennia of Sustainable Cultivation of the Tropical Woodlands* Walnut Creek, CA: Left Coast Press.

Fossil Free. n.d. "1000+ Divestment Commitments." https://gofossilfree.org /divestment/commitments.

Foxen, Patricia. 2007. *In Search of Providence: Transnational Mayan Identities.* Nashville: Vanderbilt University Press.

Frachetti, Michael D. 2011. "Migration Concepts in Central Eurasian Archaeology." *Annual Review of Anthropology* 40:195–212.

Fraser, Nancy. 1992. "Rethinking the Public Sphere: A Contribution to the Critique of Actually Existing Democracy." In *Habermas and the Public Sphere*, edited by Craig Calhoun, 109–142. Cambridge, MA: MIT Press.

Galarneau, T. J., Jr., C. A. Davis, and M. A. Shapiro. 2013. "Intensification of Hurricane Sandy (2012) through Extratropical Warm Core Seclusion." *Monthly Weather Review* 141:4296–4321.

Galtung, Johan. 1980. "'A Structural Theory of Imperialism'—Ten Years Later." *Millennium: Journal of International Studies* 9(3):181–196.

Gálvez, Alyshia. 2018. *Eating NAFTA: Trade, Food Policies, and the Destruction of Mexico*. Berkeley: University of California Press.

Gambino, Lauren. 2018. "Latino Turnout Up 174% in 2018 Midterms Elections, Democrats Say." *Guardian*, November 14. www.theguardian.com/us-news/2018/nov/14/latino-turnout-up-174-in-2018-midterms-elections-democrats-say.

Gamble, Clive. 1988. "Hunter-Gatherers and the Origin of States." In *States in History*, edited by John A. Hall, 22–47. Oxford: Basil Blackwell.

Garza, Alicia. 2014. "A Herstory of the #BlackLivesMatter Movement by Alicia Garza." *Feminist Wire*, October 7. https://thefeministwire.com/2014/10/blacklivesmatter-2.

Gershon, Ilana. 2011. "Neoliberal Agency." *Current Anthropology* 52(4):537–555.

Gibbons, Ann. 2009. "A New Kind of Ancestor: *Ardipithecus* Unveiled." *Science* 326:36–50.

———. 2017. World's Oldest *Homo Sapiens* Fossils Found in Morocco." *Science*, June 7. www.sciencemag.org/news/2017/06/world-s-oldest-homo-sapiens-fossils-found-morocco.

Gilmore, Ruth Wilson, and Craig Gilmore. 2016. "Beyond Bratton." In *Policing the Planet: Why the Policing Crisis Led to Black Lives Matter*, edited by Jordan T. Camp and Christina Heatherton. New York: Verso.

Giroux, Henry. 2007. *University in Chains: Confronting the Military-Industrial-Academic Complex*. New York: Paradigm.

———. 2013. *Neoliberalism's War on Higher Education*. Chicago: Haymarket Books.

Gitlin, Todd. 1995. *The Twilight of Common Dreams: Why America Is Wracked by Culture Wars*. New York: Metropolitan Books.

Gladstone, Rick. 2017. "After Bringing Cholera to Haiti, U.N. Can't Raise Money to Fight It." *New York Times*, March 19. www.nytimes.com/2017/03/19/world/americas/cholera-haiti-united-nations.html.

Glick Schiller, Nina, and Georges Fouron. 2001. *Georges Woke Up Laughing: Long Distance Nationalism and the Search for Home*. Edited by Gilbert Joseph and Emily Rosenberg. Durham, NC: Duke University Press.

Glover, Kaiama L. 2016. "'Written with Love': Intimacy and Relation in Katherine Dunham's *Island Possessed*." In *The Haiti Exception: Anthropology and the Predicament of Narrative*, edited by Alessandra Benedicty-Kokken, Kaiama L. Glover, Mark Schuller, and Jhon Picard Byron, 93–109. Cambridge: Cambridge University Press.

Goldrick-Rab, Sara, and Katharine M. Broton. 2015. "Hungry, Homeless and in College." *New York Times*, December 4. http://www.nytimes.com/2015/12/x04/opinion/hungry-homeless-and-in-college.html.

Gomberg-Muñoz, Ruth. 2017. *Becoming Legal: Immigration Law and Mixed-Status Families*. New York: Oxford University Press.

Gomberg-Muñoz, Ruth, and Laura Nussbaum-Barberena. 2011. "Is Immigration Policy Labor Policy? Immigration Enforcement, Undocumented Workers, and the State." *Human Organization* 70(4):366–375.

Gomez, Alan. 2017. "Trump Immigration Agency Wants to Kick 50,000 Haitians Out of the USA." *USA Today*, April 20. www.usatoday.com/story/news/world /2017/04/20/trump-agency-temporary-protection-haitians-united-states /100709428.

Gonzáles, Roberto G. 2016. *Lives in Limbo: Undocumented and Coming of Age in America*. Berkeley: University of California Press.

Gonzáles, Roberto G., and Leo R. Chavez. 2012. "'Awakening to a Nightmare': Abjectivity and Illegality in the Lives of Undocumented 1.5-Generation Latino Immigrants in the United States." *Current Anthropology* 53(3):255–281.

González, Roberto J. 2004. *Anthropologists in the Public Sphere: Speaking Out on War, Peace, and American Power*. Austin: University of Texas Press.

———. 2009. *American Counterinsurgency: Human Science and the Human Terrain*. Chicago: Prickly Paradigm.

Goodman, Alan, Yolanda T. Moses, and American Anthropological Association. 2012. *RACE: Are We So Different?* Washington, DC: American Anthropological Association.

Gowricharn, Ruben. 2006. *Caribbean Transnationalism: Migration, Pluralization, and Social Cohesion*. Lanham, MD: Lexington Books.

Gramsci, Antonio. 1971. *Selections from the Prison Notebooks of Antonio Gramsci*. Edited and translated by Quintin Hoare and Geoffrey Nowell Smith. New York: International.

Gray, Rosie. 2017. "Trump Defends White-Nationalist Protesters: 'Some Very Fine People on Both Sides.'" *Atlantic*, August 15. www.theatlantic.com/politics/archive /2017/08/trump-defends-white-nationalist-protesters-some-very-fine-people-on -both-sides/537012.

Greyser, Naomi, and Margot Weiss. 2012. "Introduction: Left Intellectuals and the Neoliberal University." *American Quarterly* 64(4):787–793.

Griffin, Jake. 2017. "Spending per Student Ranges from $8,500 to $32,000 in Suburbs." *Daily Herald*, April 19. www.dailyherald.com/news/20170419/spending-per -student-ranges-from-8500-to-32000-in-suburbs-.

Gusterson, Hugh. 2017. "Homework: Toward a Critical Ethnography of the University, AES Presidential Address, 2017." *American Ethnologist* 44(3):435–450.

Gutiérrez y Muhs, Gabriella, Yolanda Flores Niemann, Carmen G. González, and Angela P. Harris. 2012. *Presumed Incompetent: The Intersections of Race and Class for Women in Academia*. Boulder, CO: Utah State University Press.

"Haiti—Economy: Impacts of Remittances from Diaspora on the National Economy." 2017. *Haiti Libre*, April 4. www.haitilibre.com/en/news-20563-haiti-economy -impacts-of-remittances-from-diaspora-on-the-national-economy.html.

Hale, Charles R. 2006. "Activist Research v. Cultural Critique: Indigenous Land Rights and the Contradictions of Politically Engaged Anthropology." *Cultural Anthropology* 21(1):96–120.

Haley, Alex. 1976. *Roots: The Saga of an American Family*. Garden City, NY: Doubleday.

Hansberry, Lorraine. 1959. *A Raisin in the Sun*. New York: Plume.

Hansen, James. 2009. *Storms of My Grandchildren: The Truth about the Coming Climate Catastrophe and Our Last Chance to Save Humanity*. New York: Bloomsbury.

Haraway, Donna. 2015. "Anthropocene, Capitalocene, Plantationocene, Chthulucene: Making Kin." *Environmental Humanities* 6:159–165.

Hardesty, Donald L. 2007. "Perspectives on Global-Change Archaeology." *American Anthropologist* 109(1):1–7.

Hardoon, Deborah. 2017. *An Economy for the 99%*. London: Oxfam International.

Harney, Stefano, and Fred Moten. 2013. *The Undercommons: Fugitive Planning & Black Study*. Brooklyn, NY: Autonomedia.

Harrison, Faye Venetia. 1997. "The Gendered Politics and Violence of Structural Adjustment: A View from Jamaica." In *Situated Lives: Gender and Culture in Everyday Life*, edited by Louise Lamphere, Helen Ragone, and Patricia Zavella, 451–468. New York: Routledge.

———. 2002. "Race and Globalization: Global Apartheid, Foreign Policy, and Human Rights." *Souls: A Critical Journal of Black Politics, Culture, and Society* 4(3):48–68.

———. 2008. *Outsider Within: Reworking Anthropology in the Global Age*. Urbana: University of Illinois Press.

———. [1991] 2010. *Decolonizing Anthropology: Moving Further toward an Anthropology for Liberation*. 3rd ed. Arlington, VA: Association of Black Anthropologists, American Anthropological Association.

———. 2012a. "Critical Analysis: Writing the Anthropological Imagination for Public Engagement." *North American Dialogue* 15(2):50–60.

———. 2012b. "Race, Racism, and Antiracism: Implications for Human Rights." In *Race: Are We So Different?*, edited by Alan Goodman, Yolanda T. Moses and Joseph L. Jones, 237–244. Malden, MA: Wiley-Blackwell.

Harrison, Faye Venetia, and Ira Harrison. 1999. "Introduction: Anthropology, African Americans, and the Emancipation of a Subjugated Knowledge." In *African-American Pioneers in Anthropology*, edited by Ira Harrison and Faye Venetia Harrison, 1–36. Urbana: University of Illinois Press.

Harrison, Ira E., Deborah Johnson-Simon, and Erica Lorraine Williams. 2018. *The Second Generation of African American Pioneers in Anthropology*. Champaign: University of Illinois Press.

Harris-Perry, Melissa. 2017. "How #SquadCare Saved My Life." *Elle*, July 24. https://www.elle.com/culture/career-politics/news/a46797/squad-care-melissa-harris-perry/.

Harvey, David. 2014. *Seventeen Contradictions and the End of Capitalism*. Oxford: Oxford University Press.

Hervey, Ginger. 2016. "To Pay for College, More Students Are Becoming Sugar Babies." *USA Today*, July 21. http://college.usatoday.com/2016/07/21/to-pay-forcollege-more-students-are-becoming-sugar-babies/.

Hetey, Rebecca C., and Jennifer L. Eberhardt. 2018. "The Numbers Don't Speak for Themselves: Racial Disparities and the Persistence of Inequality in the Criminal Justice System." *Current Directions in Psychological Science* 27(3):183–187.

Heyman, Josiah McC. 1998. *Finding a Moral Heart for U.S. Immigration Policy. An Anthropological Perspective*. Arlington, VA: American Anthropological Association.

———. 2012. "Capitalism and US Policy at the Mexican Border." *Dialectical Anthropology* 36(3/4):263–277.

Heyman, Josiah McC, Maria Cristina Morales, and Guillermina Gina Núñez. 2009. "Engaging with the Immigrant Human Rights Movement in a Besieged Border Region: What Do Applied Social Scientists Bring to the Policy Process?" *NAPA Bulletin* 31:13–29.

Higher Ed Jobs. 2020. "Administrators in Higher Education Salaries." www.higheredjobs.com/salary/salarydisplay.cfm?surveyid=22.

Hilker, Lynday McLean. 2012. "Rwanda's 'Hutsi': Intersections of Ethnicity and Violence in the Lives of Youth of 'Mixed' Heritage." *Identities: Global Studies in Culture and Power* 19(2):229–247.

Hing, Julianne. 2013. "Undocumented Youth Pay Tribute to the Original DREAMers." *Colorlines*, March 29. http://colorlines.com/archives/2013/03/undocumented_youth_pay_tribute_to_the_original_dreamers.html.

Hirschkind, Charles, and Saba Mahmood. 2002. "Feminism, the Taliban, and Politics of Counter-insurgency." *Anthropological Quarterly* 75(2):339–354.

Holland, Greg, and Cindy Bruyère. 2014. "Recent Intense Hurricane Response to Global Climate Change." *Climate Dynamics* 42:617–627.

Holmes, Seth. 2013. *Fresh Fruit, Broken Bodies: Migrant Farmworkers in the United States*. Berkeley: University of California Press.

Hornsby, Alton. 1986. "Martin Luther King, Jr. 'Letter from a Birmingham Jail.'" *Journal of Negro History* 71(1/4):38–44.

Horton, Sarah Bronwen. 2016. *They Leave Their Kidneys in the Fields: Illness, Injury, and Illegality among U.S. Farmworkers*. Berkeley: University of California Press.

Howe, Cymene. 2015. "Latin America in the Anthropocene: Energy Transitions and Climate Change Mitigations." *Journal of Latin American and Caribbean Anthropology* 20(2):231–241.

Hsu, Kaiting Jessica, and Jean-Claudy Aristil. 2014. "Reconstruction or Haiti's Latest Disaster? Tourism Development on Île-à-Vache Island." *Toward Freedom*, July 21. https://towardfreedom.org/story/archives/americas/reconstruction-or-haiti-s-latest-disaster-tourism-development-on-ile-a-vache-island/

Huelsman, Mark, Tamara Draut, Tatjana Meschede, Lars Dietrich, Thomas Shapiro, and Laura Sullivan. 2015. "Less Debt, More Equity: Lowering Student Debt While Closing the Black-White Wealth Gap." *Demos*, November 24. www.demos.org/publication/less-debt-more-equity-lowering-student-debt-while-closing-black-white-wealth-gap.

Human Rights Watch. 2017. "Croatia: Asylum Seekers Forced Back to Serbia." January 20. www.hrw.org/news/2017/01/20/croatia-asylum-seekers-forced-back-serbia.

Hurston, Zora Neale. [1938] 1990. *Tell My Horse: Voodoo and Life in Haiti and Jamaica*. Edited by Henry Louis Gates Jr. New York: Harper & Row.

Hutchinson, Janis Faye. 2005. *The Coexistence of Race and Racism: Can They Become Extinct Together?* Washington, DC: University Press of America.

Hyatt, Susan Brin, Boone W. Shear, and Susan Wright. 2015. *Learning under Neoliberalism: Ethnographies of Governance in Higher Education*. New York: Berghahn Books.

Immigrant Legal Resource Center. 2017. "Economic Contributions by Salvadoran, Honduran, and Haitian TPS Holders." www.ilrc.org/report-tps-economic-cost.

Inda, Jonathan X. 2006. *Targeting Immigrants. Government, Technology, and Ethics.* London: Blackwell.

Indigenous Action. 2014. "Accomplices, not Allies: Abolishing the Ally Industrial Complex, an Indigenous Perspective." Indigenous Action Media.

Inikori, Joseph E. 1976. "Measuring the Atlantic Slave Trade: An Assessment of Curtin and Anstey." *Journal of African History* 17(2):197–223.

Inikori, Joseph E., and Stanley L. Engerman. 1992. *The Atlantic Slave Trade: Effects on Economies, Societies and Peoples in Africa, the Americas, and Europe.* Durham, NC: Duke University Press.

International Organization for Migration. 2020. "Migration, Environment and Climate Change (MECC) Division." www.iom.int/definitional-issues.

Isser, Mindy, and interview with Adam Burch. 2020. "Minneapolis Bus Driver: 'It's Imperative That Unions Fight for All Workers.'" *Jacobin*, May 31. https://jacobinmag.com/2020/05/minneapolis-bus-drivers-unions-george-floyd-protest-police.

Jacques, Peter J., Riley E. Dunlap, and Mark Freeman. 2008. "The Organization of Denial: Conservative Think Tanks and Environmental Scepticism." *Environmental Politics* 17:349–385.

Jaschik, Scott. 2015. "Embedded Conflicts." *Inside Higher Ed*, July 7. www.insidehighered.com/news/2015/07/07/army-shuts-down-controversial-human-terrain-system-criticized-many-anthropologists.

Jean-Baptiste, Chenet. 2012. "Haiti's Earthquake: A Further Insult to Peasants' Lives." In *Tectonic Shifts: Haiti since the Earthquake*, edited by Mark Schuller and Pablo Morales, 97–100. Sterling, VA: Kumarian Press.

Johnson, Jake. 2018. "Calling Out Trump Denial, Durbin Confirms President Said 'Those Hate-Filled' Words 'Repeatedly.'" *Common Dreams*, January 12. www.commondreams.org/news/2018/01/12/calling-out-trump-denial-durbin-confirms-president-said-those-hate-filled-words.

Johnston, Barbara Rose. 2011. *Half-Lives and Half-Truths: Confronting the Radioactive Legacies of the Cold War.* Santa Fe, NM: School of American Research Press.

Jordan, Miriam. 2018. "'Why Did You Leave Me?' The Migrant Children Left Behind as Parents Are Deported." *New York Times*, July 27. www.nytimes.com/2018/07/27/us/migrant-families-deportations.html.

Kaplan, Sarah. 2019. "The North Pole Is Mysteriously Moving, and the U.S. Government Finally Caught Up." *Washington Post*, February 6. www.washingtonpost.com/science/2019/02/05/north-pole-is-mysteriously-moving-us-government-finally-caught-up/?noredirect=on.

Kawa, Nicholas C., José A. Clavijo Michelangeli, Jessica L. Clark, Daniel Ginsberg, and Christopher McCarty. 2018. "The Social Network of US Academic Anthropology and Its Inequalities." *American Anthropologist* 121:14–29.

Kehoe, Alice Beck, and Paul L. Doughty. 2012. *Expanding American Anthropology, 1945–1980: A Generation Reflects.* Tuscaloosa: University of Alabama Press.

Kelley, Colin P., Shahrzad Mohtadi, Mark A. Cane, Richard Seager, and Yochanan Kushnir. 2015. "Climate Change in the Fertile Crescent and Implications of the Recent Syrian Drought." *Proceedings of the National Academy of Sciences* 112:3241–3246.

Kelley, Robin D. G. 2002. *Freedom Dreams: The Black Radical Imagination*. Boston: Beacon.

Kennedy, Robert F. 2018. "Ripple of Hope." YouTube, January 14. www.youtube.com /watch?v=h7gAM9xTLKU.

Kerr, Emma. 2019. "10 Universities with the Biggest Endowments." *U.S. News & World Report*, September 24. www.usnews.com/education/best-colleges/the-short -list-college/articles/2017-09-28/10-universities-with-the-biggest-endowments.

Khan-Cullors, Patrisse, and Asha Bandele. 2017. *When They Call You a Terrorist: A Black Lives Matter Memoir*. New York: St. Martin's.

Kibicho, Karanja. 2016. "As the Kenyan Minister for National Security, Here's Why I'm Shutting the World's Biggest Refugee Camp." *Independent*, May 9. www .independent.co.uk/voices/as-the-kenyan-minister-for-national-security-heres-why -im-shutting-the-worlds-biggest-refugee-camp-a7020891.html.

King, Charles. 2019. *The Reinvention of Humanity: A Story of Race, Sex, Gender and the Discovery of Culture*. London: The Bodley Head.

King, Martin Luther. 1968. *Why We Can't Wait*. New York: New American Library.

Kishore, Nishant, et al. 2018. "Mortality in Puerto Rico after Hurricane Maria." *New England Journal of Medicine* 379:162–170.

Klein, Naomi. 2014. *This Changes Everything: Capitalism vs. the Climate*. New York: Simon & Schuster.

Klugh, Elgin. 2018. "Delmos Jones and the End of Neutrality." In *The Second Generation of African American Pioneers in Anthropology*, edited by Ira E. Harrison, Deborah Johnson-Simon, and Erica Lorraine Williams, 52–67. Champaign: University of Illinois Press.

Köhler, Gernot. 1978. "Global Apartheid." In *Talking about People: Readings in Contemporary Cultural Anthropology*, edited by William A. Haviland and Robert J. Gordon, 262–268. Mountain View, CA: Mayfield.

Kotlowitz, Alex. 1991. *There Are No Children Here: The Story of Two Boys Growing Up in the Other America*. New York: Doubleday.

Kranish, Michael, and Robert O'Harrow Jr. 2016. "Inside the Government's Racial Bias Suit against Donald Trump's Company, and How He Fought It." *The Washington Post*, January 23.

Kuklick, Henrika. 2006. "'Humanity in the Chrysalis State': Indigenous Australians in the Anthropological Imagination, 1899–1926." *British Journal for the History of Science* 39(4):535–568.

Lacy, Sarah H., and Ashton Rome. 2017. "(Re)Politicizing the Anthropologist in the Age of Neoliberalism and #Blacklivesmatter." *Transforming Anthropology* 25(2): 171–184.

LaDuke, Winona. 1999. *All Our Relations: Native Struggles for Land and Life*. Boston: South End Press and Honor the Earth.

LaDuke, Winona, with Sean Aaron Cruz. 2017. *The Militarization of Indian Country (2017 Edition), with News from Standing Rock*. Minneapolis: Honor the Earth.

Laguerre, Michel. 1998. *Diasporic Citizenship: Haitian Americans in Transnational America*. New York: St. Martin's.

Lamphere, Louise. 1993. "The Domestic Sphere of Women and the Public World of Men: The Strengths and Limitations of an Anthropological Dichotomy." In *Gender in Cross Cultural Perspective*, edited by Caroline Brottel and Carolyn Sergent, 67–77. Englewood Cliffs, NJ: Prentice Hall.

———. 2018. "2017 Malinowski Award Lecture: The Transformation of Ethnography: From Malinowki's Tent to the Practice of Collaborative/Activist Anthropology." *Human Organization* 77(1):64–76.

Landy, Benjamin. 2013. "Graph: Don't Blame Teachers for Rising College Tuition." Century Foundation, September 11. https://tcf.org/content/commentary/graph-dont-blame-teachers-for-rising-college-tuition.

LeCompte, Margaret D. 2014. "Collisions of Culture: Academic Culture in the Neoliberal University." *Learning and Teaching* 7(1):57–78.

Levin, Sam. 2017. "No African Citizens Granted Visas for African Trade Summit in California." *Guardian*, March 20. www.theguardian.com/us-news/2017/mar/20/no-african-citizens-visas-california-annual-trade-summit.

Logan, Erin B. 2018. "Interior Secretary Blames Intensity of California Wildfires on 'Environmental Terrorist Groups.'" *Los Angeles Times*, August 16. www.latimes.com/politics/la-na-pol-zinke-wildfires-20180816-story.html.

López, Edwin. 2018. "Water Is Life at Standing Rock: A Case of First World Resistance to Global Capitalism." *Perspectives on Global Development and Technology* 17(1–2):139–157.

López-Marrero, Tania, and Tamara Heartill Scalley. 2012. "Get Up, Stand Up: Environmental Situation, Threats, and Opportunities in the Insular Caribbean." *Caribbean Studies* 40(2):3–14.

López-Marrero, Tania, and Ben Wisner. 2012. "Not in the Same Boat: Disasters and Differential Vulnerability in the Insular Caribbean." *Caribbean Studies* 40(2):129–168.

Lord, Debbie. 2018. "What Happened at Charlottesville: Looking Back on the Rally That Ended in Death." *Atlanta Journal-Constitution*, August 10. www.ajc.com/news/national/what-happened-charlottesville-looking-back-the-anniversary-the-deadly-rally/fPpnLrbAtbxSwNI9BEy93K.

Low, Setha, and Sally Engle Merry. 2010. "Engaged Anthropology: Diversity and Dilemmas. An Introduction to Supplement 2." *Current Anthropology* 51(Suppl. 2):S203–S226.

Lowen, Rebecca S. 1997. *Creating the Cold War University: The Transformation of Stanford*. Berkeley: University of California Press.

Lucas, George R. 2009. *Anthropologists in Arms: The Ethics of Military Anthropology*. Lanham, MD: Alta Mira.

Lyman, Rick. 2015. "Hungary Seals Border with Croatia in Migrant Crackdown." *New York Times*, October 16. www.nytimes.com/2015/10/17/world/europe/hungary-croatia-refugees-migrants.html.

Lyon-Callo, Vincent. 2015. "To Market, to Market, to Buy a ... Middle Class Life? Insecurity, Anxiety, and Neoliberal Education in Michigan." In *Learning under Neoliberalism: Ethnographies of Governance in Higher Education*, edited by Susan Brin Hyatt, Boone W. Shear, and Susan Wright, 79–102. New York: Berghahn Books.

MacDonald, Fiona. 2016. "New Study Shows How Rapidly Earth's Magnetic Field Is Changing." *Science Alert*, May 11. www.sciencealert.com/new-study-shows-that-earth-s-magnetic-field-is-weakening-more-rapidly-than-we-thought.

Macdonald, Isabel, and Isabeau Doucet. 2011. "The Shelters That Clinton Built." *The Nation*, July 11. www.thenation.com/article/shelters-clinton-built.

Magloire, Gérarde, and Kevin A. Yelvington. 2005. "Haiti and the Anthropological Imagination." *Gradhiva [en ligne]* 1. http://gradhiva.revues.org/335.

Malcolm X. 1992. *By Any Means Necessary*. New York: Pathfinder Press.

Maldonado, Julie Koppel. 2018. *Seeking Justice in an Energy Sacrifice Zone: Standing on Vanishing Land in Coastal Louisiana*. New York: Routledge.

Maldonado, Julie Koppel, Christine Shearer, Robin Bronen, Kristina Peterson, and Heather Lazrus. 2013. "The Impact of Climate Change on Tribal Communities in the US: Displacement, Relocation, and Human Rights." *Climatic Change* 120:601–614.

Mamdani, Mahmood. 2005. *Good Muslim, Bad Muslim: America, the Cold War, and the Roots of Terror*. New York: Three Leaves.

Mandela, Nelson. 1994. *Long Walk to Freedom: The Autobiography of Nelson Mandela*. New York: Little, Brown.

Mangan, Dan. 2019. "FBI Releases Files on President Trump's Late Lawyer, Roy Cohn." *CNBC*, September 27. www.cnbc.com/2019/09/27/fbi-releases-file-on -trumps-late-lawyer-roy-cohn.html.

Marable, Manning. [1983] 2000. *How Capitalism Underdeveloped Black America: Problems in Race, Political Economy, and Society*. Boston: South End Press.

———. 2011. *Malcolm X: A Life of Reinvention*. New York: Penguin.

Marcotte, Amanda. 2015. "Hillary Clinton Defies Right-Wing Critics, Endorses Universal Pre-K." *Slate*, June 18. https://slate.com/human-interest/2015/06 /conservatives-hate-it-takes-a-village-hillary-clinton-embraces-it-by-endorsing -universal-pre-k.html.

Marcuse, Harold. 2016. "The Origin and Reception of Martin Niemöller's Quotation, 'First They Came for Communists. . . .'" In *Remembering for the Future: Armenia, Auschwitz, and Beyond*, edited by Michael Berenbaum, Richard Libowitz, and Marcia Sache Littell, 173–199. St. Paul, MN: Paragon House.

Marino, Elizabeth. 2015. *Fierce Climate Sacred Ground: An Ethnography of Climate Change in Shishmaref, Alaska*. Fairbanks: University of Alaska Press.

Marino, Elizabeth, and Heather Lazrus. 2016. "'We Are Always Getting Ready': How Diverse Notions of Time and Flexibility Build Adaptive Capacity in Alaska and Tuvalu." In *Contextualizing Disaster*, edited by Gregory V. Button and Mark Schuller, 153–170. New York: Berghahn Books.

Maskovsky, Jeff. 2012. "Beyond Neoliberalism: Academia and Activism in a Nonhegemonic Moment." *American Quarterly* 64(4):819–822.

Maseko, Zola. 1998. *The Life and Times of Sara Baartman: "The Hottentot Venus."* Brooklyn, NY: Icarus Films.

Masters, James, and Euan McKirdy. 2017. "Head to Head: How Le Pen and Macron Compare" *CNN*, May 3. https://www.cnn.com/2017/04/24/europe/how-le-pen -and-macron-compare/index.html.

Maurer, Bill. 2003. "Comment: Got Language? Law, Property, and the Anthropological Imagination." *American Anthropologist* 105:775–781.

McAnany, Patricia A., and Norman Yoffee. 2009. *Questioning Collapse: Human Resilience, Ecological Vulnerability, and the Aftermath of Empire*. Cambridge: Cambridge University Press.

McElrath, Suzy, Rahsaan Mahadeo, and Stephen Suh. 2014. "'Crimmigration,' with Tanya Golash-Boza, Ryan King, and Yolanda Vázquez." *Society Pages*, February 24. https://thesocietypages.org/roundtables/crimmigration.

McKinney, Cynthia. 2013. "Cultural Dimensions of Leading Change." www.academia .edu/38209820/Cultural_Dimensions_of_Leading_Change.doc.

McKittrick, Katherine. 2013. "Plantation Futures." *Small Axe* 17(3):1–15.

Mead, Margaret. [1928] 2001. *Coming of Age in Samoa: A Psychological Study of Primitive Youth for Western Civilisation*. New York: Perennial Classics.

Mendez, Jennifer Bickham. 2002. "Gender and Citizenship in a Global Context: The Struggle for Maquila Workers' Rights in Nicaragua." *Identities: Global Studies in Culture and Power* 9(1):7–38.

Middleton Manning, Beth Rose. 2011. *Trust in the Land: New Directions in Tribal Conservation*. Tucson: University of Arizona Press.

———. 2018. *Upstream: Trust Lands and Power on the Feather River*. Tucson: University of Arizona Press.

Mikell, Gwendolyn. 1999. "Feminism and Black Culture in the Ethnography of Zora Neale Hurston." In *African American Pioneers in Anthropology*, edited by Ira E. Harrison and Faye V. Harrison, 51–69. Champaign: University of Illinois Press.

Millard, Ann V., and Jorge Chapa. 2004. *Apple Pie and Enchiladas: Latino Newcomers in the Rural Midwest*. Austin: University of Texas Press.

Mills, C. Wright. 1959. *The Sociological Imagination*. New York: Oxford University Press.

Mintz, Sidney J. 1977. *Was the Plantation Slave a Proletarian?* Working papers; Seminar 1. Binghamton: Fernand Braudel Center for the Study of Economies, Historical Systems Civilizations, State University of New York at Binghamton.

———. 1984. *Labor Needs and Ethnic Ripening in the Caribbean Region*. Washington, DC: Wilson Institute for International Relations.

Mitchell, Bruce, and Juan Franco. 2018. "HOLC 'Redlining' Maps: The Persistent Structure of Segregation and Economic Inequality." NCRC, March 20. https://ncrc.org/holc.

Mohanty, Chandra Talpade. 1988. "Under Western Eyes: Feminist Scholarship and Colonial Discourses." *Feminist Review* 30:61–88.

Moore, Jason W. 2016. *Anthropocene or Capitalocene? Nature, History, and the Crisis of Capitalism*. Oakland, CA: PM Press.

Moore, Sophie Sapp, Monique Allewaert, Pablo Gòmez, and Gregg Mitman. 2019. "Plantation Legacies." *Edge Effects*. http://edgeeffects.net/plantation-legacies-plantationocene.

Moraga, Cherrie L., and Gloria E. Anzaldua. 1983. *This Bridge Called My Back: Writings by Radical Women of Color*. New York: Kitchen Table: Women of Color Press.

Moran, Emilio F. 2006. *An Introduction to Human Ecological Relations*. Malden, MA: Blackwell.

Moyneur, Sarah. 2013. *Meet the Flintstones: A critical essay on the perpetuation of the 'caveman' stereotype, from the late 1800's to today.*, Archaeology and Ancient History, Lund University, Lund.

Mullings, Leith. 2005. "Interrogating Racism: Toward an Antiracist Anthropology." *Annual Review of Anthropology* 34:667–694.

Mumm, Jesse. 2008. "Redoing Chicago: Gentrification, Race, and Intimate Segregation." *North American Dialogue* 11(1):16–19.

Murphy, Hannah. 2017. "Macron's Policies on Europe, Trade, Immigration and Defence." *Financial Times*, May 7. www.ft.com/content/37223e92-3319-11e7-bce4-9023f8cofd2e.

Nader, Laura. 2002. "Breaking the Silence: Politics and Professional Autonomy." *Anthropological Quarterly* 75(1):160–169.

NASA. 2003a. "Earth's Inconstant Magnetic Field." December 29. www.nasa.gov /vision/earth/lookingatearth/29dec_magneticfield.html.

———. 2003b. "Solar Radiation and Climate Experiment (SORCE)." https:// earthobservatory.nasa.gov/features/SORCE/sorce_04.php.

———. 2011. "2012: Magnetic Pole Reversal Happens All the (Geologic) Time." November 30. www.nasa.gov/topics/earth/features/2012-poleReversal.html.

National Black Justice Coalition. 2011. "Injustice at Every Turn: A Look at Black Respondents to the Transgender Discrimination Survey." Washington, DC: National Black Justice Coalition, National Center for Trans-gender Equality, National Gay and Lesbian Task Force.

National Partnership for Women & Families. 2019. "Beyond Wages: Effects of the Latina Wage Gap." www.nationalpartnership.org/research-library/workplace -fairness/fair-pay/latinas-wage-gap.pdf.

———. 2020. "Black Women and the Wage Gap." March. www.nationalpartnership .org/research-library/workplace-fairness/fair-pay/african-american-women-wage -gap.pdf.

National Public Radio. 2006. "'White Money' and Black Studies Departments." January 30. www.npr.org/templates/story/story.php?storyId=5179249.

———. 2016. "Why America's Schools Have a Money Problem." April 18. www.npr .org/2016/04/18/474256366/why-americas-schools-have-a-money-problem.

Navarro, Sharon Ann. 2002. "*Las Mujeres Invisibles:* The Invisible Women." In *Women's Activism and Globalization: Linking Local Struggles and International Politics*, edited by Nancy A. Naples and Manisha Desai, 83–98. London: Routledge.

Navarro, Tami, Bianca C. Williams, and Attiya Ahmad. 2013. "Sitting at the Kitchen Table: Fieldnotes from Women of Color in Anthropology." *Cultural Anthropology* 28(3):443–463.

Newfield, Christopher. 2008. *Unmaking the Public University: The Forty-Year Assault on the Middle Class*. Cambridge, MA: Harvard University Press.

"New Zealand Mosque Attacks Suspect Praised Trump in Manifesto." 2019. *Al Jazeera*, March 16. www.aljazeera.com/news/2019/03/zealand-mosques-attack -suspect-praised-trump-manifesto-190315100143150.html.

Nguyen, Tram. 2005. *We Are All Suspects Now: Untold Stories from Immigrant Communities after 9/11*. Boston: Beacon.

Nicholls, Walter J. 2013. *The DREAMers: How the Undocumented Youth Movement Transformed the Immigrant Rights Debate*. Stanford, CA: Stanford University Press.

Nixon, Rob. 2011. *Slow Violence and the Environmentalism of the Poor*. Cambridge, MA: Harvard University Press.

Northern Illinois University, University Council. 2018. "Executive Summary and Recommendations: 2015–16 Faculty Salary Study." www.niu.edu/u_council /reports/faculty-salary-study/fss-final-report-03-16-18.pdf.

Norwegian Refugee Council. n.d. "Disaster and Climate Change." www.nrc.no/what -we-do/speaking-up-for-rights/climate-change.

Ntarangwi, Mwenda. 2010. *Reversed Gaze: An African Ethnography of American Anthropology*. Urbana, IL: University of Illinois Press.

"Omarosa Confirms Trump Called Nigeria a 'Shithole' Country." 2018. *Daily Beast*, April 30. www.thedailybeast.com/omarosa-confirms-trump-called-nigeria-a-shithole-country.

O'Neal, Lonnae. 2016. "The 53 Percent Issue." *Undefeated*, December 20. https://the undefeated.com/features/black-women-say-white-feminists-have-a-trump-problem.

Ong, Aihwa. 1996. "Cultural Citizenship as Subject-Making: Immigrants Negotiate Racial and Cultural Boundaries in the United States." *Current Anthropology* 37(5):737–762.

"Open Letter to UN Secretary-General: Current Scientific Knowledge Does Not Substantiate Ban Ki-Moon Assertions on Weather and Climate, Say 125-Plus Scientists." 2012. *Financial Post*, November 29. https://business.financialpost.com /opinion/open-climate-letterto-un-secretary-general-current-scientific-knowledge -does-not-substantiate-ban-ki-moonassertions-on-weather-and-climate-say-125 -scientists.

Operation Ghetto Storm. 2014. "2012 Annual Report on the Extrajudicial Killings of 313 Black People by Police, Security Guards, and Vigilantes." November. www .operationghettostorm.org/uploads/1/9/1/1/19110795/new_all_14_11_04.pdf.

Orent, Amnon. 1970. "Dual Organizations in Southern Ethiopia: Anthropological Imagination or Ethnographic Fact." *Ethnology* 9(3):228–233.

Park, Madison. 2017. "In a Trump-Defying Move, California's Senate Passes Sanctuary State Bill." *CNN*, April 4. www.cnn.com/2017/04/04/politics/california -sanctuary-state-bill-sb-54/index.html.

Patterson, Orlando. 1982. *Slavery and Social Death: A Comparative Study*. Cambridge, MA: Harvard University Press.

Pearl, Betsy. 2018. "Ending the War on Drugs: By the Numbers." Center for American Progress, June 27. www.americanprogress.org/issues/criminal-justice/reports/2018 /06/27/452819/ending-war-drugs-numbers.

Peck, Raoul. 2013. *Assistance Mortelle*. Arte France.

Pentón, Mario J. 2020. "Fears of a Total Ban on U.S. Flights to Cuba Lead to a Run on Tickets." *Miami Herald*, January 16. www.miamiherald.com/news/nation-world /world/americas/cuba/article239327793.html.

Perkins, John. 2006. *Confessions of an Economic Hit Man*. New York: Plume Books.

Perlstein, Rick. 2012. "Exclusive: Lee Atwater's Infamous 1981 Interview on the Southern Strategy." *The Nation*, November 13. www.thenation.com/article /exclusive-lee-atwaters-infamous-1981-interview-southern-strategy.

Perry, Keisha-Khan Y. 2020. "The Resurgent Far Right and the Black Feminist Struggle for Social Democracy in Brazil." *American Anthropologist* 122(1):157–162.

Petersen, Eva Bendix, and Bronwyn Davies. 2010. "In/Difference in the Neoliberalised University." *Learning and Teaching* 3(2):92–109.

Petterson, John S., Laura D. Stanley, Edward Glazier, and James Philipp. 2006. "A Preliminary Assessment of Social and Economic Impacts Associated with Hurricane Katrina." *American Anthropologist* 108(4):643–670.

Pew Research Center. 2011. "Unauthorized Immigrant Population: National and State Trends, 2010." February 1. www.pewhispanic.org/2011/02/01/unauthorized -immigrant-population-brnational-and-state-trends-2010.

———. 2012. "Up to 1.7 Million Unauthorized Immigrant Youth May Benefit from New Deportation Rules." August 14. www.pewhispanic.org/2012/08/14/up-to-1-7 -million-unauthorized-immigrant-youth-may-benefit-from-new-deportation-rules.

———. 2018a. "An Examination of the 2016 Electorate, Based on Validated Voters." August 9. www.people-press.org/2018/08/09/an-examination-of-the-2016 -electorate-based-on-validated-voters.

———. 2018b. "Key Takeaways about Latino Voters in the 2018 Midterm Elections." November 9. www.pewresearch.org/fact-tank/2018/11/09/how-latinos-voted-in -2018-midterms.

———. 2019. "5 Facts about Illegal Immigration in the U.S." June 12. www.pewresearch .org/fact-tank/2017/04/27/5-facts-about-illegal-immigration-in-the-u-s.

Pierre, Jemima. 2013. *The Predicament of Blackness: Postcolonial Ghana and the Politics of Race*. Chicago: University of Chicago Press.

———. 2020. "The Racial Vernaculars of Development: A View from West Africa." *American Anthropologist* 122(1):86–98.

Pierre-Louis, François. 2006. *Haitians in New York City: Transnationalism and Hometown Associations*. Gainesville: University Press of Florida.

Polanyi, Karl. [1944] 2001. *The Great Transformation: The Political and Economic Origins of Our Time*. Boston: Beacon.

Posecznik, Alex. 2014. "Introduction: On Theorising and Humanising Academic Complicity in the Neoliberal University." *Learning and Teaching* 7(1):1–11.

Powell, Benjamin. 2012. "The Law of Unintended Consequences: Georgia's Immigration Law Backfires." *Forbes*, May 17. www.forbes.com/sites/realspin/2012/05/17 /the-law-of-unintended-consequences-georgias-immigration-law-backfires /#3863ebb7492a.

Powell, James L. 2011. *The Inquisition of Climate Science*. New York: Columbia University Press.

Prashad, Vijay. 2007. *The Darker Nations: A People's History of the Third World*. New York: New Press.

Price, David. 2004. *Threatening Anthropology: McCarthyism and the FBI's Surveillance of Activist Anthropologists*. Durham, NC: Duke University Press.

———. 2008. *Anthropological Intelligence: The Deployment and Neglect of American Anthropology in the Second Cold War*. Durham, NC: Duke University Press.

———. 2011. *Weaponizing Anthropology*. Petrolia, CA: Counterpunch and AK Press.

Prison Policy Initiative. 2012. "United States Incarceration Rates by Race and Ethnicity, 2010." www.prisonpolicy.org/graphs/raceinc.html.

"Projected GDP Ranking." 2020. Statistics Times, February 20. http://statisticstimes .com/economy/projected-world-gdp-ranking.php.

Puig González, Miguel Ángel, José Ernesto Benacourt Lavastida, and Rolando Álvarez Cedeño. 2010. *Fortalezas frente a Huracanes*. La Habana: Editorial Científico-Técnica.

Purvis, Bryant. 2015. *My Story as a Jena 6*. Scotts Valley, CA: CreateSpace.

Quijano, Anibal. 2000. "Coloniality of Power, Eurocentrism, and Latin America." *Nepantla* 1(3):533–580.

Rabben, Linda. 2016. *Sanctuary and Asylum: A Social and Political History*. Seattle: University of Washington Press.

Rahier, Jean Mutaba. 2003. "Introduction: Mestizaje, mulataje, mestiçagem in Latin American Ideologies of National Identities." *Journal of Latin American Anthropology* 8(1):40–51.

Ramos Guadalupe, Luis Enrique. 2005. *Instituto de Meteorlogía: Expresión de una ciencia en Revolución*. Habana: Editorial Academia.

Rana, Junaid. 2020. "Anthropology and the Riddle of White Supremacy." *American Anthropologist* 122(1):99–111.

Randall, Alex. n.d. "Climate Refugees: How Many Are There? How Many Will There Be?" http://climatemigration.org.uk/climate-refugees-how-many.

Ransby, Barbara. 2016. "Black Study, Black Struggle." *Boston Review*, March 7. http://bostonreview.net/forum/black-study-black-struggle/barbara-ransby-barbara -ransby-response-robin-kelley.

———. 2018. *Making All Black Lives Matter: Reimagining Freedom in the Twenty-First Century*. Berkeley: University of California Press.

Rapoza, Kenneth. 2016. "U.S. 'Hostage' to China and Saudi Arabia, but Only One Seems to Matter." *Forbes*, April 22.

Rediker, Marcus. 2007. *The Slave Ship: A Human History*. New York: Viking.

Reed, Adolph. 2008. "Class Inequality, Liberal Bad Faith, and Neoliberalism: The True Disaster of Katrina." In *Capitalizing on Catastrophe: Neoliberal Strategies in Disaster Reconstruction*, edited by Nandini Gunewardena and Mark Schuller, 147–154. Lanham, MD: Alta Mira Press.

Reiter, Rayna. 1975. *Toward an Anthropology of Women*. New York: Monthly Review Press.

Remnick, David. 2017. "A Conversation with Mark Lilla on His Critique of Identity Politics." *New Yorker*, August 25. www.newyorker.com/news/news-desk/a -conversation-with-mark-lilla-on-his-critique-of-identity-politics.

Renda, Mary. 2001. *Taking Haiti: Military Occupation and the Culture of U.S. Imperialism, 1915–1940*. Chapel Hill: University of North Carolina Press.

Richardson, Matt. 2015. "Killed Outright or Left to Die: Black (Trans)Women and the Police State." *Hot Spots*, June 29. https://culanth.org/fieldsights/killed-outright -or-left-to-die-black-transwomen-and-the-police-state.

Ritchie, Andrea J. 2017. *Invisible No More: Police Violence Against Black Women and Women of Color*. Boston: Beacon.

Robinson, Cedric J. [1983] 2000. *Black Marxism: The Making of the Black Radical Tradition*. Chapel Hill: University of North Carolina Press.

Robotham, Don. 1998. "Transnationalism in the Caribbean: Formal and Informal." *American Ethnologist* 25(2):307–321.

Rodney, Walter. 1972. *How Europe Underdeveloped Africa*. Washington, DC: Howard University Press.

Rosa, Jonathan D. 2012. "Contesting Representations of Immigration." *Anthropology News* 53(8):s13–s14.

———. 2013. "Learning Ethnolinguistic Borders: Language and Diaspora in the Socialization of U.S. Latinas/os." In *Diaspora Studies in Education: Toward a Framework for Understanding the Experiences of Transnational Communities*, edited by Rosalie Rólon-Dow and Jason G. Irrizary, 39–60. New York: Peter Lang.

Rosa, Jonathan, and Yarimar Bonilla. 2017. "Deprovincializing Trump, Decolonizing Diversity, and Unsettling Anthropology." *American Ethnologist* 44(2):201–208.

Rosa, Jonathan, and Vanessa Díaz. 2020. "Raciontologies: Rethinking Anthropologi- cal Accounts of Institutional Racism and Enactments of White Supremacy in the United States." *American Anthropologist* 122(1):120–132.

Rosaldo, Michelle Zimbalist, Joan Bamberger, and Louise Lamphere. 1974. *Woman, Culture, and Society*. Stanford, CA: Stanford University Press.

Rosaldo, Renato. 1994. "Cultural Citizenship in San José, California." *Political and Legal Anthropological Review* 17(2):57–64.

Rosas, Gilberto. 2018a. "Fugitive Work: On the Criminal Possibilities of Anthropology." *Hot Spots*, September 26. https://culanth.org/fieldsights/1529-fugitive-work -on-the-criminal-possibilities-of-anthropology.

———. 2018b. "Refusing Refuge at the United States-Mexico Border." *Humanity* 8(3). http://humanityjournal.org/issue8-3/refusing-refuge-at-the-united-states-mexico -border/.

Roscoe, Paul. 2014. "A Changing Climate for Anthropological and Archaeological Research? Improving the Climate-Change Models." *American Anthropologist* 116(3):535–548.

Rosentiel, Tom. 2008. "Inside Obama's Sweeping Victory." Pew Research Center, November 5. www.pewresearch.org/2008/11/05/inside-obamas-sweeping-victory.

Running, Steven W. 2006. "Is Global Warming Causing More, Larger Wildfires?" *Science* 313:927–928.

"Russian Hacking and Influence in the U.S. Election." 2020. *New York Times*, April 30. www.nytimes.com/news-event/russian-election-hacking.

Ruth, Alyssa. 2018. "Attaining the College Dream: The Effects of Politics on the Social Capital of First-Generation Undocumented Immigrant Students." *Human Organization* 77(1):22–31.

Sacks, Karen. 1975. "Engels Revisited: Women, the Organization of Production, and Private Property." In *Toward an Anthropology of Women*, edited by Rayna Reiter. New York: Monthly Review Press.

Sadowski, Dennis. 2018. "Church Teaching Leads Catholic Entities to Divest from Fossil Fuels." *Crux*, April 23. https://cruxnow.com/church-in-the-usa/2018/04/23 /church-teaching-leads-catholic-entities-to-divest-from-fossil-fuels.

Sahlins, Marshall. 1999. "What Is Anthropological Enlightenment? Some Lessons of the Twentieth Century." *Annual Reviews of Anthropology* 28:i–xxiii.

Said, Edward. 1979. *Orientalism*. New York: Vintage.

Salaita, Stephen. 2006. *Anti-Arab Racism in the USA: Where It Comes from and What It Means for Politics Today*. London: Pluto Press.

———. 2014. "Normatizing State Power: Uncritical Ethical Praxis and Zionism." In *The Imperial University: Academic Repression and Scholarly Dissent*, edited by Piya Chatterjee and Sunaina Maira. Minneapolis: University of Minnesota Press.

Sanday, Peggy Reeves. 1998. "Skeletons in the Anthropological Closet: The Life Work of William S. Willis, Jr.," in *African-American Pioneers in Anthropology*, edited by Ira E. Harrison and Faye V. Harrison. Champaign: University of Illinois Press.

Sandoval, Chela. 2000. *Methodology of the Oppressed*. Minneapolis: University of Minnesota Press.

Sassen, Saskia. 2001. *The Global City: New York, London, Tokyo*. 2nd ed. Princeton, NJ: Princeton University Press.

Savransky, Rebecca. 2016. "Michael Moore: 5 Reasons Trump Will Be President." *The Hill*, July 25. http://thehill.com/blogs/blog-briefing-room/news/donald-trump -michael-moore-hillary-clinton-prediction-victory-election-5-reasons-why.

Sayre, Nathan F. 2012. "The Politics of the Anthropogenic." *Annual Review of Anthropology* 41:57–70.

Schambach, Emma. 2019. "Nine White Students Show Up for a 'White Consciousness' Discussion." *College Fix*, September 20. www.thecollegefix.com/on-campus-of-30000-students-less-than-10-attend-universitys-white-privilege-workshop.

Schamisso, Ben. 2017. "Why This DACA Recipient Refuses to Be Called a 'Dreamer.'" *Newsy*, November 6. www.newsy.com/stories/daca-recipient-refuses-to-be-called-a-dreamer.

Schlosser, Eric. 1998. "The Prison Industrial Complex." *Atlantic Monthly*, December, 51–77.

Schmidt, Hans. 1971. *The United States Occupation of Haiti, 1915–1934*. New Brunswick, NJ: Rutgers University Press.

Schoenfeld, Bruce. 2011. "How the Farm-to-Table Movement Is Helping Grow the Economy." *Entrepreneur*, September 21. www.entrepreneur.com/article/220357.

Schrecker, Ellen W. 1986. *No Ivory Tower: McCarthyism and the Universities*. New York: Oxford University Press.

Schuller, Mark. 2016. *Humanitarian Aftershocks in Haiti*. New Brunswick, NJ: Rutgers University Press.

Schuller, Mark, and Julie Koppel Maldonado. 2016. "Disaster Capitalism." *Annals of Anthropological Practice* 40(1):61–72.

Scott, James C. 1985. *Weapons of the Weak: Everyday Forms of Peasant Resistance*. New Haven, CT: Yale University Press.

———. 2009. *The Art of Not Being Governed: An Anarchist History of Upland Southeast Asia*. New Haven, CT: Yale University Press.

———. 2014. *Two Cheers for Anarchism: Six Easy Pieces on Autonomy, Dignity, and Meaningful Work and Play*. Princeton, NJ: Princeton University Press.

Semuels, Alana. 2016. "Good School, Rich School; Bad School, Poor School: The Inequality at the Heart of America's Education System." *Atlantic*, August 25.

Sen, Rinku. 2003. *Stir It Up: Lessons in Community Organizing and Advocacy*. San Francisco: Jossey-Bass.

Sharpe, Christina. 2010. *Monstrous Intimacies: Making Post-Slavery Subjects (Perverse Modernities)*. Durham, NC: Duke University Press.

Sharpley-Whiting, Tracy Denean. 1999. *Black Venus: Sexualized Savages, Primal Fears, and Primitive Narratives in French*. Durham, NC: Duke University Press.

Sharratt, Nicola. 2016. "Collapse and Cohesion: Building Community in the Aftermath of Tiwanaku State Breakdown." *World Archaeology* 48(1):144–163.

Shear, Boone W., and Susan Brin Hyatt. 2015. "Introduction. Higher Education, Engaged Anthropology and Hegemonic Struggle." In *Learning under Neoliberalism: Ethnographies of Governance in Higher Education*, edited by Susan Brin Hyatt, Boone W. Shear, and Susan Wright, 1–29. New York: Berghahn Books.

Shear, Michael D., and Julie Hirschfeld Davis. 2017. "Stoking Fears, Trump Defied Bureaucracy to Advance Immigration Agenda." *New York Times*, December 23. www.nytimes.com/2017/12/23/us/politics/trump-immigration.html.

Shearer, Christine. 2011. *Kivalina: A Climate Change Story*. Chicago: Haymarket Books.

Sheller, Mimi. 2018. "Caribbean Futures in the Offshore Anthropocene: Debt, Disaster, and Duration"*Environment and Planning D: Society and Space* 36(6):971–986.

Shore, Cris, and Susan Wright. 2000. "Coercive Accountability: The Rise of Audit Culture in Higher Education." In *Audit Cultures: Anthropological Studies in*

Accountability: Ethics and the Academy, edited by Marilyn Strathern, 57–89. London: Routledge.

Shostak, Marjorie, and Nisa. [1981] 2000. *Nisa, the Life and Words of a !Kung Woman.* Cambridge, MA: Harvard University Press.

Simmons, David. 2010. "Structural Violence as Social Practice: Haitian Agricultural Workers, Anti-Haitianism, and Health in the Dominican Republic." *Human Organization* 69(1):10–18.

Simmons, Kimberly Eison. 2009. *Reconstructing Racial Identity and the African Past in the Dominican Republic.* Gainesville: University Press of Florida.

Slocum, Sally. 1975. "Women the Gatherer." In *Toward an Anthropology of Women*, edited by Rayna Reiter, 36–50. New York: Monthly Review Books.

Slotta, James. 2014. "Revelations of the World: Transnationalism and the Politics of Perception in Papua New Guinea." *American Anthropologist* 116(3):626–642.

Smedley, Audrey, and Janis Faye Hutchinson. 2012. "Racism in the Academy: The New Millennium." Washington, DC: American Anthropological Association.

Smith, Linda Tuhiwai. 2013. *Decolonizing Methodologies: Research and Indigenous Peoples.* 2nd ed. New York: Zed Books.

Smith, Neil. 1984. *Uneven Development: Nature, Capital, and the Production of Space.* Oxford: Blackwell.

———. 1996. *The New Urban Frontier: Gentrification and the Revanchist City.* New York: Routledge.

Sohn, Heeju. 2017. "Racial and Ethnic Disparities in Health Insurance Coverage: Dynamics of Gaining and Losing Coverage over the Life-Course." *Population Research and Policy Review* 36(2):181–201.

Sontag, Deborah. 2012. "Earthquake Relief Where Haiti Wasn't Broken." *New York Times*, July 5. www.nytimes.com/2012/07/06/world/americas/earthquake-relief -where-haiti-wasnt-broken.html.

Speakman, Robert J., Carla S. Hadden, Matthew H. Colvin, Justin Cramb, K. C. Jones, Travis W. Jones, Isabelle Lulewicz, Katharine G. Napora, Katherine L. Reinberger, Brandon T. Ritchison, Alexandra R. Edwards, and Victor D. Thompson. 2018. "Market Share and Recent Hiring Trends in Anthropology Faculty Positions." *PLOS ONE* 13(9):1–19.

Spillers, Hortence J. 1987. "Mama's Baby, Papa's Maybe: An American Grammar Book." *Diacritics* 17(2):64–81.

Stephen, Lynn. 2007. *Transborder Lives: Indigenous Oaxacans in Mexico, California, and Oregon.* Durham, NC: Duke University Press.

Stocking, George W. 1971. "What's in a Name? Origins of the Royal Anthropological Institute (1837–71)." *Man* 6(3):371–390.

Stolberg, Sheryl Gay. 2019. "At Historic Hearing, House Panel Explores Reparations." *New York Times*, June 19. www.nytimes.com/2019/06/19/us/politics/slavery -reparations-hearing.html.

"Stop Breaking Up Families at the Border." 2018. *New York Post*, June 17. https:// nypost.com/2018/06/17/stop-breaking-up-families-at-the-border.

Stovall, David Omotoso. 2016. *Born out of Struggle: Critical Race Theory, School Creation, and the Politics of Interruption.* Albany: State University of New York Press.

Strathern, Marilyn. 2000. *Audit Cultures: Anthropological Studies in Accountability, Ethics, and the Academy.* London: Routledge.

Stringer, E. T. 1996. *Action Research: A Handbook for Practitioners*. Thousand Oaks, CA: Sage.

Stuesse, Angela. 2016. *Scratching Out a Living: Latinos, Race, and Work in the Deep South*. Berkeley: University of California Press.

Stuesse, Angela, Cheryl Staats, and Andrew Grant-Thomas. 2017. "As Others Pluck Fruit off the Tree of Opportunity: Immigration, Racial Hierarchies, and Intergroup Relations Efforts in the United States." *Du Bois Review* 14(1):245–271.

Stumpf, Juliet. 2006. "The Crimmigration Crisis: Immigrants, Crime, and Sovereign Power." *American University Law Review* 56(2):367–417.

Sudbury, Julia. 2008. "Rethinking Global Justice: Black Women Resist the Transnational Prison Industrial Complex." *Souls: A Critical Journal of Black Politics, Culture, and Society* 10(4):344–360.

Sullivan, Kevin, and Rosalind S. Helderman. 2015. "Role of Hillary Clinton's Brother in Haiti Gold Mine Raises Eyebrows." *Washington Post*, March 20.

Tahi, Mahi. 2018. "A Response, and Second Open Letter to the Hau Journal's Board of Trustees." Association of Social Anthropologists of Aotearoa/New Zealand, June 21. www.asaanz.org/blog/2018/6/21/a-response-and-second-open-letter-to-the-hau-journals-board-of-trustees.

Tallbear, Kim. 2015. "Dossier: Theorizing Queer Inhumanisms: An Indigenous Reflection on Working Beyond the Human/Not Human." *GLQ: A Journal of Lesbian and Gay Studies* 21(2–3):230–235. https://doi.org/10.1215/10642684-2843323.

Taub, Ben. 2017. "Lake Chad: The World's Most Complex Humanitarian Disaster." *New Yorker*, November 27. www.newyorker.com/magazine/2017/12/04/lake-chad-the-worlds-most-complex-humanitarian-disaster.

Taylor, Keeanga-Yamahtta. 2016. *From #BlackLivesMatter to Black Liberation*. Chicago: Haymarket Books.

———. 2017. *How We Get Free: Black Feminism and the Combahee River Collective*. Chicago: Haymarket Books.

———. 2020. "The Black Plague." *The New Yorker*, April 16. https://www.newyorker.com/news/our-columnists/the-black-plague.

Taylor, Michael A., Tannecia S. Stephenson, A. Anthony Chen, and Kimberly A. Stephenson. 2012. "Climate Change and the Caribbean." *Caribbean Studies* 40(2):169–200.

Taylor, Sarah. 2015. "The Construction of Vulnerability along the Zarumilla River Valley in Prehistory." *Human Organization* 74(4):296–307.

Terkel, Studs. 1967. *Division Street: America*. New York: Pantheon Books.

———. 1986. *Chicago*. New York: Pantheon Books.

Thomas, Deborah, and Kamari Maxine Clarke. 2013. "Globalization and Race: Structures of Inequality, New Sovereignties, and Citizenship in a Neoliberal Era." *Annual Review of Anthropology* 42:305–325.

Thompson, Ginger. 2018. "Families Are Still Being Separated at the Border, Months after 'Zero Tolerance' Was Reversed." *ProPublica*, November 27. www.propublica.org/article/border-patrol-families-still-being-separated-at-border-after-zero-tolerance-immigration-policy-reversed.

Thompson, Martha, with Izaskun Gaviria. 2004. *Weathering the Storm: Lessons in Risk Reduction from Cuba*. Boston: Oxfam America.

Thornton, Margaret. 2015. *Through a Glass Darkly: The Social Sciences Look at the Neoliberal University*. Canberra: Australia National University.

Thu, Kendall, and E. Paul Durrenberger. 1998. *Pigs, Profits, and Rural Communities*. Albany: State University of New York Press.

Thu, Kendall, Mark Schuller, Tiara Huggins, and Valarie Redmond. 2017. "'Being Heard, Not Only Seen': Intersections of Tea Partyism, Racism, and Classism in a Low-Income Housing Struggle in DeKalb, Illinois." *Human Organization* 76(4):348–357.

Tiano, Susan. 1992. "Maquiladora Women: A New Category of Workers?" In *Women Workers and Global Restructuring*, edited by Kathryn B. Ward, 193–223. Ithaca, NY: Cornell University Press.

Timmer, Andria. 2017. "Advertising Populism in Hungary." *Anthropology News* (May/June). https://anthrosource.onlinelibrary.wiley.com/doi/abs/10.1111/AN.429.

Timmer, Andria, Joseph Sery, Sean Thomas Connable, and Jennifer Billinson. 2018. "A Tale of Two Paranoids: A Critical Analysis of the Use of the Paranoid Style and Public Secrecy by Donald Trump and Viktor Orbán." *Secrecy and Society* 1(2). https://scholarworks.sjsu.edu/secrecyandsociety/vol1/iss2/3.

Tobias, Jimmy. 2017. "These Cities Are Pulling Billions from the Banks That Support the Dakota Access Pipeline." *The Nation*, March 20. www.thenation.com/article/these-cities-are-divesting-from-the-banks-that-support-the-dakota-access-pipeline.

Todd, Zoe. 2015. "Decolonial Dreams: Unsettling the Academy through Namewak." In *The New (New) Corpse*, edited by Carolyn Picard, 104–117. Chicago: Green Lantern Press.

Toppin, E. J. 2019. "Blog: Reforming Anti-Tax Prop 13 Is a Racial Justice Issue." https://belonging.berkeley.edu/blog-reforming-anti-tax-prop-13-racial-justice-issue.

Torrence, Robin. 2016. "Social Resilience and Long-Term Adaptation to Volcanic Disasters: The Archaeology of Continuity and Innovation in the Willamauz Peninsula, Papua New Guinea." *Quaternary International* 394:6–16.

———. 2018. "Social Responses to Volcanic Eruptions: A Review of Key Concepts." *Quaternary International*.

Traube, Elizabeth. 1993. "Family Matters: Postfeminist Constructions of a Contested Site." *Visual Anthropology Review* 9(1):56–73.

Trouillot, Michel-Rolph. 1995. *Silencing the Past: Power and the Production of History*. Boston: Beacon.

———. 1997. "A Social Contract for Whom? Haitian History and Haiti's Future." In *Haiti Renewed: Political and Economic Prospects*, edited by Robert I. Rotberg, 47–59. Cambridge, MA: World Peace Foundation / Brookings Institution Press.

———. 2003. *Global Transformations: Anthropology and the Modern World*. New York: Palgrave Macmillan.

"Trump's Travel Ban Could Hurt U.S. College Revenue." 2017. *Newsweek*, February 1. www.newsweek.com/donald-trump-travel-ban-college-tuitions-international-students-551442.

Tuck, Eve, and K. Wayne Wang. 2012. "Decolonization Is Not a Metaphor." *Decolonization: Indigeneity, Education & Society* 1(1):1–40.

Ullian, Adam. 2020. "Extend TPS for Haiti." www.ipetitions.com/petition/haitian-tps-renewal.

Ulysse, Gina Athena. 2003. "Cracking the Silence on Reflexivity: Negotiating Identities, Fieldwork, and the Dissertation in Kingston and Ann Arbor." In

Decolonizing the Academy: African Diaspora Studies, edited by Carole Boyce Davies. Trenton, NJ: Africa World Press.

———. 2008. *Downtown Ladies: Informal Commercial Importers, a Haitian Anthropologist, and Self-Making in Jamaica.* Chicago: University of Chicago Press.

———. 2015. *Why Haiti Needs New Narratives: A Post-Quake Chronicle. With a preface from Robin Kelley.* Middletown, CT: Wesleyan University Press.

UNAIDS. 2020. "Haiti." www.unaids.org/en/regionscountries/countries/Haiti.

United Nations. n.d. "Climate Change." www.un.org/en/sections/issues-depth/climate-change.

United Nations Development Programme. 2012. "Arab Human Development Report." www.arab-hdr.org/publications/other/ahdrps/ENGFattouhKatiriV2.pdf.

United Nations Office for the Coordination of Humanitarian Affairs. 2016. "Haiti: Hurricane Matthew—Situation Report No. 01 (as of 05 October 2016)." https://reliefweb.int/report/haiti/haiti-hurricane-matthew-situation-report-no-01-05-october-2016.

———. 2017a. "Climate Change Vulnerability Index 2017." https://reliefweb.int/sites/reliefweb.int/files/resources/verisk%20index.pdf.

———. 2017b. "Haiti: Hurricane Matthew—Situation Report No. 35 (as of 04 March 2017)." www.ijdh.org/wp-content/uploads/2016/10/OCHA-Situation-Report-35-Hurricane-Matthew-Haiti-04-March-2017.pdf.

United Nations Refugee Agency. 2012. "The State of the World's Refugees: In Search of Solidarity." www.unhcr.org/4fc5ceca9.pdf.

———. 2015. "Global Trends: Forced Displacement in 2015." www.unhcr.org/576408cd7.pdf.

———. 2016. "UNHCR Appeals to Kenya over Decision to End Refugee Hosting." www.unhcr.org/57308e616.html.

———. 2020. "Refugee Statistics." www.unrefugees.org/refugee-facts/statistics.

United Nations Secretary-General. 2013. "Secretary-General's Remarks to High-Level Dialogue on International Migration and Development." www.un.org/sg/en/content/sg/statement/2013-10-03/secretary-generals-remarks-high-level-dialogue-international.

United Nations University. 2015. "5 Facts on Climate Migrants." https://ehs.unu.edu/blog/5-facts/5-facts-on-climate-migrants.html.

Van Gelder, Sarah. 2015. "Rev. Sekou on Today's Civil Rights Leaders: 'I Take My Orders from 23-Year-Old Queer Women.'" *Yes*, July 22. www.yesmagazine.org/peace-justice/black-lives-matter-s-favorite-minister-reverend-sekou-young-queer.

Vélez-Vélez, Roberto. 2010. "Reflexivity in Mobilization: Gender and Memory as Cultural Features of Women's Mobilization in Vieques, 1999–2003." *Mobilization: An International Quarterly* 15(1):81–97.

Vélez-Vélez, Roberto, and Jaqueline Villarrubia-Mendoza. 2018. "Cambio desde abajo y desde adentro: Notes on Centros de Apoyo Mutuo in post-María Puerto Rico." *Latino Studies* 16(4):542–547.

Verma, Ritu. 2017. "Gross National Happiness: Meaning, Measure and Degrowth in a Living Development Alternative." *Journal of Political Ecology* 24(1):476–490.

Villarrubia-Mendoza, Jaqueline, and Roberto Vélez-Vélez. 2017. "Iconoclastic Dreams: Interpreting Art in the DREAMers Movement." *Sociological Quarterly* 58(3):350–372.

von Rueden, Christopher R., Daniel Redhead, Rick O'Gorman, Hillard Kaplan, and Michael Gurven. 2019. "The Dynamics of Men's Cooperation and Social Status in a Small-Scale Society." *Proceedings of the Royal Society B* 286(1908). https://royal societypublishing.org/doi/10.1098/rspb.2019.1367.

Wagner, Peter, and Alison Walsh. 2016. "States of Incarceration: The Global Context 2016." Prison Policy Initiative, June 16. www.prisonpolicy.org/global /2016.html.

Watts, Vanessa. 2013. "Indigenous Place-Thought and Agency amongst Humans and Non Humans (First Woman and Sky Woman Go on a European World Tour!)." *Decolonization: Indigeneity, Education & Society* 2(1):20–34.

Wax, Dustin. 2008. *Anthropology at the Dawn of the Cold War: The Influence of Foundations, McCarthyism and the CIA.* London: Pluto Press.

Waziyatawin, and Michael Yellow Bird. 2012. *For Indigenous Minds Only: A Decoloni- zation Handbook.* Santa Fe, NM: School of American Research Press.

Webster, P. J., G. J. Holland, J. A. Curry, and H.-R. Chang. 2005. "Changes in Tropical Cyclone Number, Duration, and Intensity in a Warming Environment." *Science* 309:1844–1846.

Weedman, Kathryn. 2006. "Gender and ethnoarchaeology." In *Handbook of Gender in Archaeology*, edited by Sarah Milledge Nelson, 237–294. Lanham, MD: Alta Mira Press.

Weisbrot, Mark, Stephan Lefebvre, and Joseph Sammut. 2014. "Did NAFTA Help Mexico? An Assessment after 20 Years." Center for Economic and Policy Research. https://cepr.net/documents/nafta-20-years-2014-02.pdf.

Weiss, Harvey. 2017. *Megadrought and Collapse: From Early Agriculture to Angkor.* New York: Oxford University Press.

Wences, Reyna, and Ruth Gomberg-Muñoz. 2018. "To Create True Sanctuary Cities, We Must End Racist Policing." *Truthout*, Mary 14. https://truthout.org/articles/to -create-true-sanctuary-cities-we-must-end-racist-policing.

West, Paige. 2018. "Introduction: From Reciprocity to Relationality." *Hot Spots*, September 26. https://culanth.org/fieldsights/1526-introduction-from-reciprocity -to-relationality.

Westerling, Anthony L., Hugo G. Hidalgo, Daniel R. Cayan, and Thomas W. Swetnam. 2006. "Warming and Earlier Spring Increase Western U.S. Forest Wildfire Activity." *Science* 313:940–943.

White, Tim, G. Suwa, and R. Asfaw. 1994. "Australopithecus Ramidus, a New Species of Early Hominid from Aramis, Ethiopia." *Nature* 371:306–312.

Whitington, Jerome. 2016. "What Does Climate Change Demand of Anthropology?" *Political and Legal Anthropology Review* 39(1):7–15.

Whitten, Norman E. 2007. "The Longue Durée of Racial Fixity and the Transforma- tive Conjunctures of Racial Blending." *Journal of Latin American and Caribbean Anthropology* 12(2):356–383.

Whyte, Kyle Powys. 2017. "Indigenous Climate Change Studies: Indigenizing Futures, Decolonizing the Anthropocene." *English Language Notes* 55(1–2):153–162.

———. 2018a. "Critical Investigations of Resilience: A Brief Introduction to Indig- enous Environmental Studies & Sciences." *Daedalus* 147(2):136–147.

———. 2018b. "Indigenous Science (Fiction) for the Anthropocene: Ancestral Dystopias and Fantasies of Climate Change Crises." *Nature and Space.*

———. 2018c. "White Allies, Let's Be Honest about Decolonization." *Yes!*, April 3. www.yesmagazine.org/issues/decolonize/white-allies-lets-be-honest-about -decolonization-20180403.

———. 2019. "Way Beyond the Lifeboat: An Indigenous Allegory of Climate Justice." In *Climate Futures: Reimagining Global Climate Justice*, edited by Kum-Kum Bhavnani, John Foran, Priya Kurian, and Debashish Munshi. London: Zed Books.

Whyte, William F. 1991. *Participatory Action Research*. Thousand Oaks, CA: Sage.

Wies, Jennifer, and Hillary Haldane. 2011. *Anthropology at the Front Lines of Gender Based Violence*. Nashville: Vanderbilt University Press.

Wildcat, Daniel R. 2009. *Red Alert! Saving the Planet with Indigenous Knowledge*. Golden, CO: Fulcrum.

Wilderson, Frank B., III. 2016. "Afro-pessimism and the End of Redemption." *The Occupied Times*, March 30. https://theoccupiedtimes.org/?p=14236.

Williams, Bianca C. 2018. *The Pursuit of Happiness: Black Women, Diasporic Dreams, and the Politics of Emotional Transnationalism*. Durham, NC: Duke University Press.

Williams, Brackette F. 1995. "The Public I/Eye: Conducting Fieldwork to Do Homework on Homelessness and Begging in Two U.S. Cities." *Current Anthropology* 36(1):25–51.

Williams, Eric Eustace. 1944. *Capitalism and Slavery*. New York: Russell & Russell.

Willis, Paul. 1981. *Learning to Labour: How Working Class Kids Get Working Class Jobs*. New York: Columbia University Press.

Willis, William S., Jr. 1972. "Anthropological Skeletons in the Closet." In *Reinventing Anthropology*, edited by Dell Hynes. New York: Pantheon Books.

Willoughby-Herard, Tiffany. 2015. *Waste of a White Skin: The Carnegie Corporation and the Racial Logic of White Vulnerability*. Berkeley: University of California Press.

Wilson, Peter. 1973. *Crab Antics: The Social Anthropology of English-Speaking Negro Societies in the Caribbean*. New Haven, CT: Yale University Press.

Wilson, William J. 1987. *The Truly Disadvantaged*. Chicago: University of Chicago Press.

Wirtz, Elizabeth, and Mark Schuller. 2017. "French Election a Step for Justice for Refugees, but Entrenched Inequalities Remain." *Huffington Post*, May 11. https:// www.huffpost.com/entry/french-election-a-step-for-justice-for-refugees-but_b _591518bee4b0bd90f8e6a3da.

Wong, Andrea, and Liz McCormick. 2016. "Saudi Arabia's Secret Holdings of U.S. Debt Are Suddenly a Big Deal." *Bloomberg*, January 21. www.bloomberg.com/news /articles/2016-01-22/u-s-is-hiding-treasury-bond-data-that-s-suddenly-become -crucial.

Wrangham, Richard W. 2019. "Hypotheses for the Evolution of Reduced Reactive Aggression in the Context of Human Self-Domestication." *Frontiers in Psychology* 10(1914):11.

Wyly, Elvin K., and Daniel J. Hammel. 2001. "Gentrification, Housing Policy, and the New Context of Urban Redevelopment." *Research in Urban Sociology* 6:211–276.

Wynter, Sylvia. 2003. "Unsettling the Coloniality of Being/Power/Truth/Freedom: Towards the Human, After Man, Its Overrepresentation—An Argument." *CR: The New Centennial Review* 3(3):257–337.

Yazzie, Melanie. 2019. "Divest & End the Occupation: The Red Nation Launches Part One of the Red Deal." *The Red Nation*, November 8. https://therednation.org/2019/11/08/divest-end-the-occupation-the-red-nation-launches-part-one-of-the-red-deal.

Yelvington, Kevin A., Alisha R. Winn, E. Christian Wells, Angela Stuesse, Nancy Romero-Daza, Lauren C. Johnson, Antoinette T. Jackson, Emelda Curry, and Heide Castañeda. 2015. "Diversity Dilemmas and Opportunities: Training the Next Generation of Anthropologists." *American Anthropologist* 117(2):387–392.

Yuval-Davis, Nira, Floya Anthias, and Eleonore Kofman. 2005. "Secure Borders and Safe Haven and the Gendered Politics of Belonging: Beyond Social Cohesion." *Ethnic & Racial Studies* 28(3):513–535. doi:10.1080/0141987042000337867.

Zavella, Patricia. 2011. *I'm Neither Here nor There: Mexicans' Quotidian Struggles with Migration and Poverty*. Durham, NC: Duke University Press.

Zinn, Howard. 1995. *A People's History of the United States: 1492–Present*. Rev. ed. New York: Harper Perennial.

Zinouri, Nazanin. 2017. "I Tried to Fly Home to the U.S. on Friday. President Trump's Travel Ban Meant I Couldn't." *Washington Post*, January 30. https://www.washingtonpost.com/posteverything/wp/2017/01/30/i-tried-to-fly-home-to-the-u-s-friday-president-trumps-new-ban-meant-i-couldnt/.

Zlolniski, Christian. 2006. *Janitors, Street Vendors, and Activists: The Lives of Mexican Immigrants in Silicon Valley*. Berkeley: University of California Press.

Index

About the Author

Activist anthropologist, MARK SCHULLER, is professor at Northern Illinois University. Supported by the National Science Foundation Senior and CAREER Grant, Bellagio Center, and others, Schuller has over forty peer-reviewed publications, and even more public media. He is the author of *Humanitarian Aftershocks in Haiti* (2016) and *Killing with Kindness* (2012, both Rutgers University Press) and co-editor of five books and two book series. He is codirector/coproducer of documentary *Poto Mitan: Haitian Women, Pillars of the Global Economy* (2009). Recipient of the Margaret Mead Award (2015) and the Anthropology in Media Award (2016), he is active in several solidarity efforts. He is currently president of the Haitian Studies Association and the United Faculty Alliance, the faculty union on his campus.